MARK WAID · JEAN DIAZ

INCORRUPTIBLE

VOLUME 1

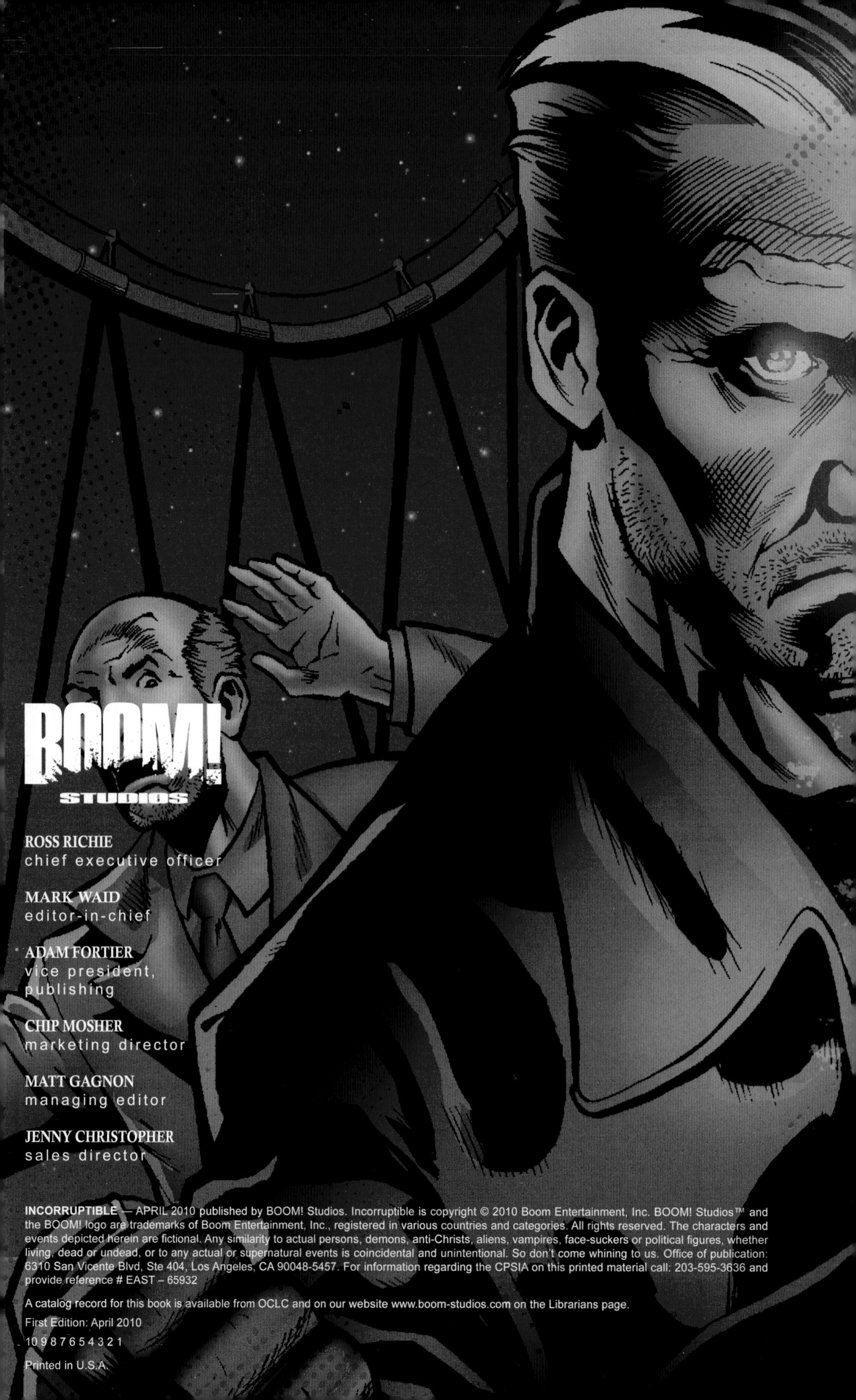

A catalog record for this book is available from OCLC and on our website www.boom-studios.com on the Librarians page.

First Edition: April 2010

10 9 8 7 6 5 4 3 2 1

Printed in U.S.A.

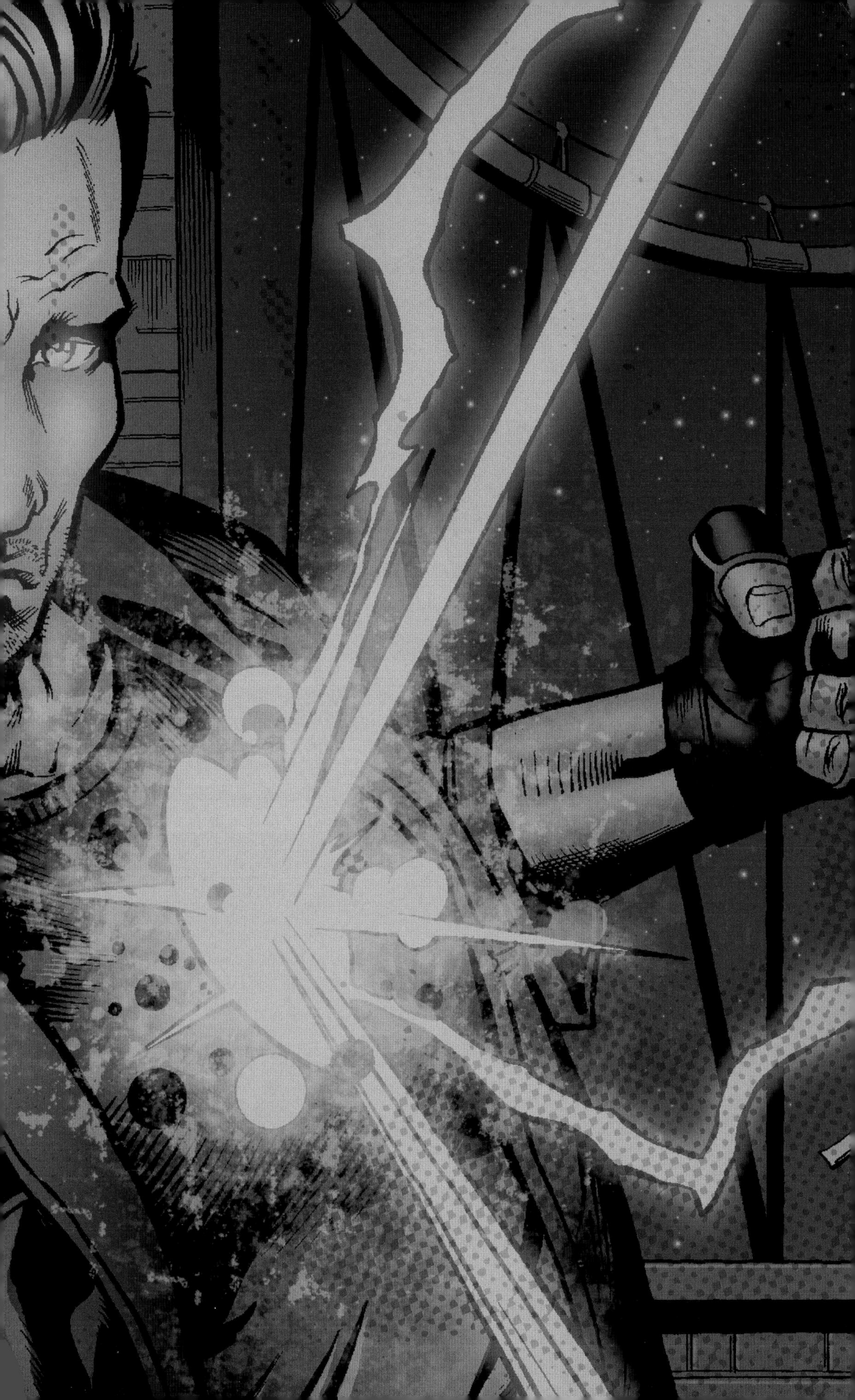

CREATED AND WRITTEN BY:
MARK WAID
ARTIST:
JEAN DIAZ

INKS: **BELARDINO BRABO**
COLORIST: **ANDREW DALHOUSE**
LETTERER: **ED DUKESHIRE**

EDITOR: **MATT GAGNON**

COVER: **JOHN CASSADAY**
COLORS: LAURA MARTIN
DESIGN: **BRIAN LATIMER**

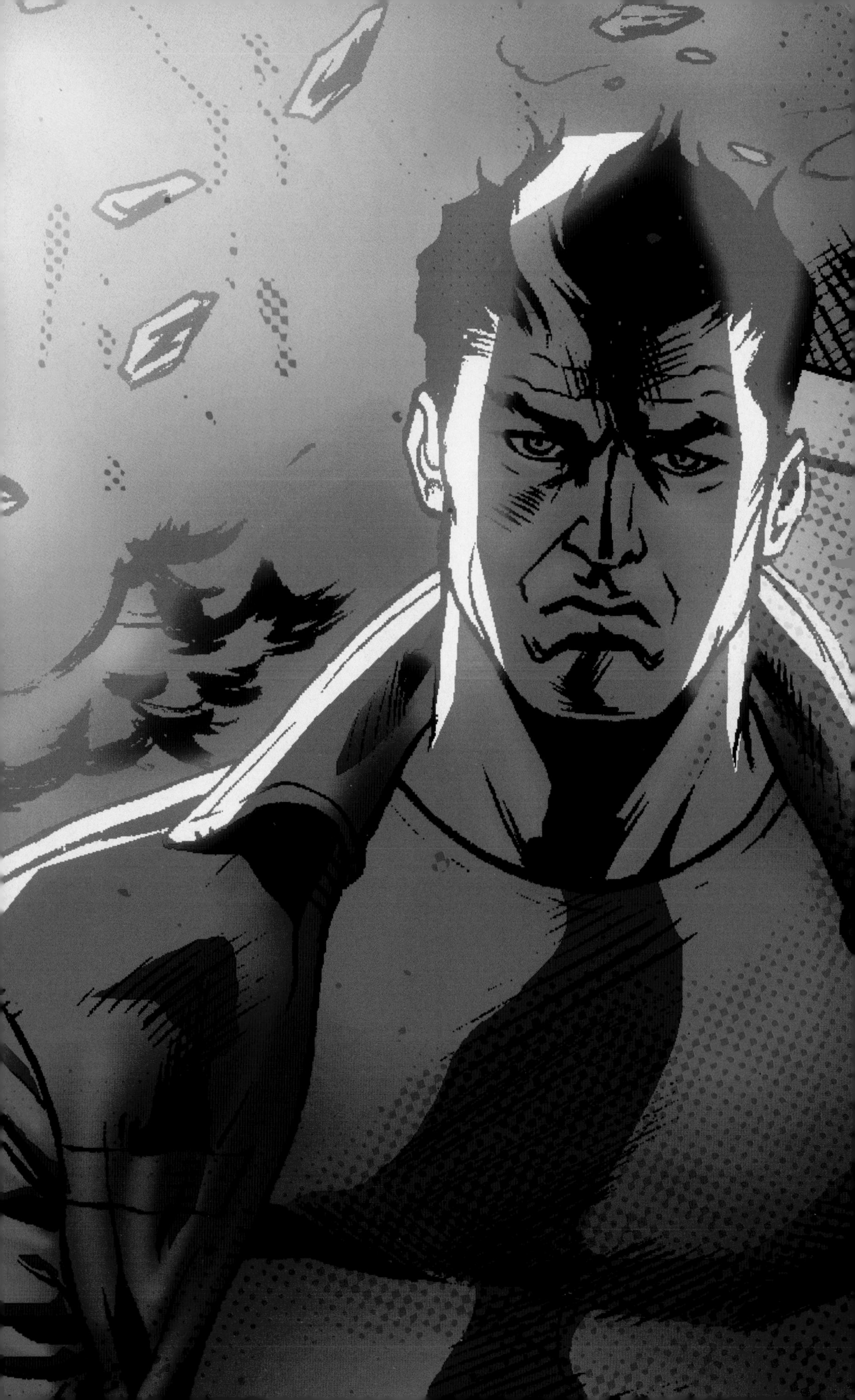

CHAPTER 1

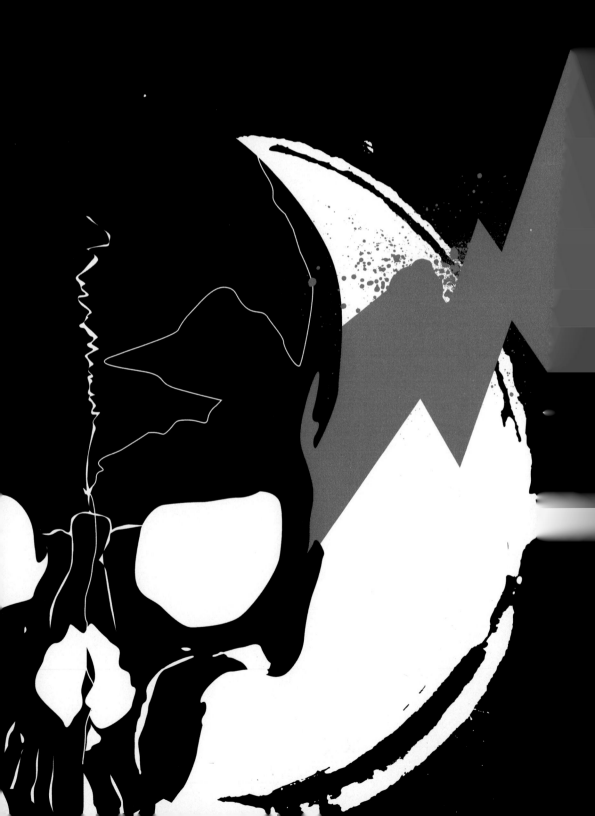

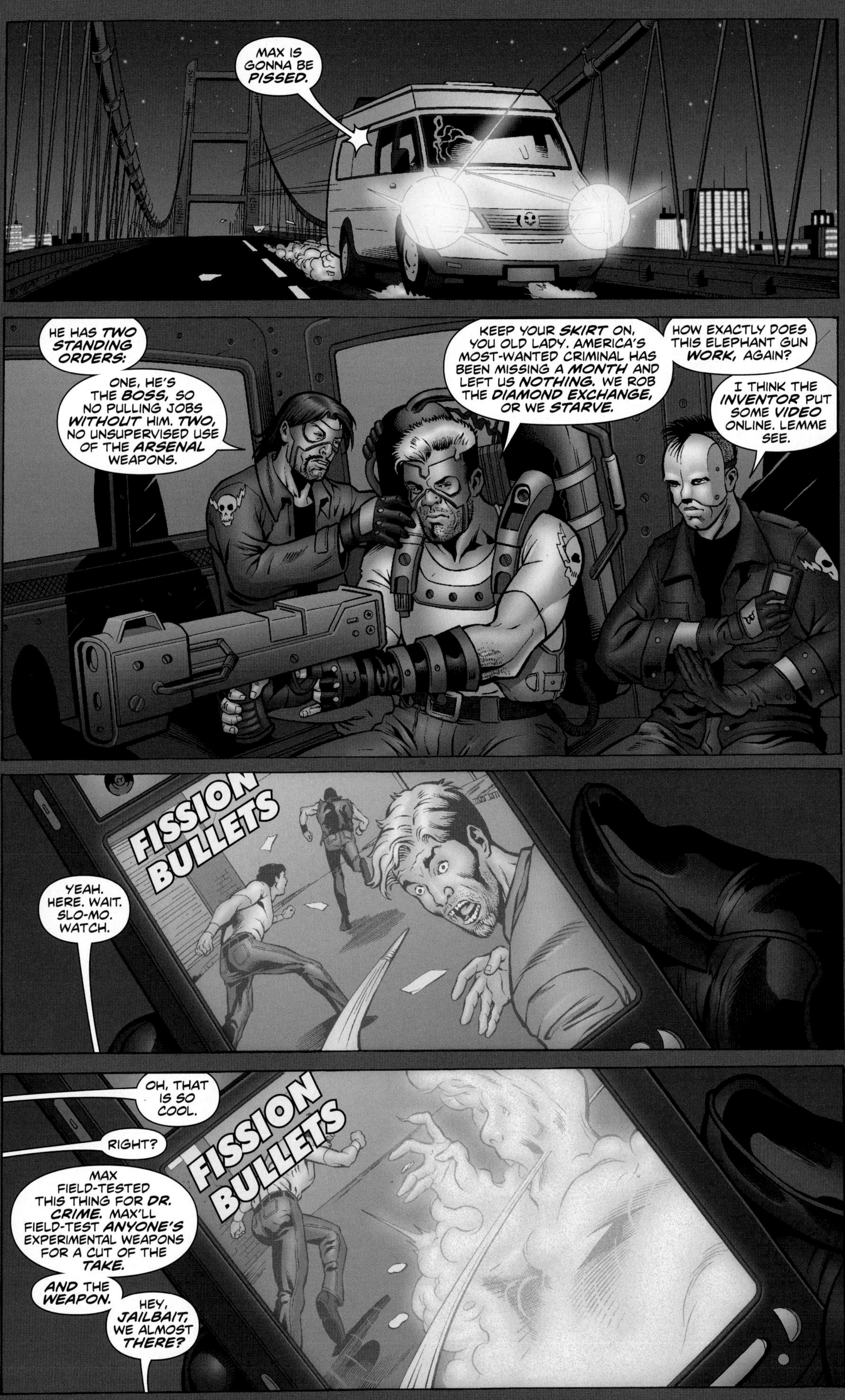
MAX IS GONNA BE PISSED.
HE HAS TWO STANDING ORDERS:
ONE, HE'S THE BOSS, SO NO PULLING JOBS WITHOUT HIM. TWO, NO UNSUPERVISED USE OF THE ARSENAL WEAPONS.
KEEP YOUR SKIRT ON, YOU OLD LADY. AMERICA'S MOST-WANTED CRIMINAL HAS BEEN MISSING A MONTH AND LEFT US NOTHING. WE ROB THE DIAMOND EXCHANGE, OR WE STARVE.
HOW EXACTLY DOES THIS ELEPHANT GUN WORK, AGAIN?
I THINK THE INVENTOR PUT SOME VIDEO ONLINE. LEMME SEE.
FISSION BULLETS
YEAH. HERE. WAIT. SLO-MO. WATCH.
OH, THAT IS SO COOL.
FISSION BULLETS
RIGHT?
MAX FIELD-TESTED THIS THING FOR DR. CRIME. MAX'LL FIELD-TEST ANYONE'S EXPERIMENTAL WEAPONS FOR A CUT OF THE TAKE.
AND THE WEAPON.
HEY, JAILBAIT, WE ALMOST THERE?

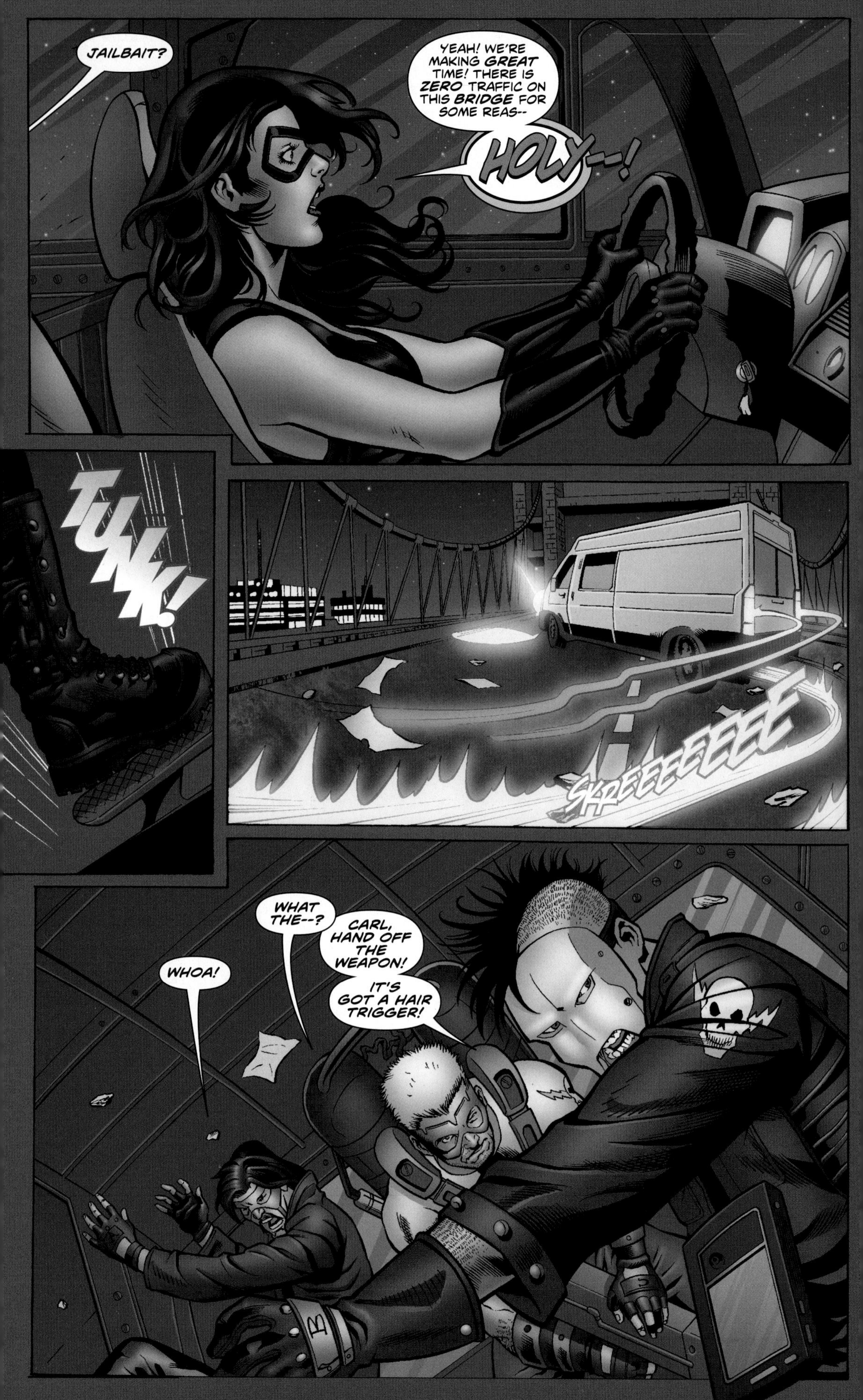
JAILBAIT?
YEAH! WE'RE MAKING GREAT TIME! THERE IS ZERO TRAFFIC ON THIS BRIDGE FOR SOME REAS--
HOLY--!
TUNK!
SKREEEEEEEEE
WHOA!
WHAT THE--?
CARL, HAND OFF THE WEAPON!
IT'S GOT A HAIR TRIGGER!

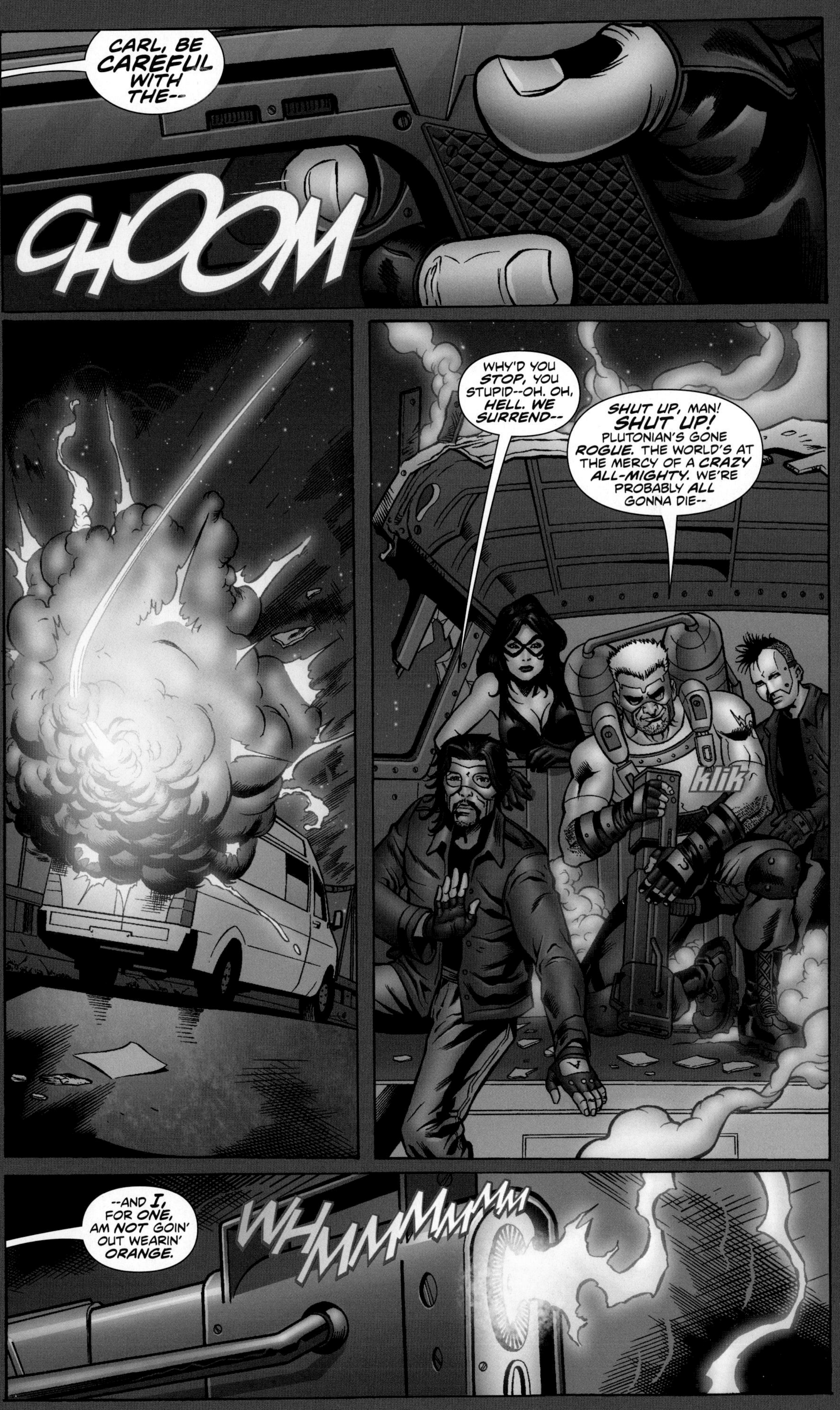
CARL, BE CAREFUL WITH THE--
CHOOM
WHY'D YOU STOP, YOU STUPID--OH. OH, HELL. WE SURREND--
SHUT UP, MAN! SHUT UP! PLUTONIAN'S GONE ROGUE. THE WORLD'S AT THE MERCY OF A CRAZY ALL-MIGHTY. WE'RE PROBABLY ALL GONNA DIE--
KLIK
--AND I, FOR ONE, AM NOT GOIN' OUT WEARIN' ORANGE.
WHMMMMMM

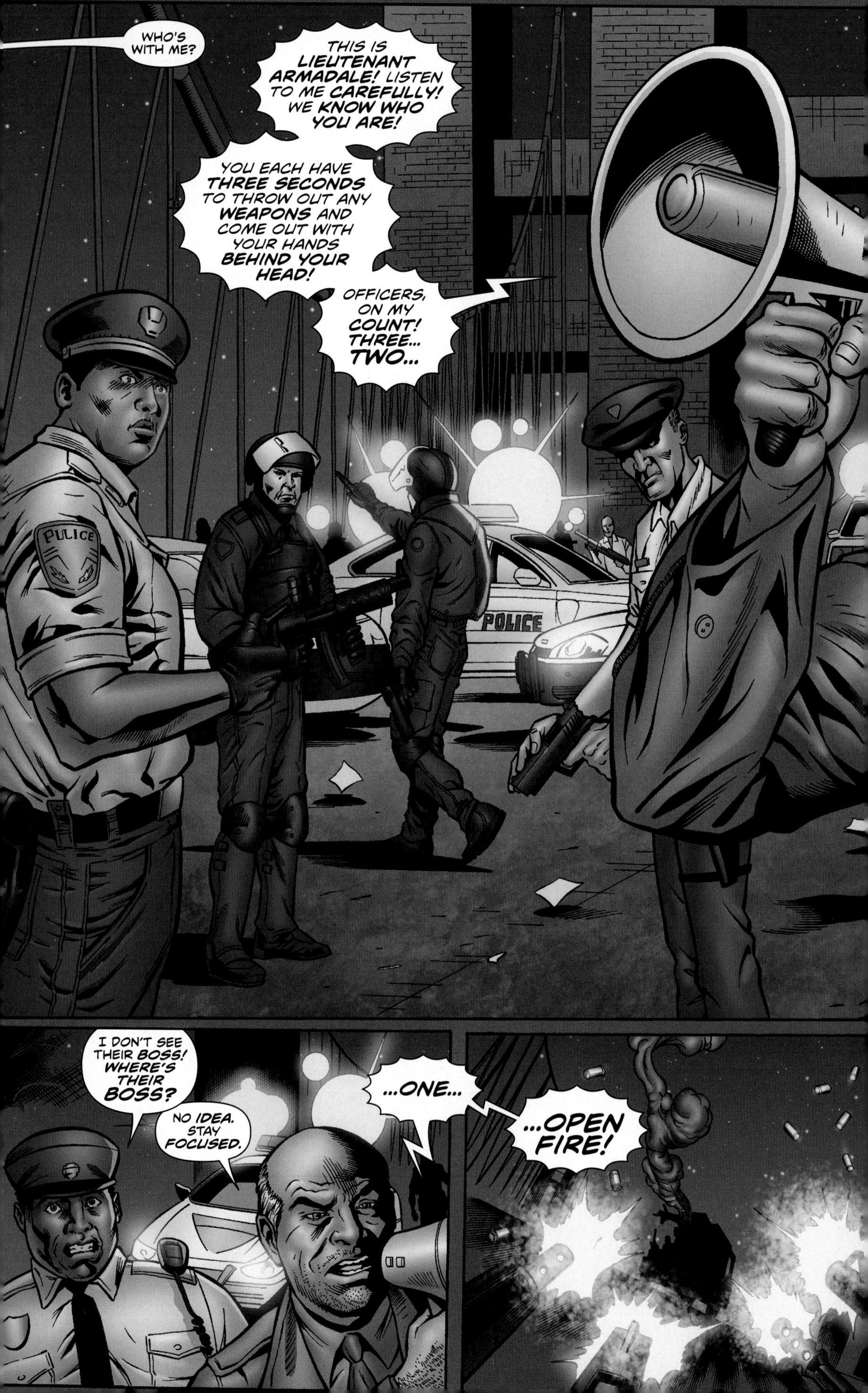
WHO'S WITH ME?
THIS IS LIEUTENANT ARMADALE! LISTEN TO ME CAREFULLY! WE KNOW WHO YOU ARE!
YOU EACH HAVE THREE SECONDS TO THROW OUT ANY WEAPONS AND COME OUT WITH YOUR HANDS BEHIND YOUR HEAD!
OFFICERS, ON MY COUNT! THREE... TWO...
POLICE
POLICE
I DON'T SEE THEIR BOSS! WHERE'S THEIR BOSS?
NO IDEA. STAY FOCUSED.
...ONE...
...OPEN FIRE!

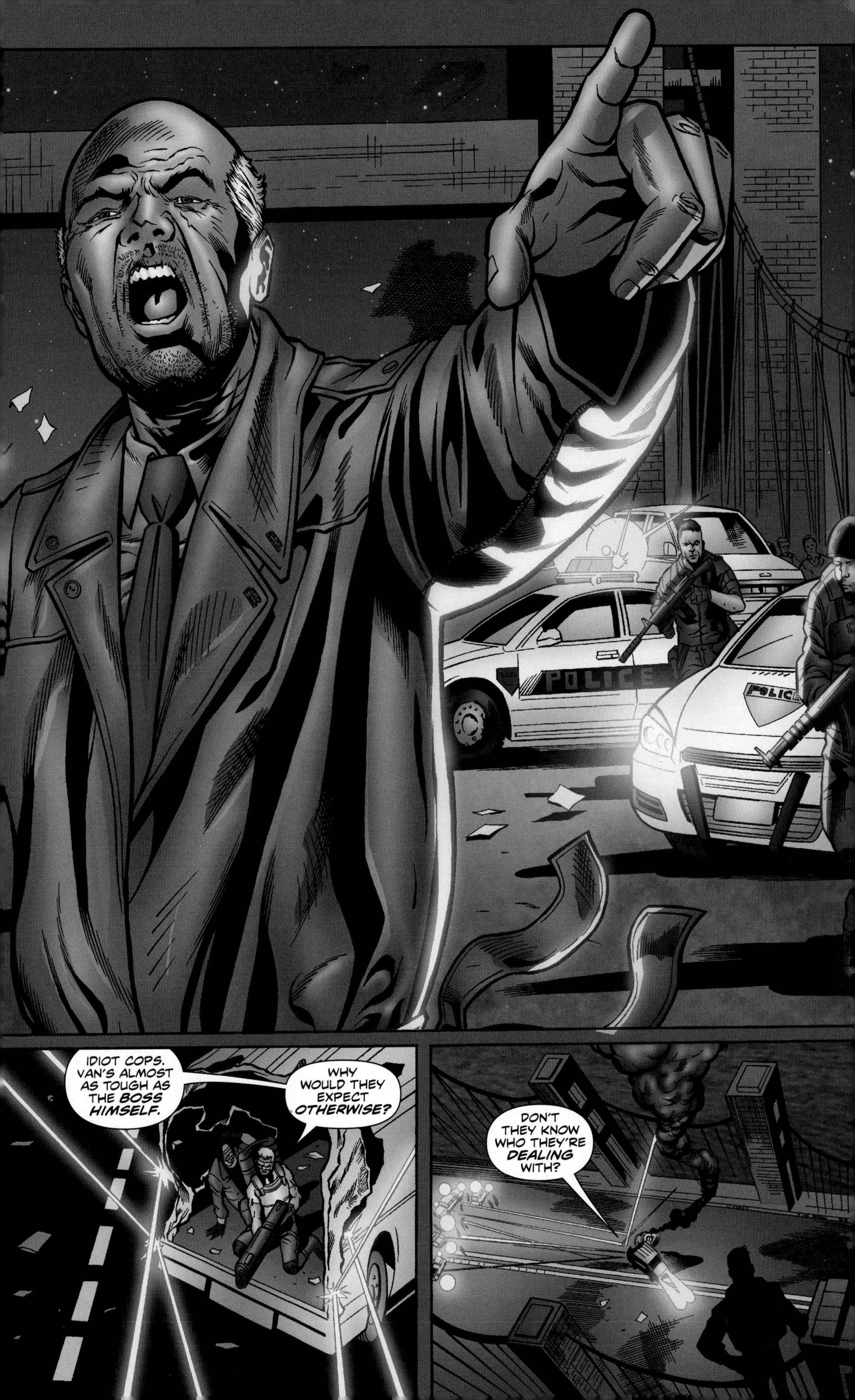
POLICE
POLICE
IDIOT COPS. VAN'S ALMOST AS TOUGH AS THE BOSS HIMSELF.
WHY WOULD THEY EXPECT OTHERWISE?
DON'T THEY KNOW WHO THEY'RE DEALING WITH?

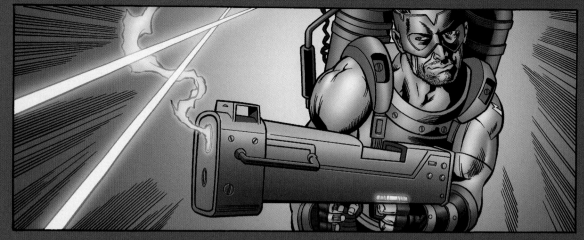

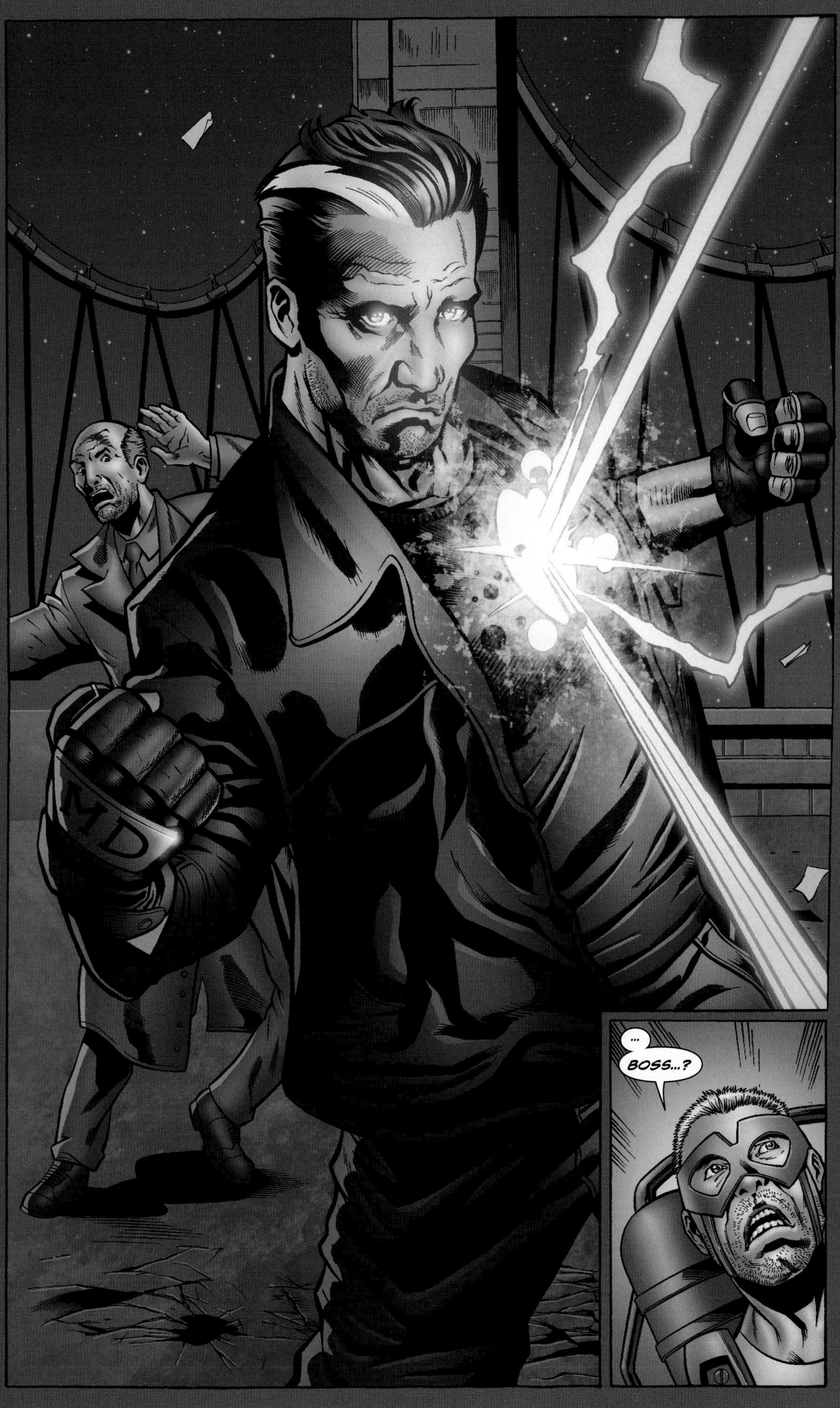
MD
...
BOSS...?

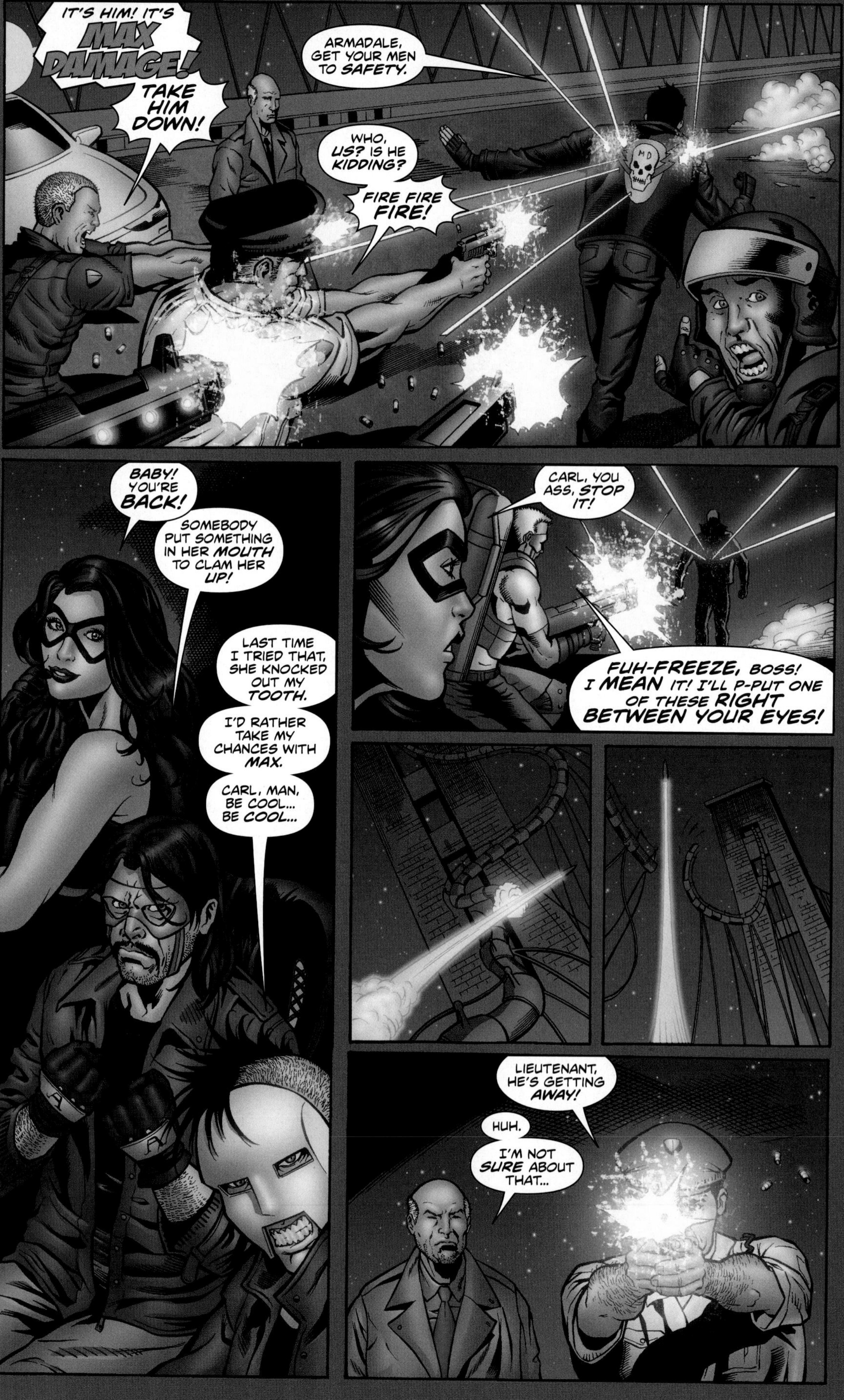
IT'S HIM! IT'S MAX DAMAGE!
TAKE HIM DOWN!
ARMADALE, GET YOUR MEN TO SAFETY.
WHO, US? IS HE KIDDING?
FIRE FIRE FIRE!
BABY! YOU'RE BACK!
SOMEBODY PUT SOMETHING IN HER MOUTH TO CLAM HER UP!
LAST TIME I TRIED THAT, SHE KNOCKED OUT MY TOOTH.
I'D RATHER TAKE MY CHANCES WITH MAX.
CARL, MAN, BE COOL... BE COOL...
CARL, YOU ASS, STOP IT!
FUH-FREEZE, BOSS! I MEAN IT! I'LL P-PUT ONE OF THESE RIGHT BETWEEN YOUR EYES!
LIEUTENANT, HE'S GETTING AWAY!
HUH.
I'M NOT SURE ABOUT THAT...

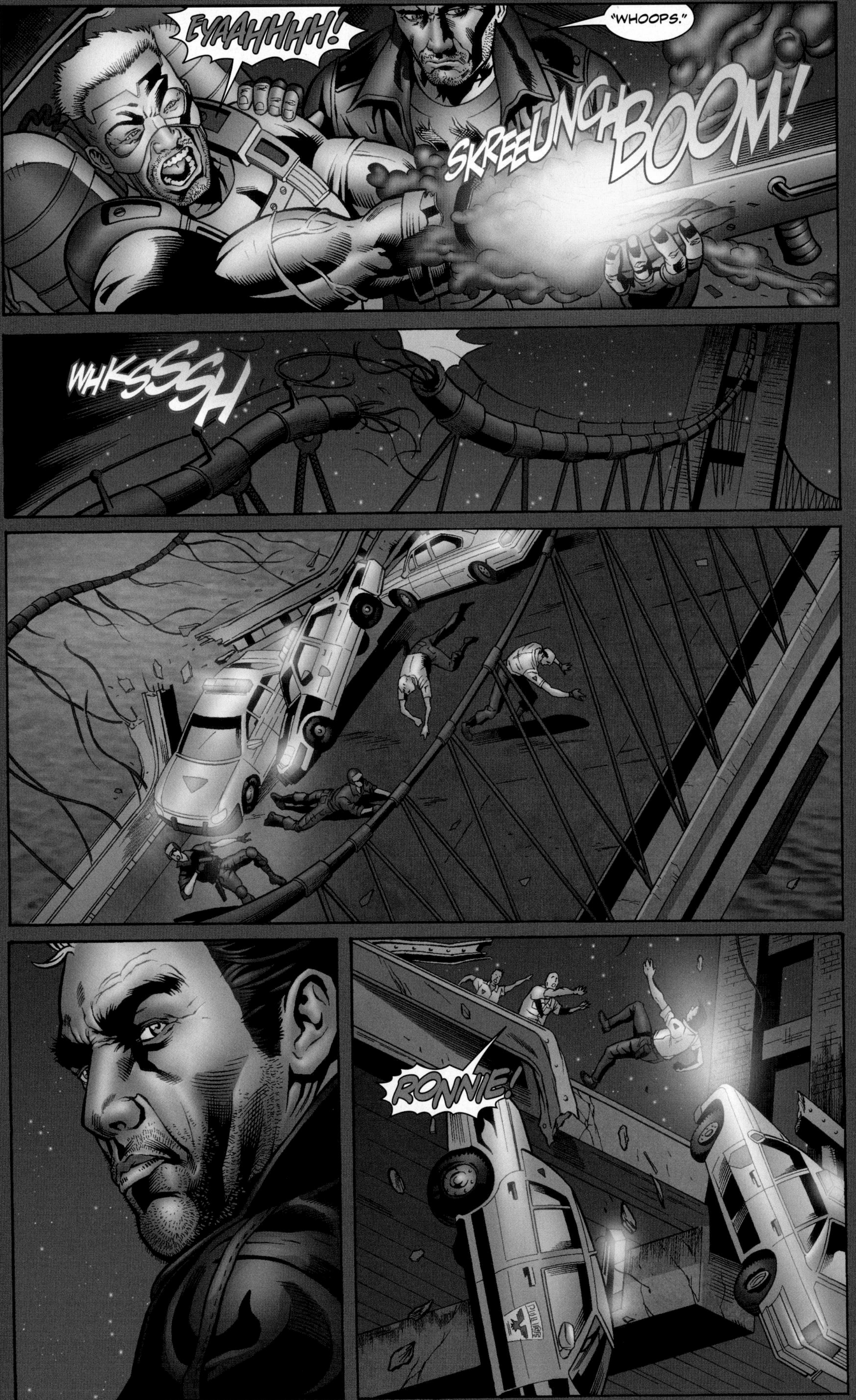
EYAAHHHH!
"WHOOPS."
SKREEUNCH
BOOM!
WHKSSSH
RONNIE!

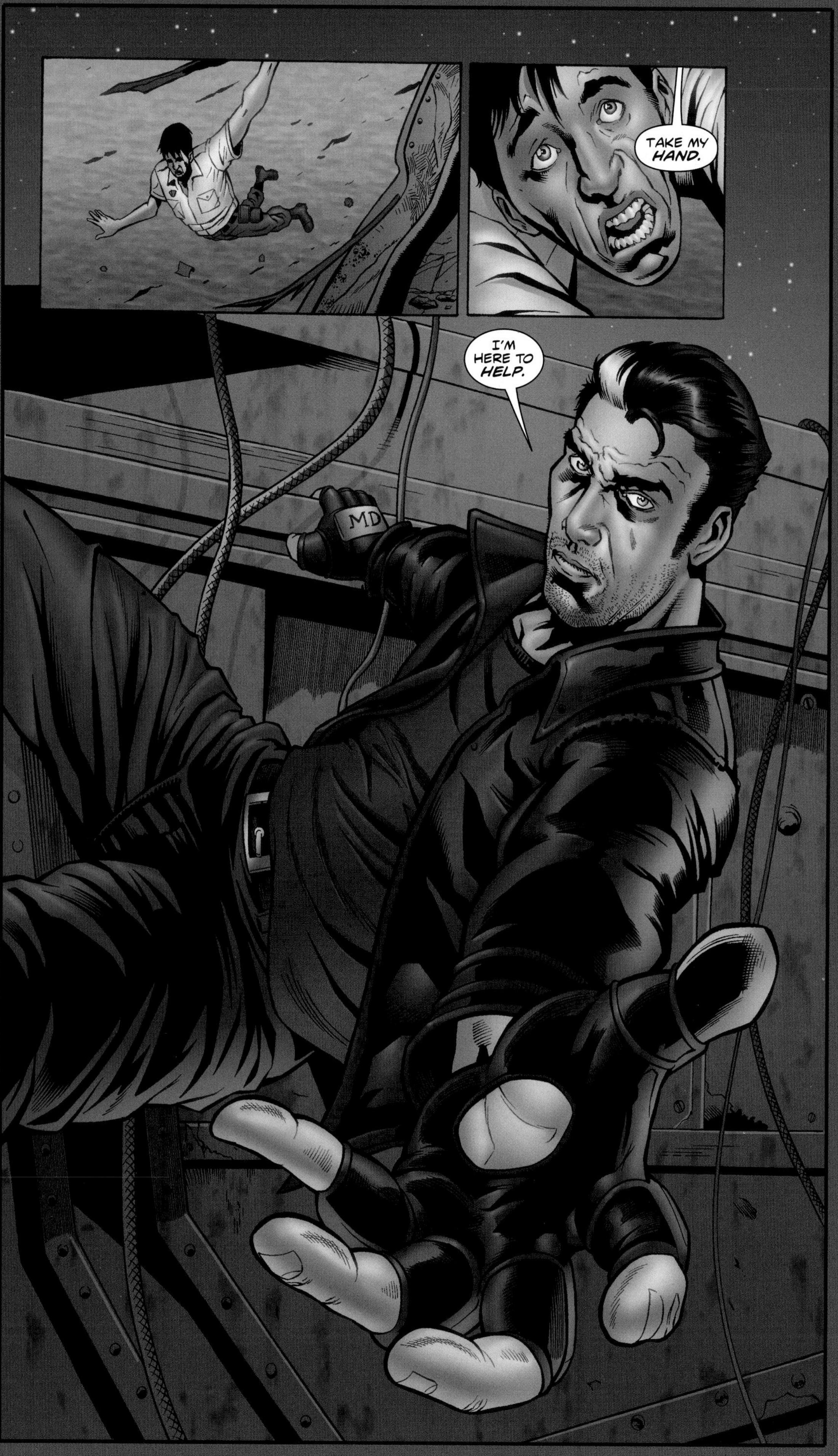
TAKE MY HAND.
I'M HERE TO HELP.

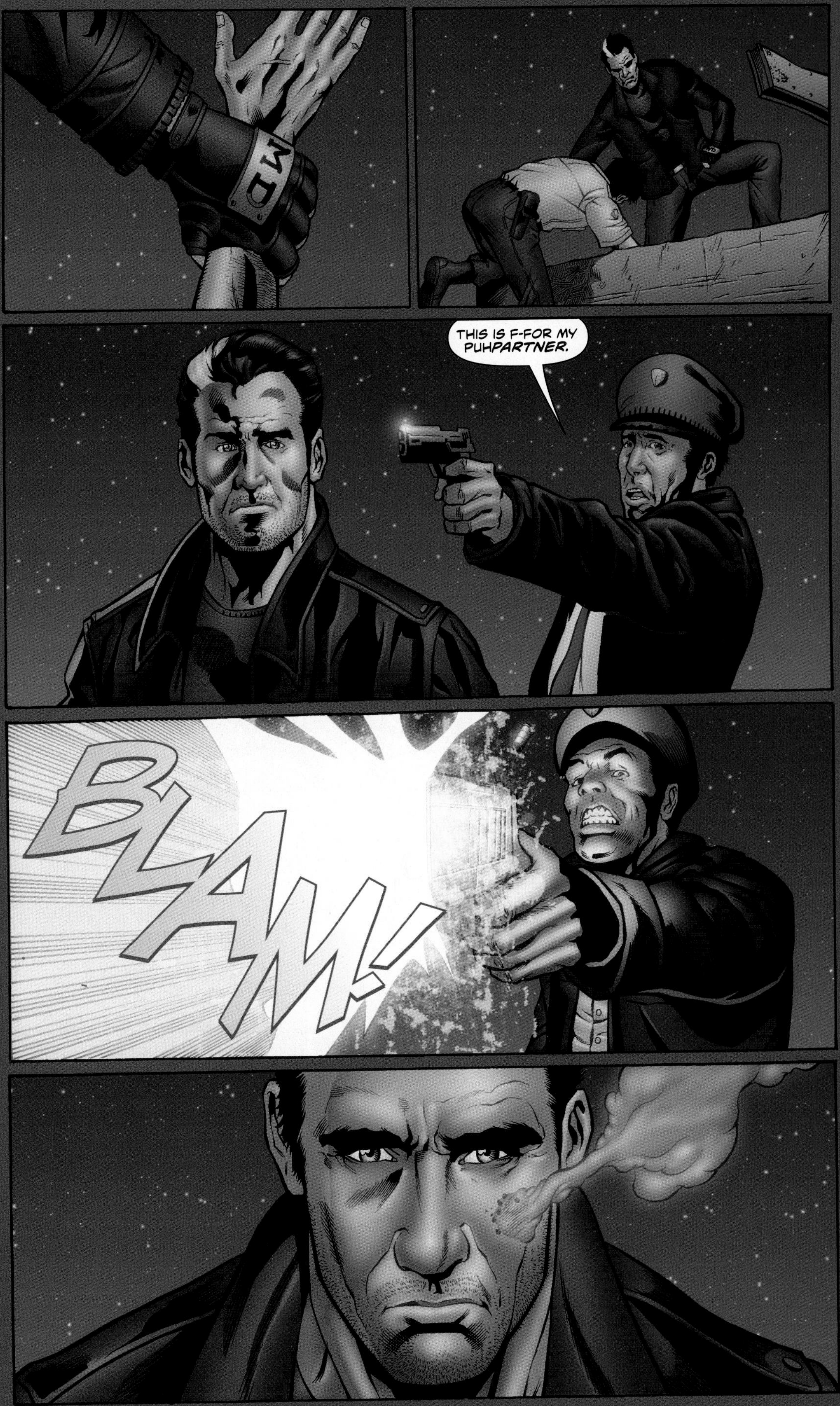
MD
THIS IS F-FOR MY PUHPARTNER.
BLAM!

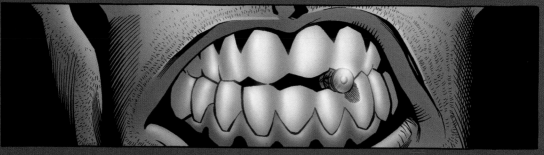

PTUH

YAAAH!

HOLD YOUR FIRE!

BUT, SIR--

YOU'RE JUST WASTING AMMO! LET'S SEE WHAT HE DOES!

B-BOSS...WE'RE SORRY...IT WAS ALL CARL'S IDEA! HE'S THE BRAINS BEHIND THIS!

BOB, CARL HAD TO BURN HIS SCHOOL DOWN TO GET OUT OF FOURTH GRADE.

WHERE'S JAILBAIT?

I--I DUNNO! SHE MUSTA SPLIT!

MAX, WE SHOULDA BEEN PATIENT, OKAY? BUT WE DIDN'T KNOW IF YOU WERE ALIVE OR DEAD OR--

MAX, YOU GOTTA SAVE US! BOSS, SAY SOMETHIN'!

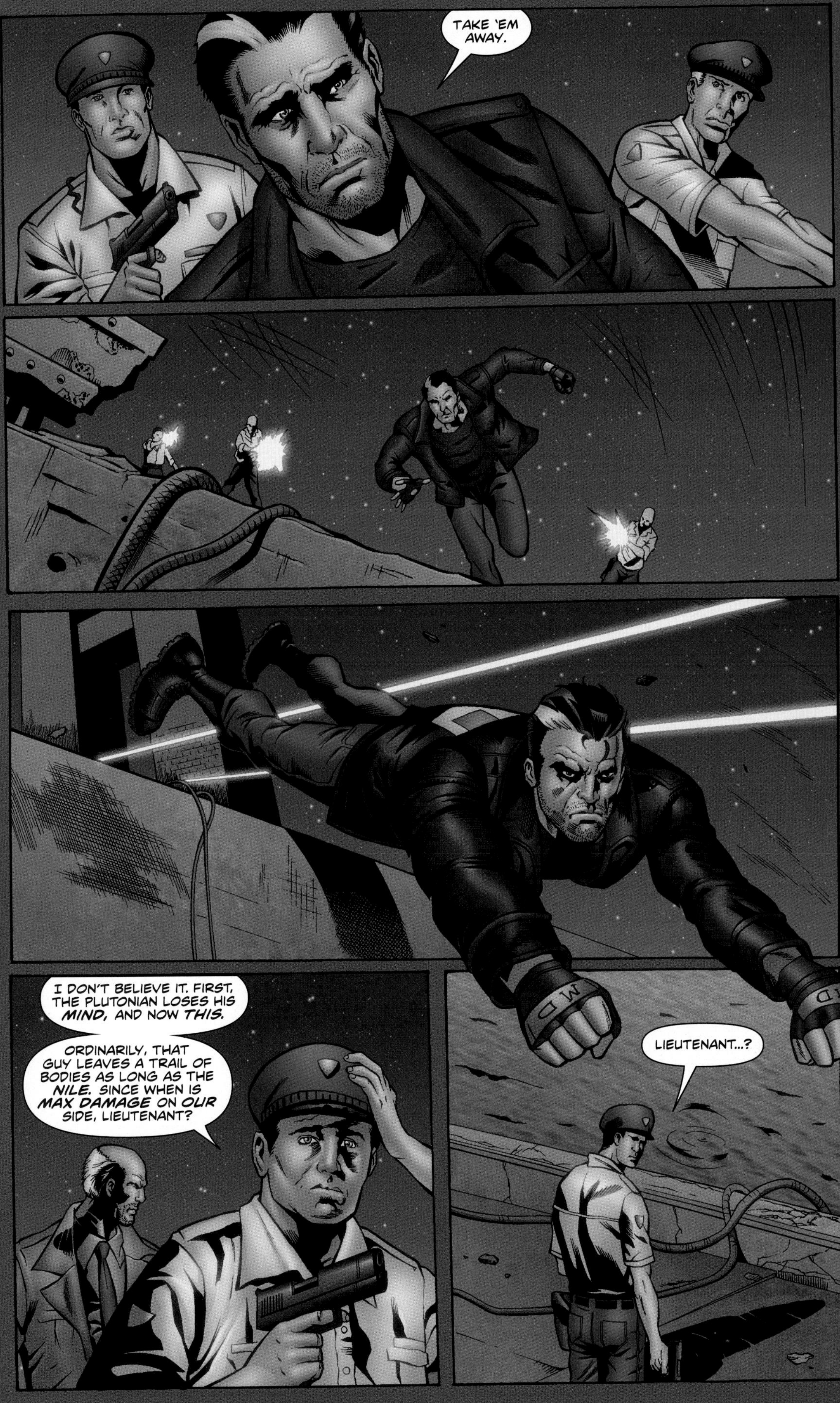
TAKE 'EM AWAY.
I DON'T BELIEVE IT. FIRST, THE PLUTONIAN LOSES HIS *MIND,* AND NOW *THIS.*
ORDINARILY, THAT GUY LEAVES A TRAIL OF BODIES AS LONG AS THE *NILE.* SINCE WHEN IS *MAX DAMAGE* ON *OUR* SIDE, LIEUTENANT?
LIEUTENANT...?

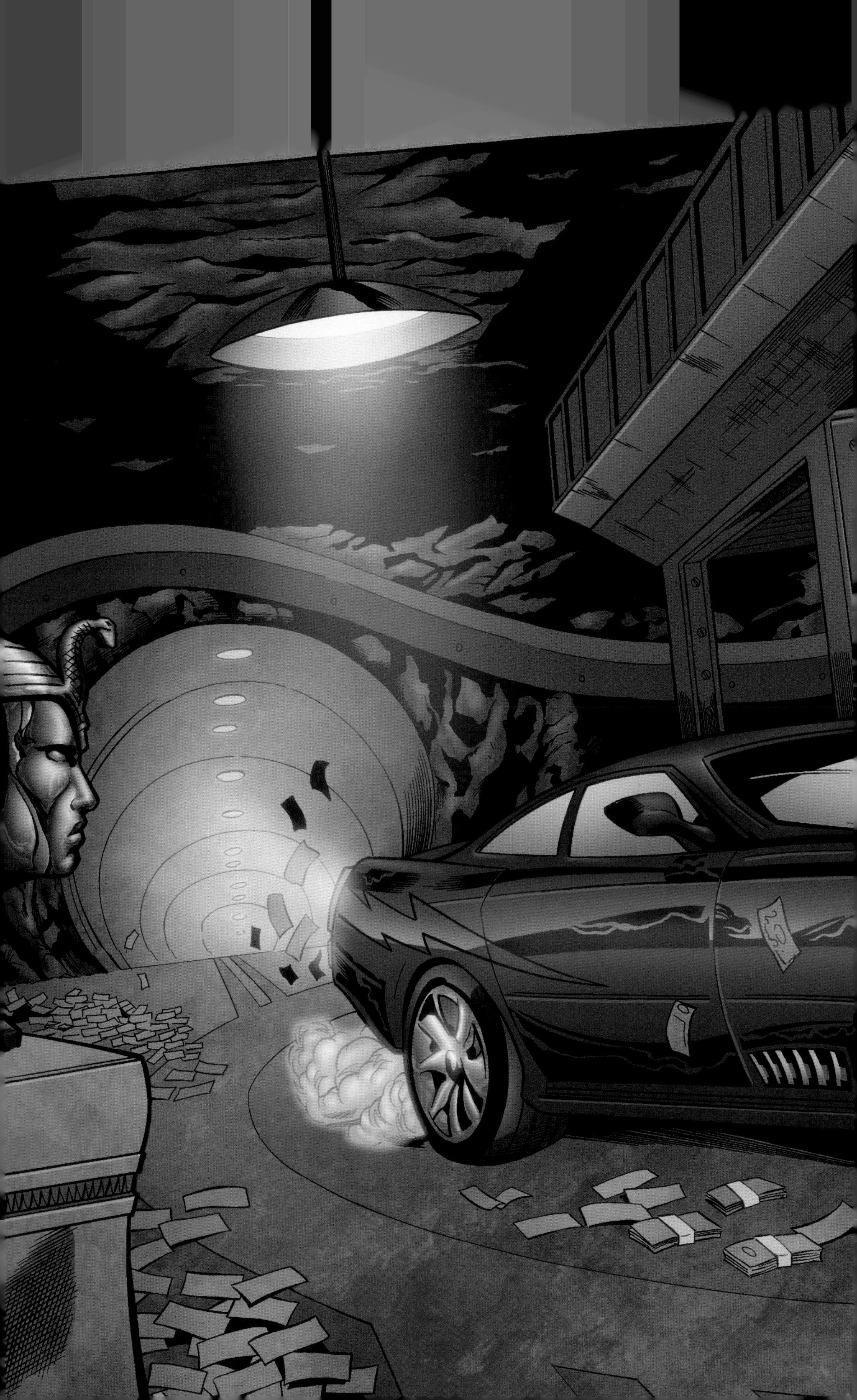

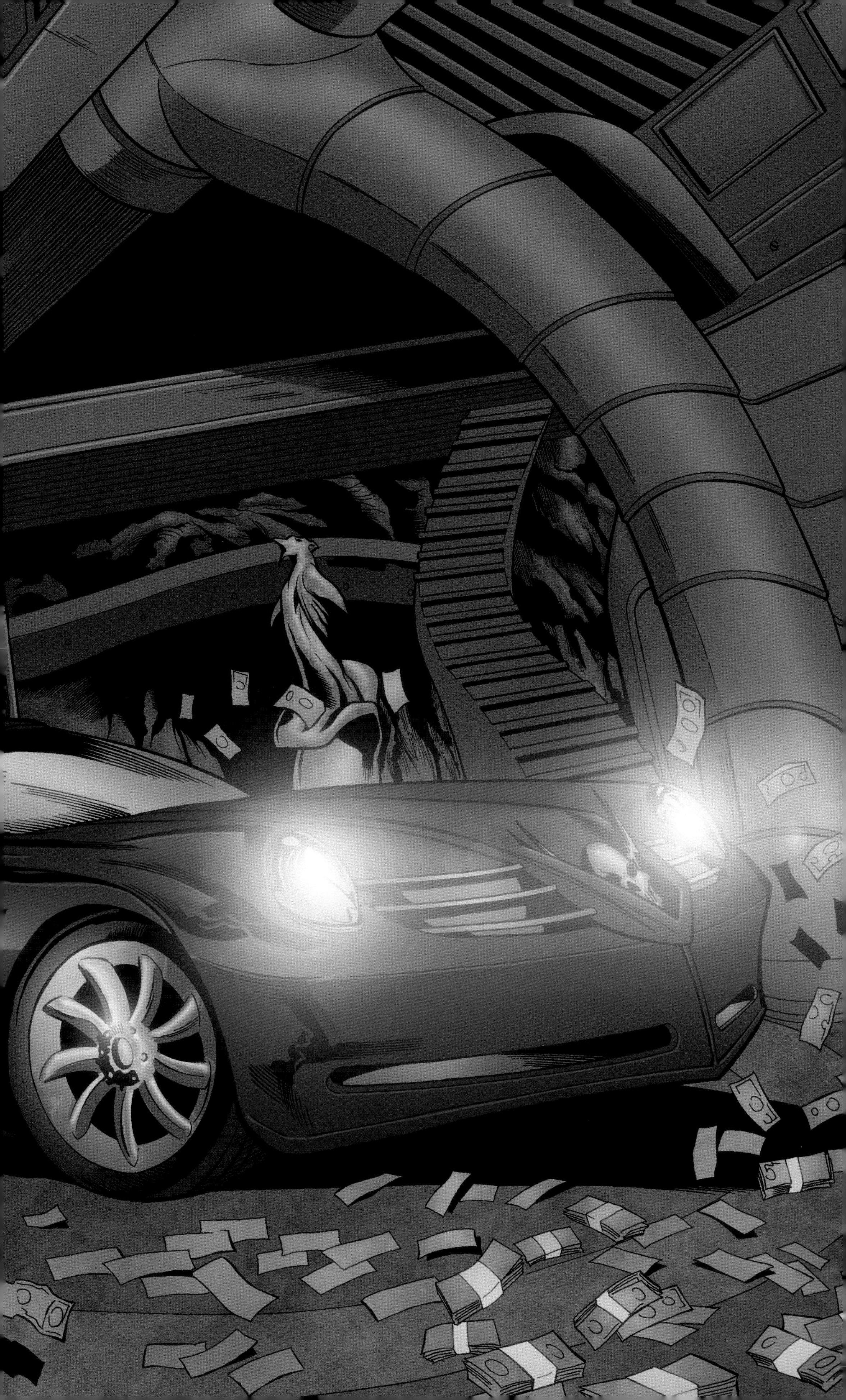

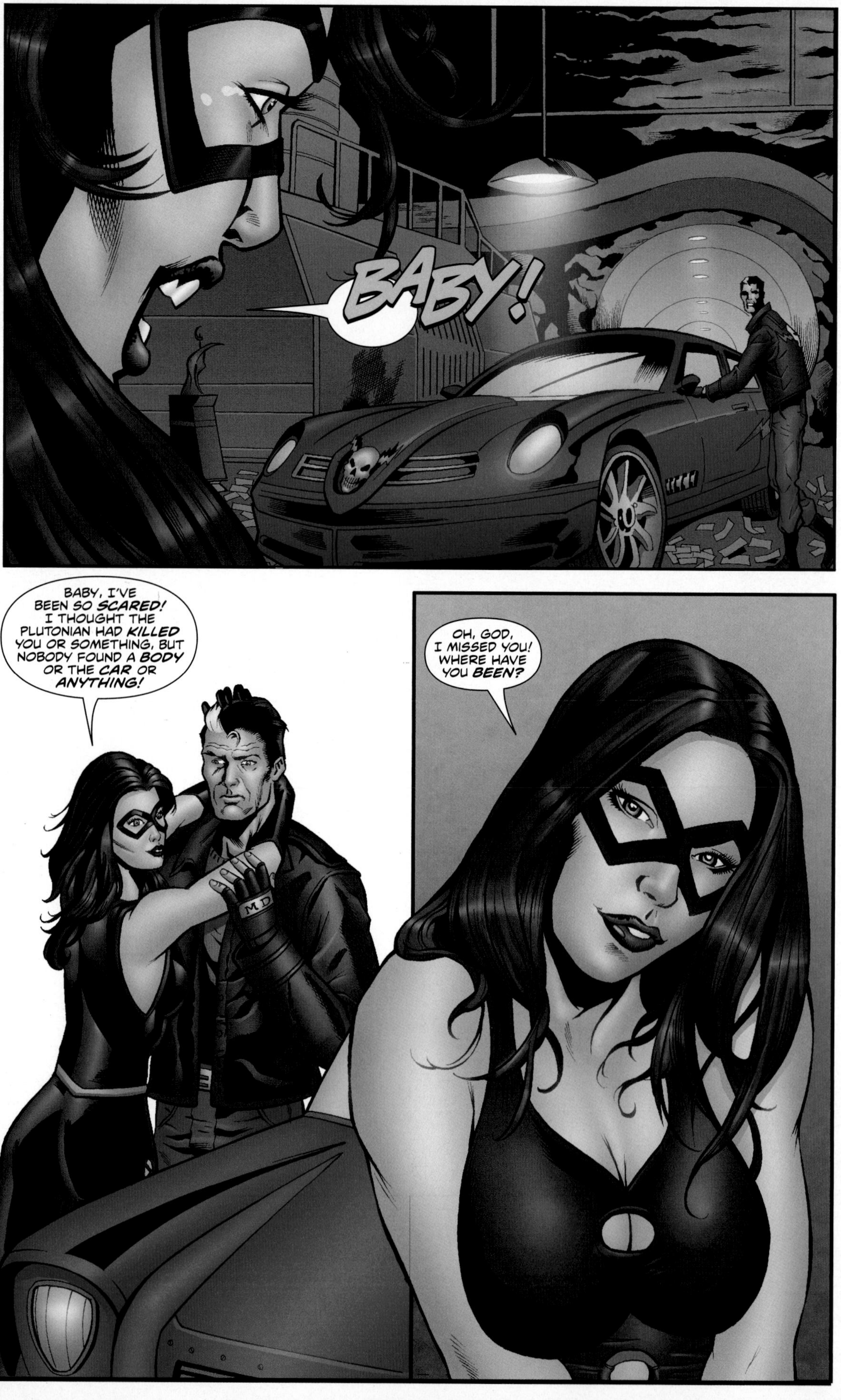
BABY!
BABY, I'VE BEEN SO SCARED! I THOUGHT THE PLUTONIAN HAD KILLED YOU OR SOMETHING, BUT NOBODY FOUND A BODY OR THE CAR OR ANYTHING!
OH, GOD, I MISSED YOU! WHERE HAVE YOU BEEN?
MD

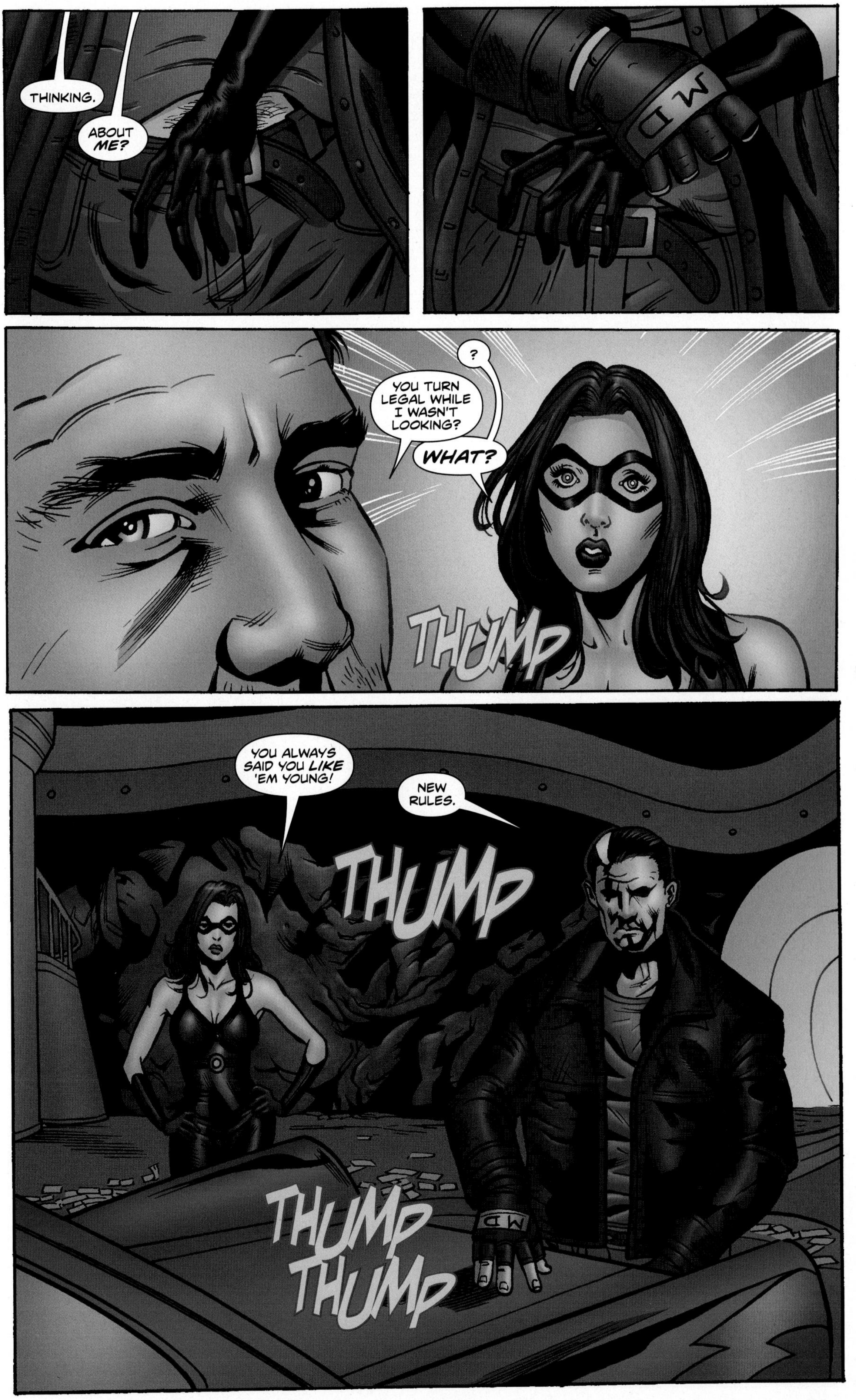
THINKING.
ABOUT *ME?*
?
YOU TURN LEGAL WHILE I WASN'T LOOKING?
WHAT?
THUMP
YOU ALWAYS SAID YOU *LIKE* 'EM YOUNG!
NEW RULES.
THUMP
THUMP THUMP

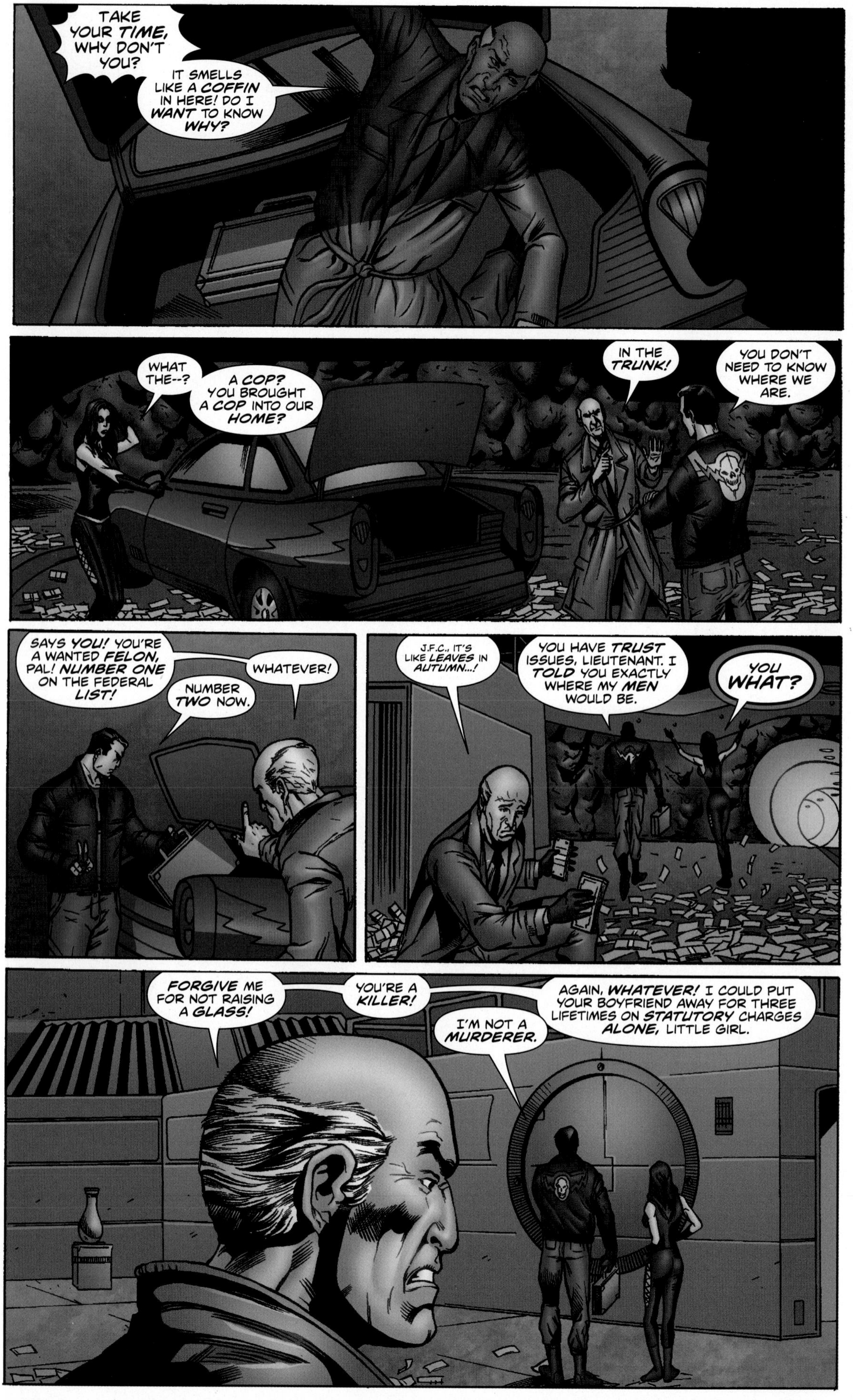
TAKE YOUR TIME, WHY DON'T YOU?
IT SMELLS LIKE A COFFIN IN HERE! DO I WANT TO KNOW WHY?
WHAT THE--?
A COP? YOU BROUGHT A COP INTO OUR HOME?
IN THE TRUNK!
YOU DON'T NEED TO KNOW WHERE WE ARE.
SAYS YOU! YOU'RE A WANTED FELON, PAL! NUMBER ONE ON THE FEDERAL LIST!
WHATEVER!
NUMBER TWO NOW.
J.F.C., IT'S LIKE LEAVES IN AUTUMN...!
YOU HAVE TRUST ISSUES, LIEUTENANT. I TOLD YOU EXACTLY WHERE MY MEN WOULD BE.
YOU WHAT?
FORGIVE ME FOR NOT RAISING A GLASS!
YOU'RE A KILLER!
AGAIN, WHATEVER! I COULD PUT YOUR BOYFRIEND AWAY FOR THREE LIFETIMES ON STATUTORY CHARGES ALONE, LITTLE GIRL.
I'M NOT A MURDERER.

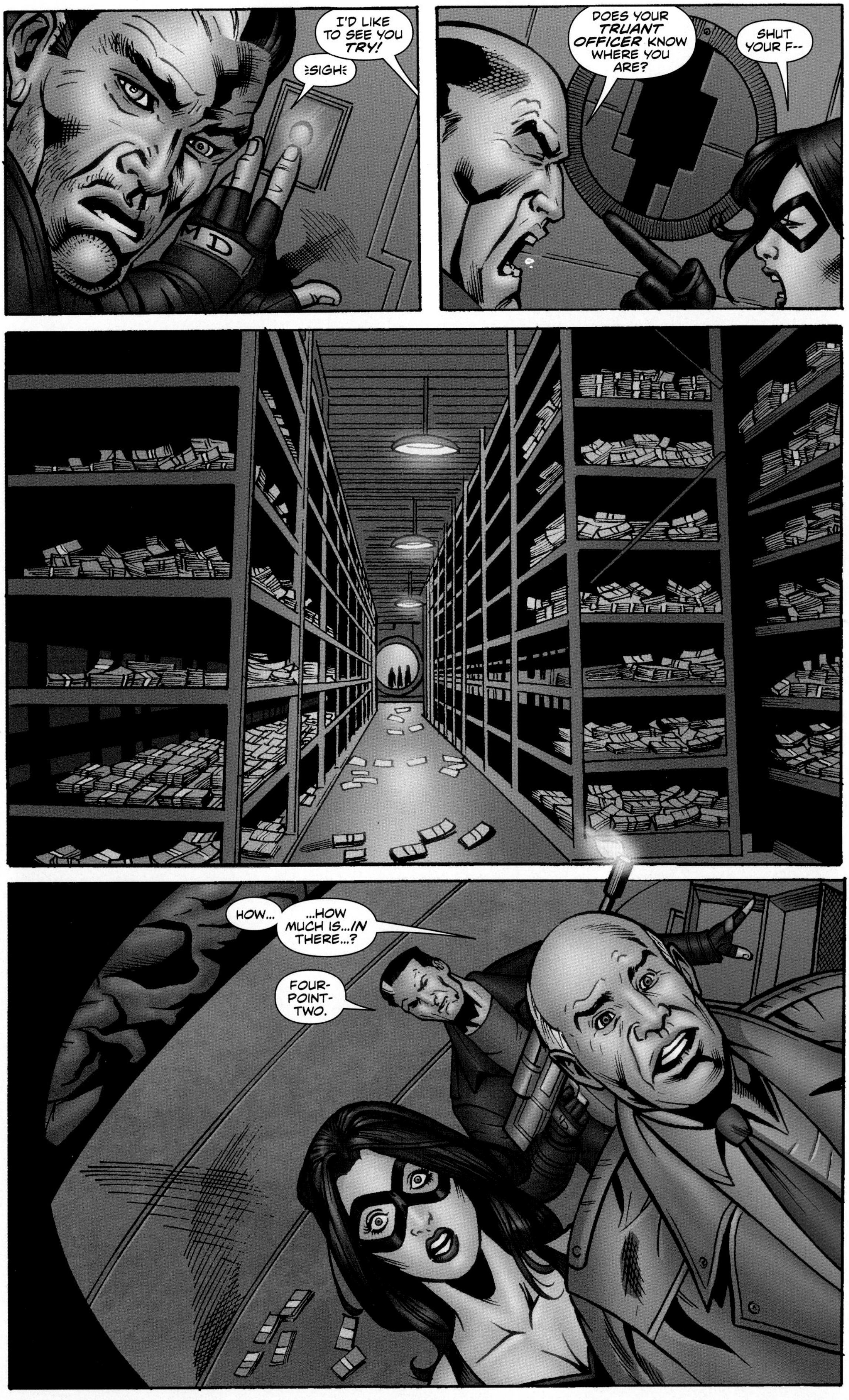
I'D LIKE TO SEE YOU TRY!
SIGH
DOES YOUR TRUANT OFFICER KNOW WHERE YOU ARE?
SHUT YOUR F--
HOW...
...HOW MUCH IS...IN THERE...?
FOUR-POINT-TWO.

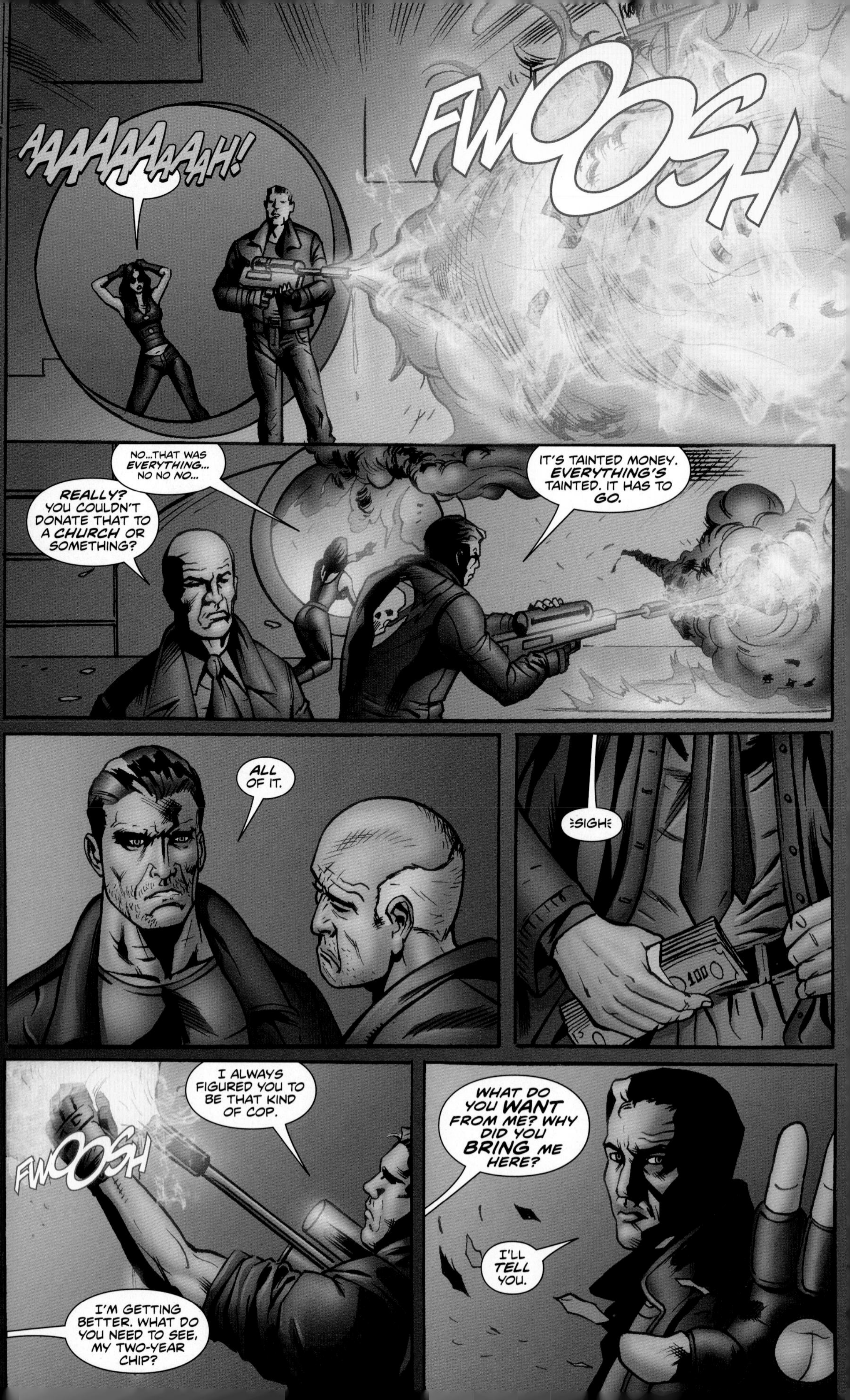
AAAAAAAAAH!
FWOOSH
NO...THAT WAS EVERYTHING... NO NO NO...
REALLY? YOU COULDN'T DONATE THAT TO A CHURCH OR SOMETHING?
IT'S TAINTED MONEY. EVERYTHING'S TAINTED. IT HAS TO GO.
ALL OF IT.
SIGH
I ALWAYS FIGURED YOU TO BE THAT KIND OF COP.
FWOOSH
I'M GETTING BETTER. WHAT DO YOU NEED TO SEE, MY TWO-YEAR CHIP?
WHAT DO YOU WANT FROM ME? WHY DID YOU BRING ME HERE?
I'LL TELL YOU.

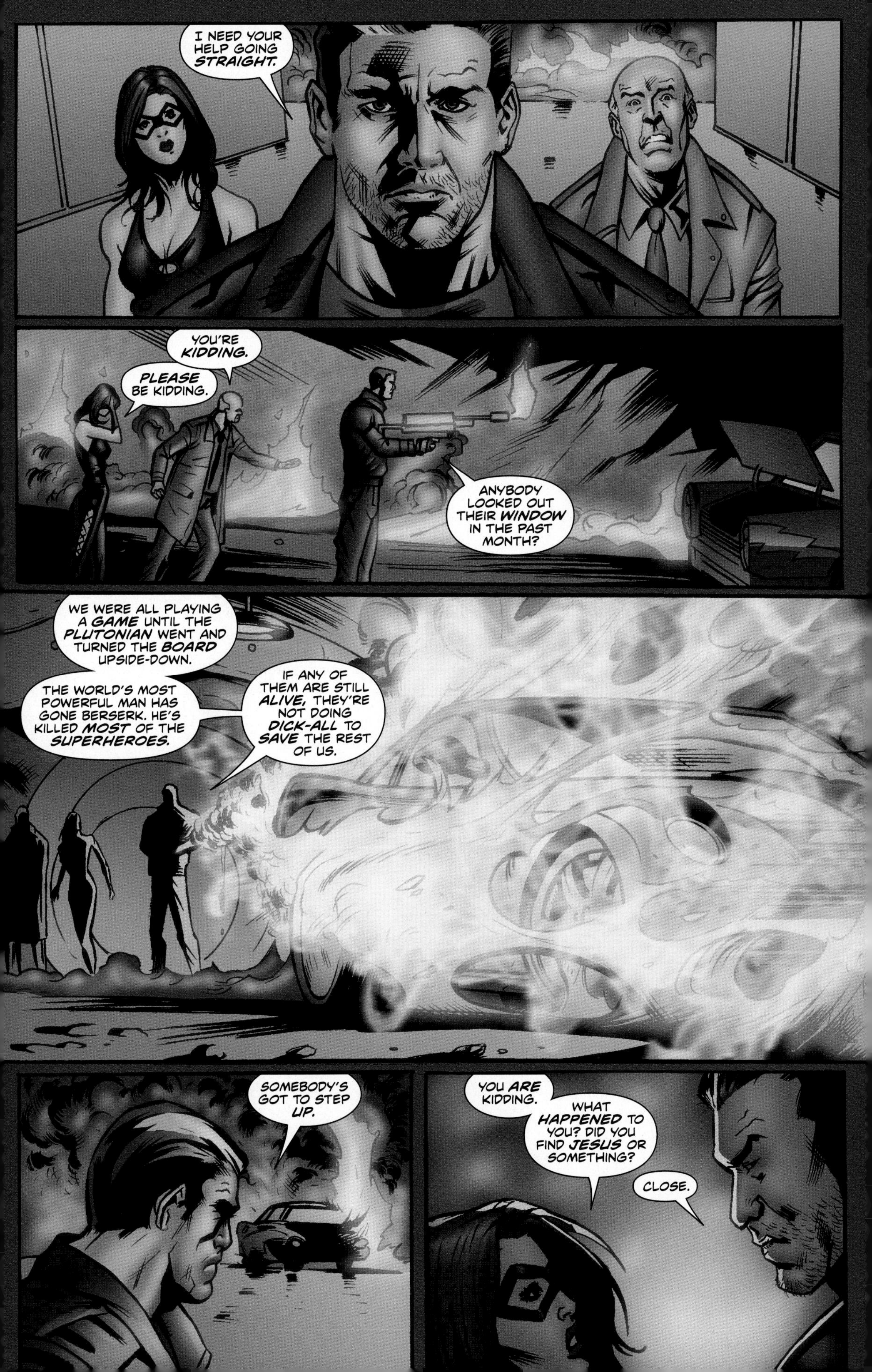
I NEED YOUR HELP GOING STRAIGHT.
YOU'RE KIDDING.
PLEASE BE KIDDING.
ANYBODY LOOKED OUT THEIR WINDOW IN THE PAST MONTH?
WE WERE ALL PLAYING A GAME UNTIL THE PLUTONIAN WENT AND TURNED THE BOARD UPSIDE-DOWN.
THE WORLD'S MOST POWERFUL MAN HAS GONE BERSERK. HE'S KILLED MOST OF THE SUPERHEROES.
IF ANY OF THEM ARE STILL ALIVE, THEY'RE NOT DOING DICK-ALL TO SAVE THE REST OF US.
SOMEBODY'S GOT TO STEP UP.
YOU ARE KIDDING.
WHAT HAPPENED TO YOU? DID YOU FIND JESUS OR SOMETHING?
CLOSE.

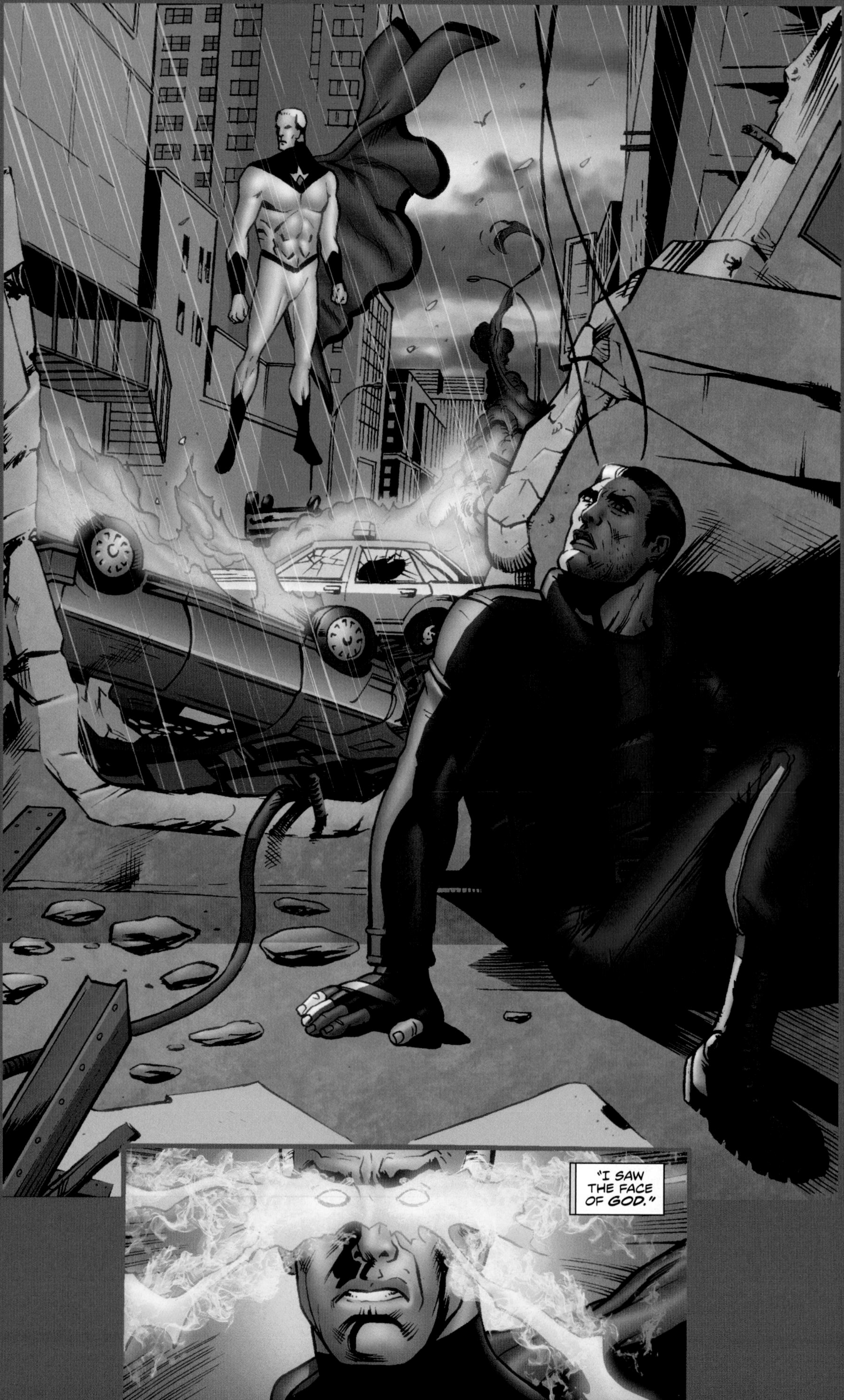
"I SAW THE FACE OF GOD."

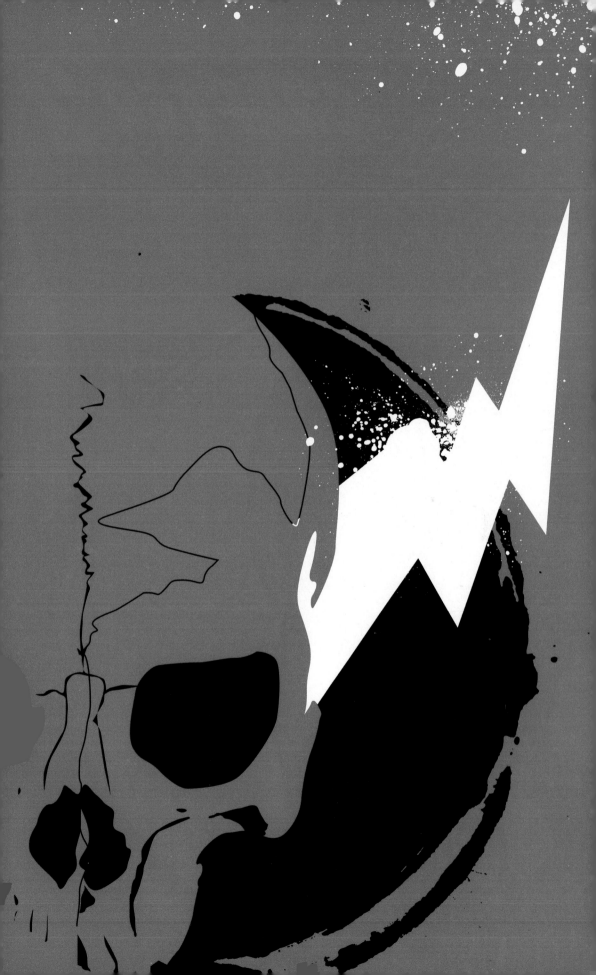

CHAPTER 2

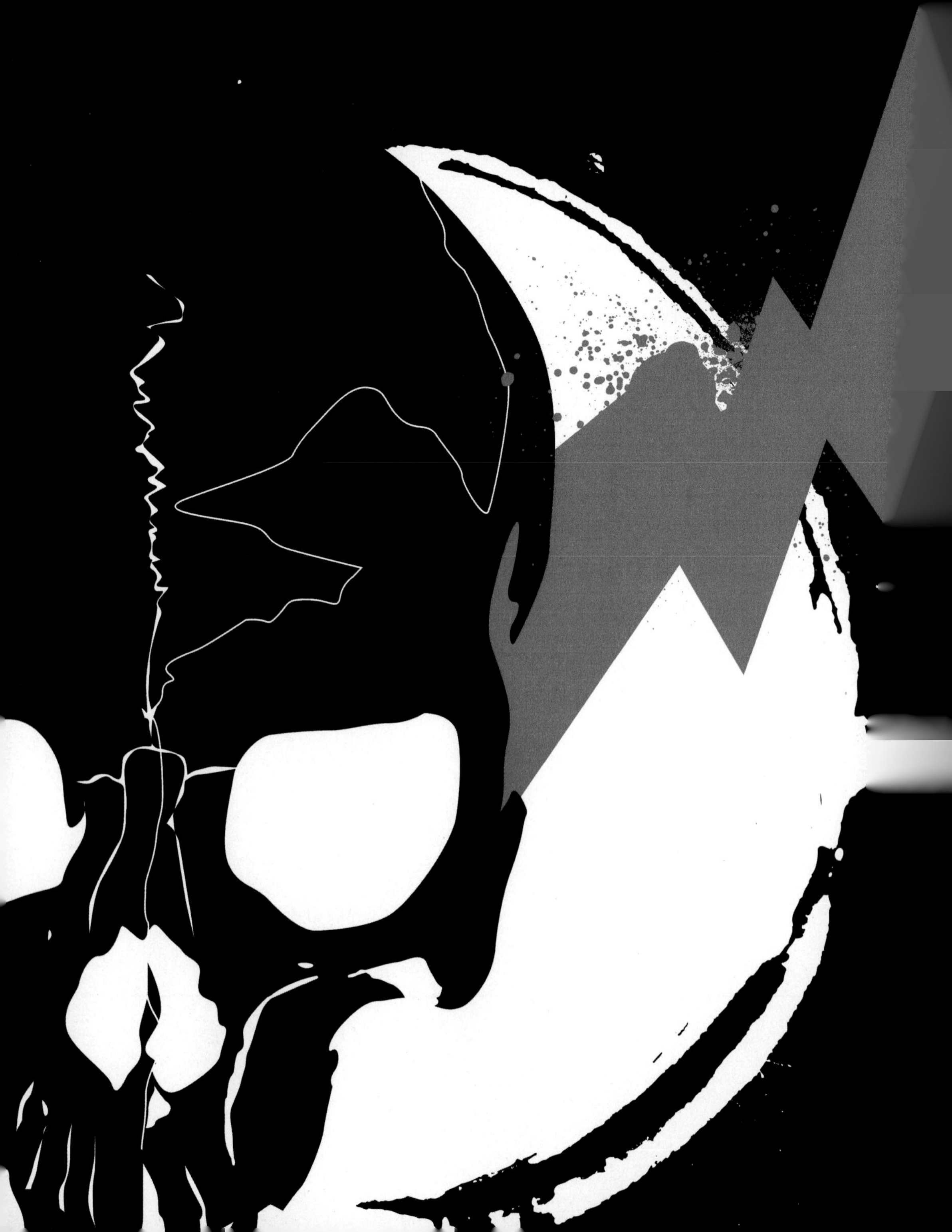

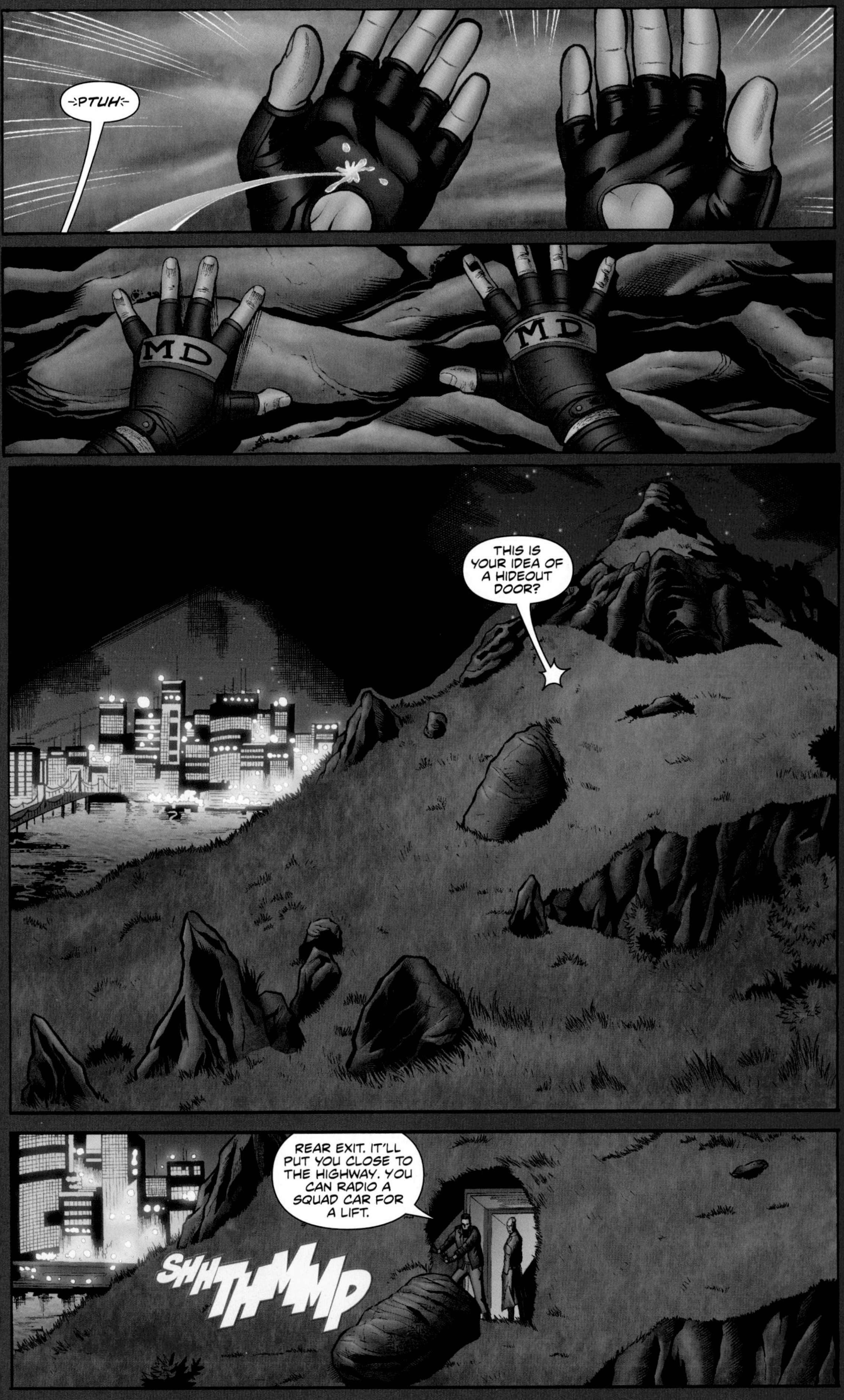
PTUH
MD
MD
THIS IS YOUR IDEA OF A HIDEOUT DOOR?
REAR EXIT. IT'LL PUT YOU CLOSE TO THE HIGHWAY. YOU CAN RADIO A SQUAD CAR FOR A LIFT.
SHHTHMMMP

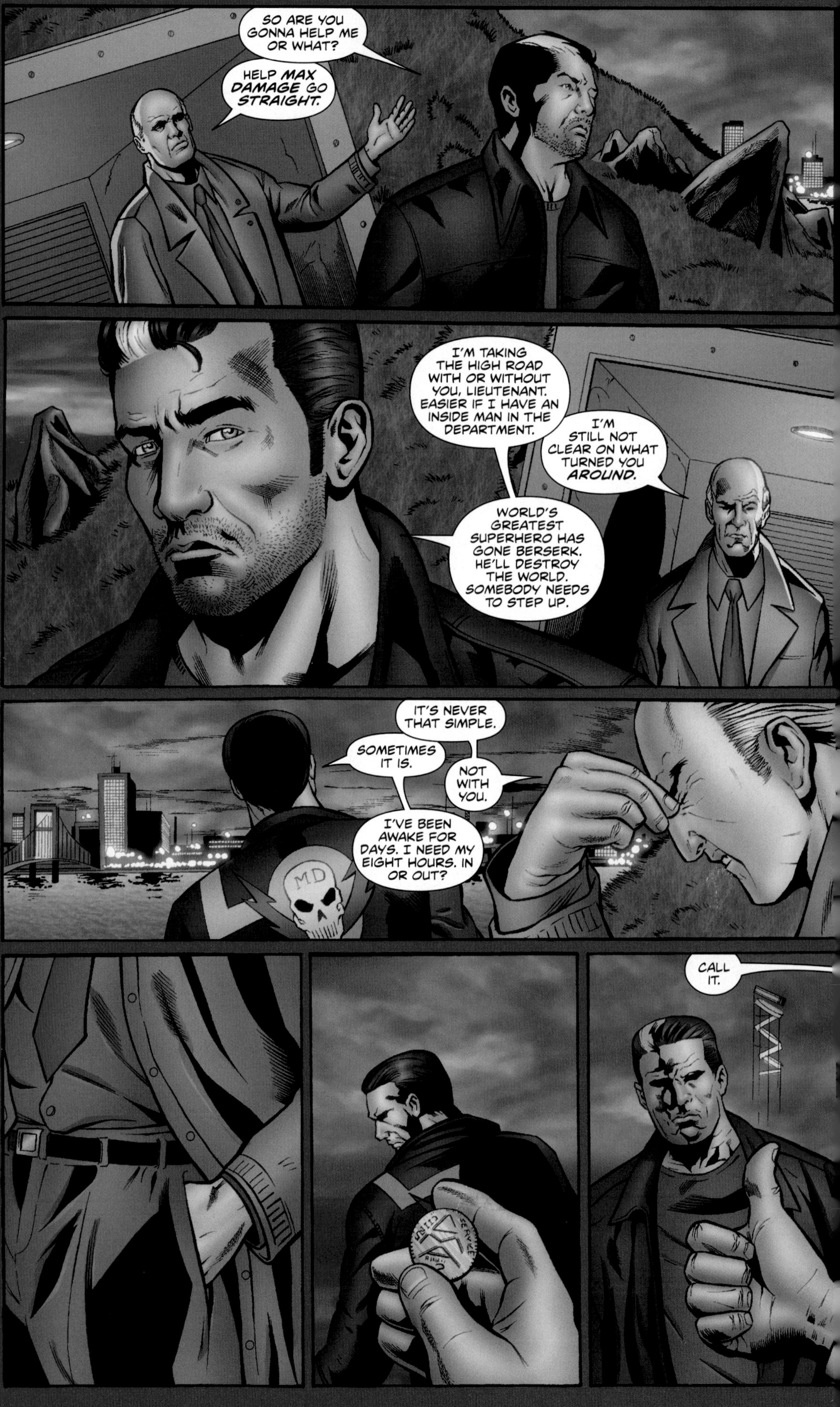
SO ARE YOU GONNA HELP ME OR WHAT?
HELP MAX DAMAGE GO STRAIGHT.
I'M TAKING THE HIGH ROAD WITH OR WITHOUT YOU, LIEUTENANT. EASIER IF I HAVE AN INSIDE MAN IN THE DEPARTMENT.
I'M STILL NOT CLEAR ON WHAT TURNED YOU AROUND.
WORLD'S GREATEST SUPERHERO HAS GONE BERSERK. HE'LL DESTROY THE WORLD. SOMEBODY NEEDS TO STEP UP.
IT'S NEVER THAT SIMPLE.
SOMETIMES IT IS.
NOT WITH YOU.
I'VE BEEN AWAKE FOR DAYS. I NEED MY EIGHT HOURS. IN OR OUT?
MD
CALL IT.

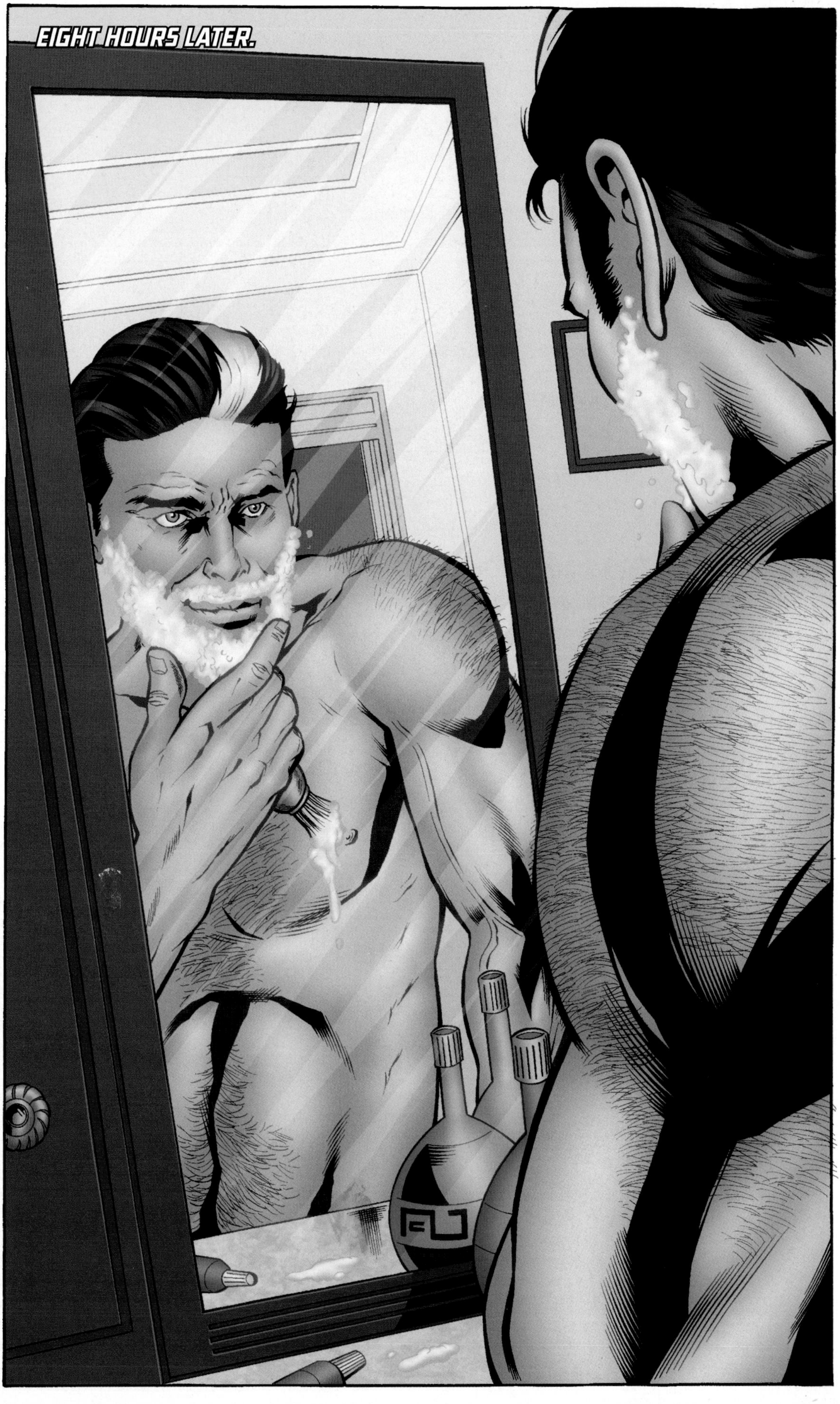
EIGHT HOURS LATER.

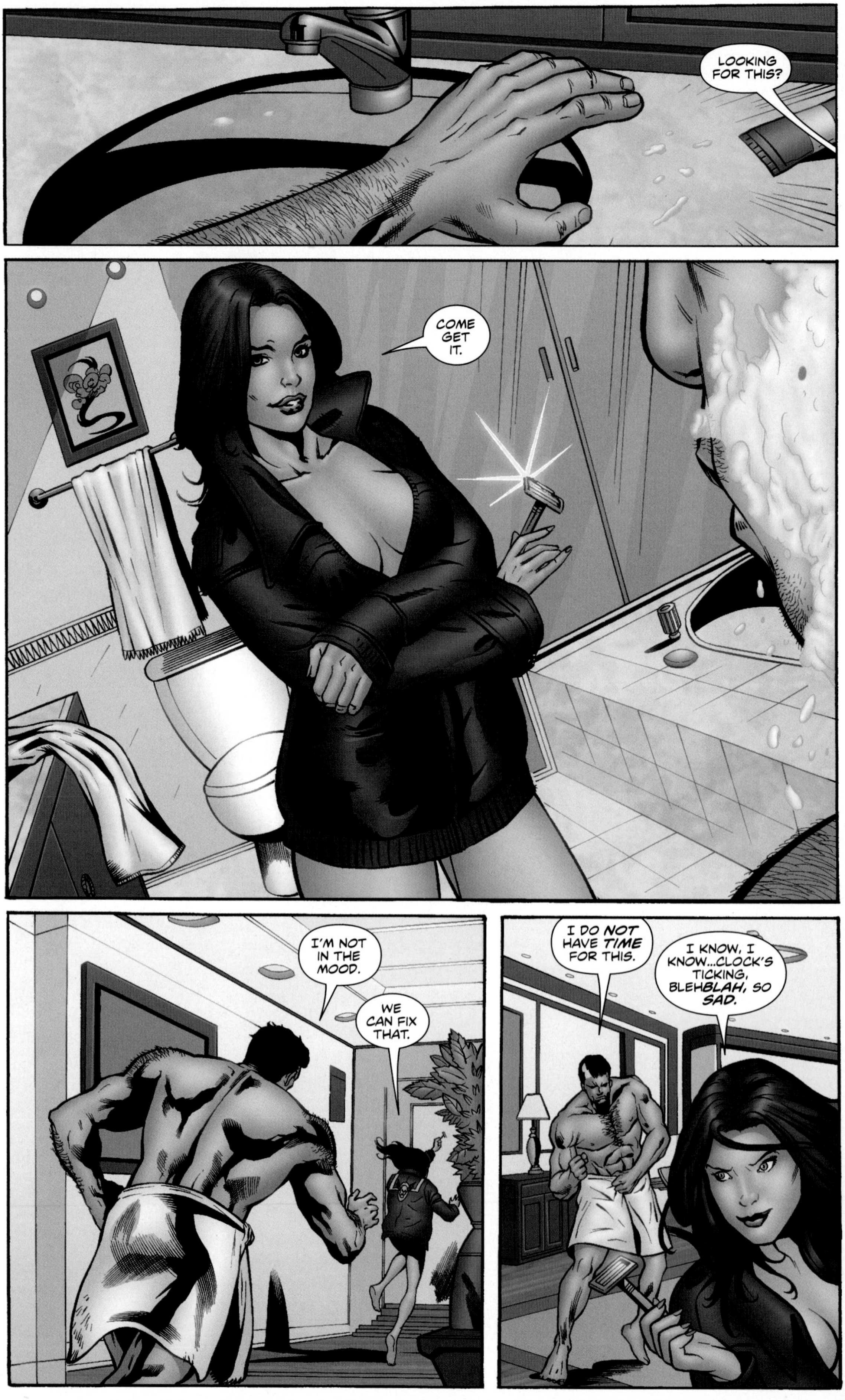
LOOKING FOR THIS?
COME GET IT.
I'M NOT IN THE MOOD.
WE CAN FIX THAT.
I DO NOT HAVE TIME FOR THIS.
I KNOW, I KNOW...CLOCK'S TICKING, BLEHBLAH, SO SAD.

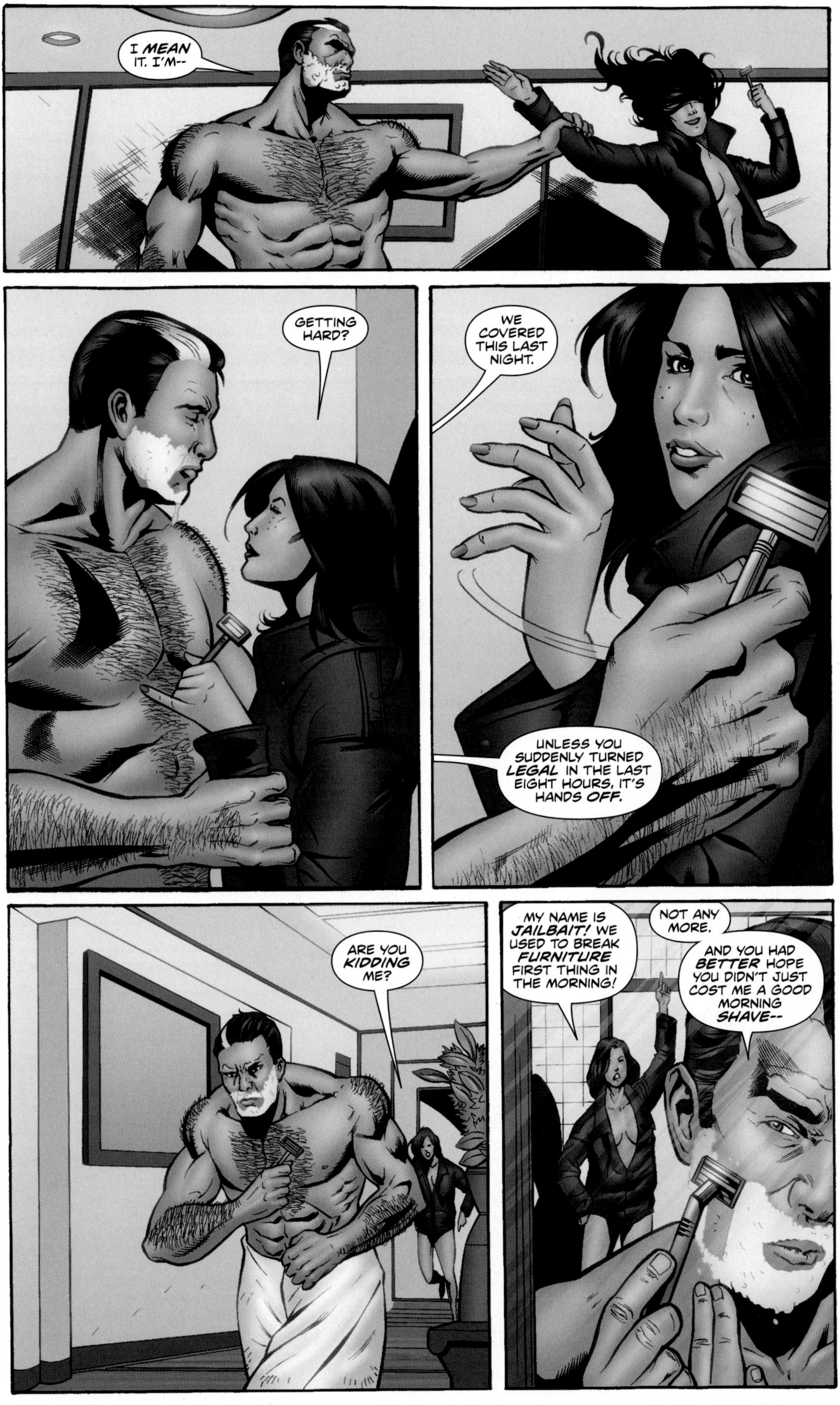
I MEAN IT. I'M--
GETTING HARD?
WE COVERED THIS LAST NIGHT.
UNLESS YOU SUDDENLY TURNED LEGAL IN THE LAST EIGHT HOURS, IT'S HANDS OFF.
ARE YOU KIDDING ME?
MY NAME IS JAILBAIT! WE USED TO BREAK FURNITURE FIRST THING IN THE MORNING!
NOT ANY MORE.
AND YOU HAD BETTER HOPE YOU DIDN'T JUST COST ME A GOOD MORNING SHAVE--

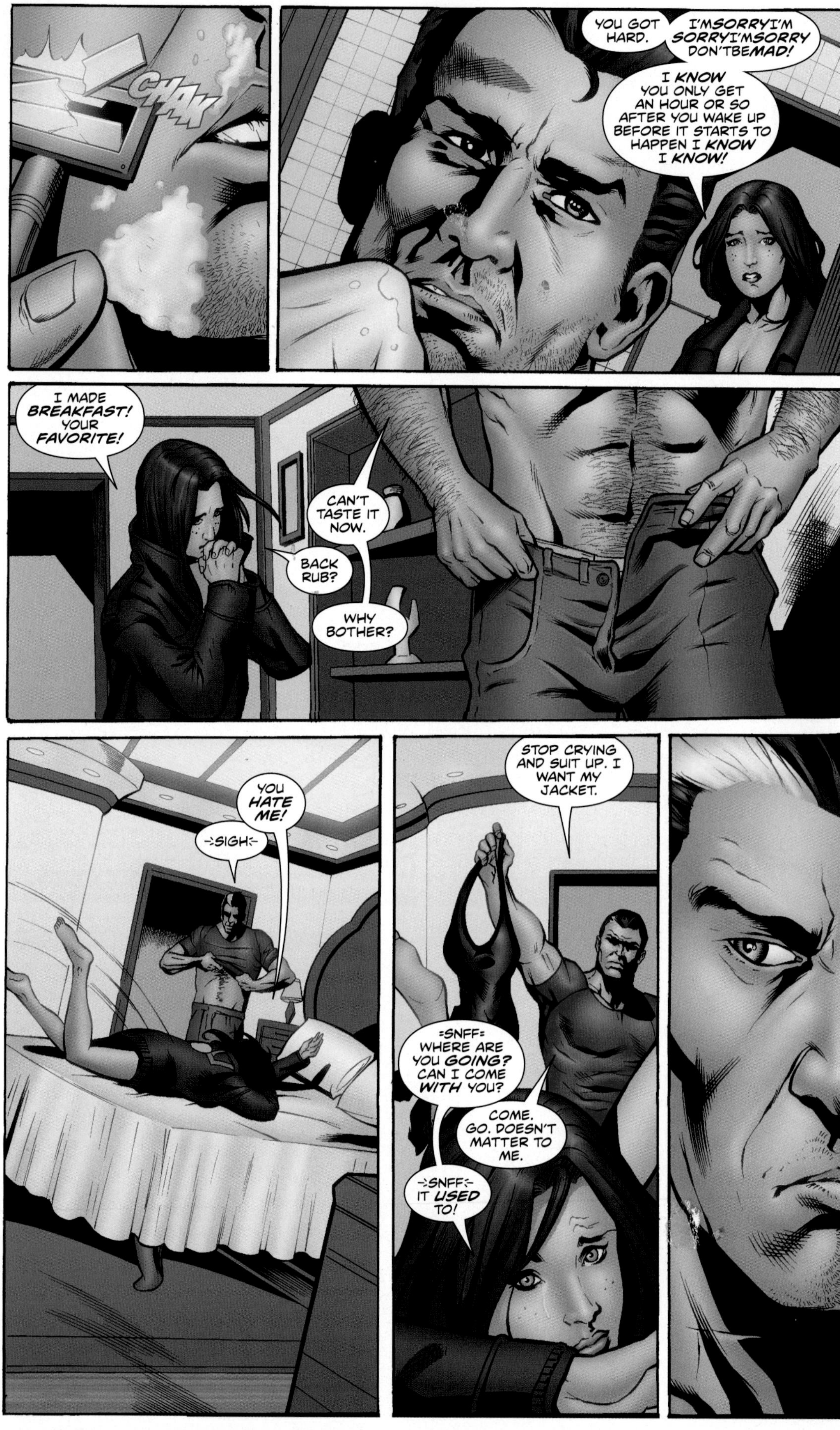
CHAK
YOU GOT HARD.
I'MSORRYI'M SORRYI'MSORRY DON'TBEMAD!
I KNOW YOU ONLY GET AN HOUR OR SO AFTER YOU WAKE UP BEFORE IT STARTS TO HAPPEN I KNOW I KNOW!
I MADE BREAKFAST! YOUR FAVORITE!
CAN'T TASTE IT NOW.
BACK RUB?
WHY BOTHER?
YOU HATE ME!
-SIGH-
STOP CRYING AND SUIT UP. I WANT MY JACKET.
=SNFF= WHERE ARE YOU GOING? CAN I COME WITH YOU?
COME. GO. DOESN'T MATTER TO ME.
-SNFF- IT USED TO!

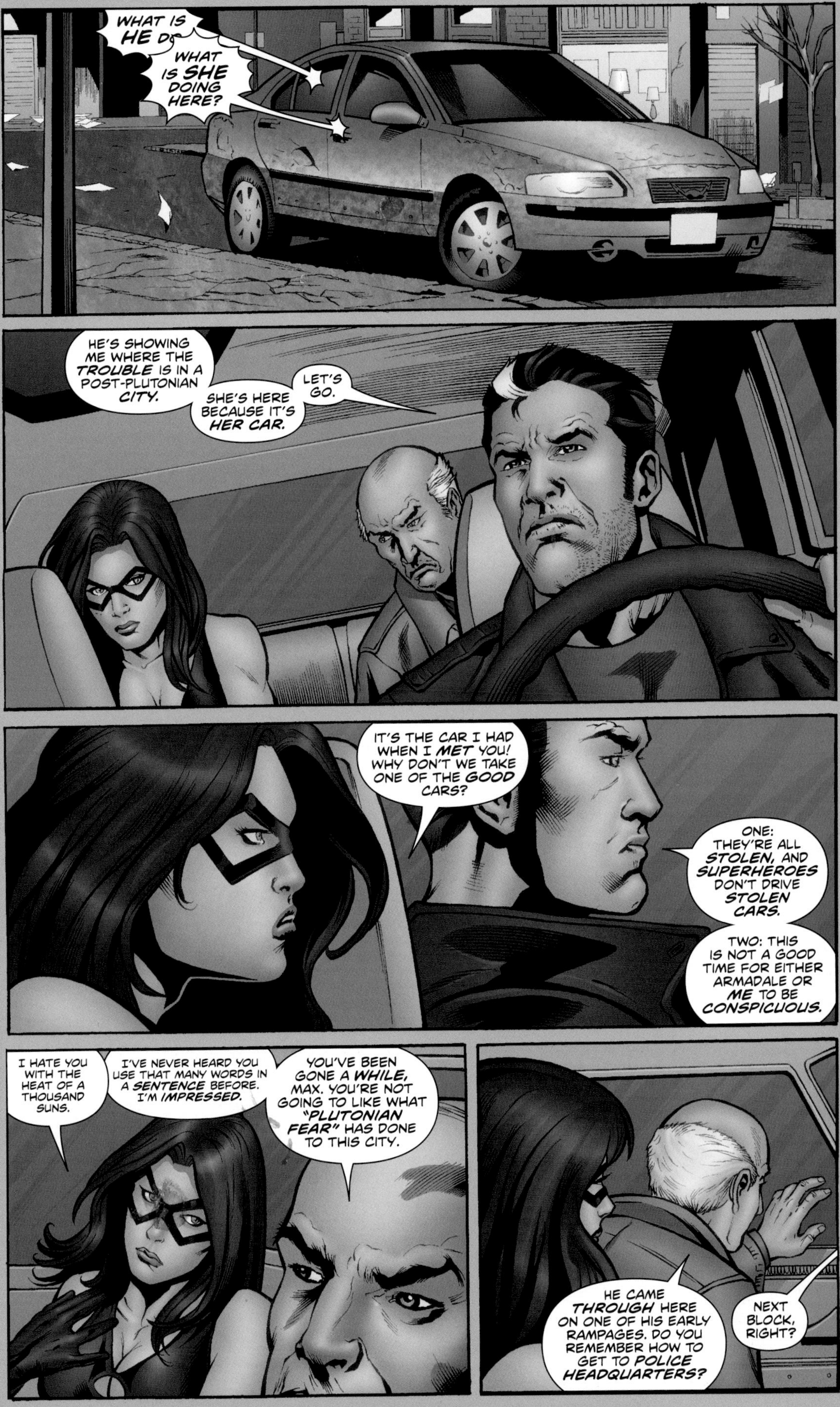
WHAT IS HE D—
WHAT IS SHE DOING HERE?
HE'S SHOWING ME WHERE THE TROUBLE IS IN A POST-PLUTONIAN CITY.
SHE'S HERE BECAUSE IT'S HER CAR.
LET'S GO.
IT'S THE CAR I HAD WHEN I MET YOU! WHY DON'T WE TAKE ONE OF THE GOOD CARS?
ONE: THEY'RE ALL STOLEN, AND SUPERHEROES DON'T DRIVE STOLEN CARS.
TWO: THIS IS NOT A GOOD TIME FOR EITHER ARMADALE OR ME TO BE CONSPICUOUS.
I HATE YOU WITH THE HEAT OF A THOUSAND SUNS.
I'VE NEVER HEARD YOU USE THAT MANY WORDS IN A SENTENCE BEFORE. I'M IMPRESSED.
YOU'VE BEEN GONE A WHILE, MAX. YOU'RE NOT GOING TO LIKE WHAT "PLUTONIAN FEAR" HAS DONE TO THIS CITY.
HE CAME THROUGH HERE ON ONE OF HIS EARLY RAMPAGES. DO YOU REMEMBER HOW TO GET TO POLICE HEADQUARTERS?
NEXT BLOCK, RIGHT?

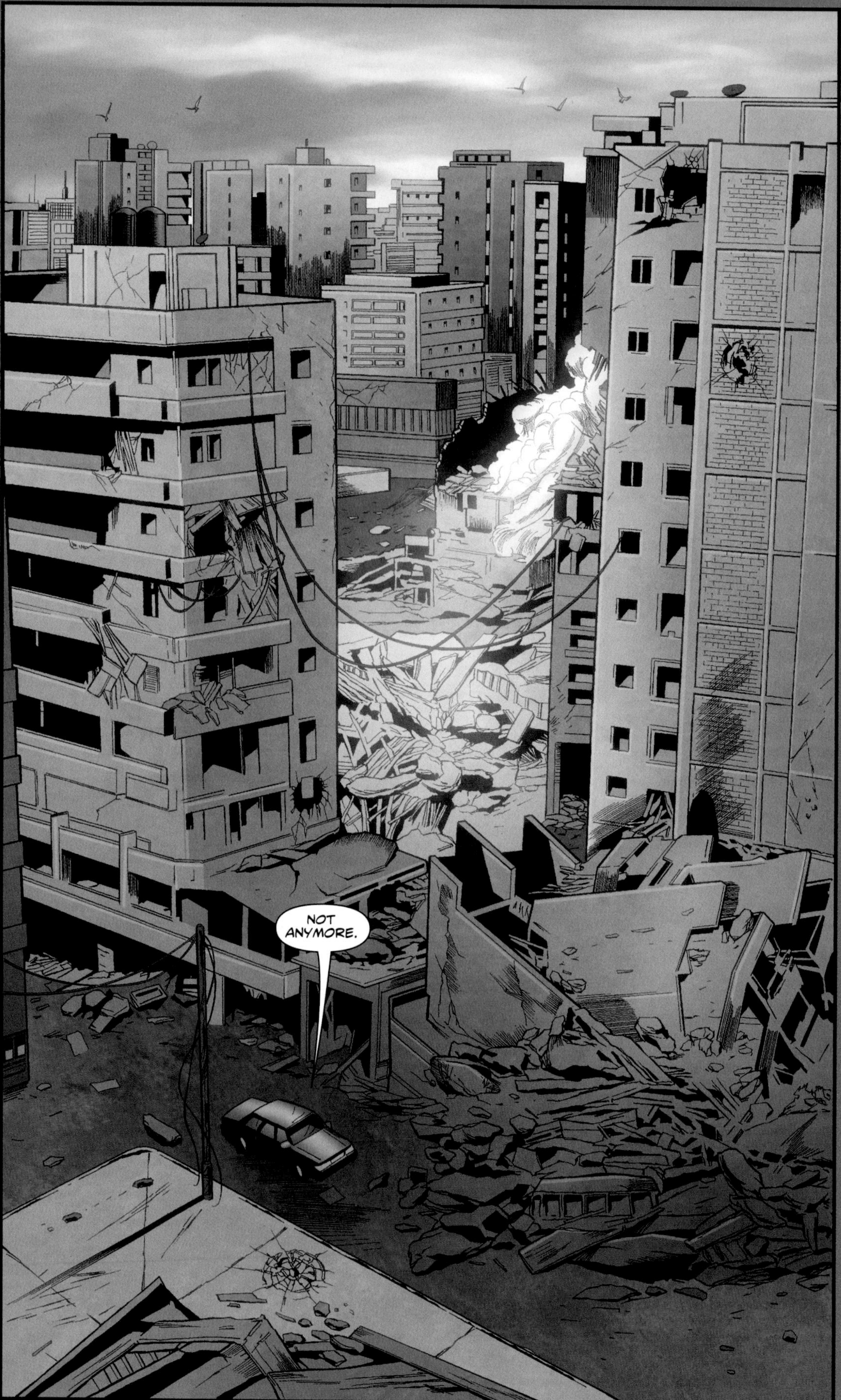
NOT ANYMORE.

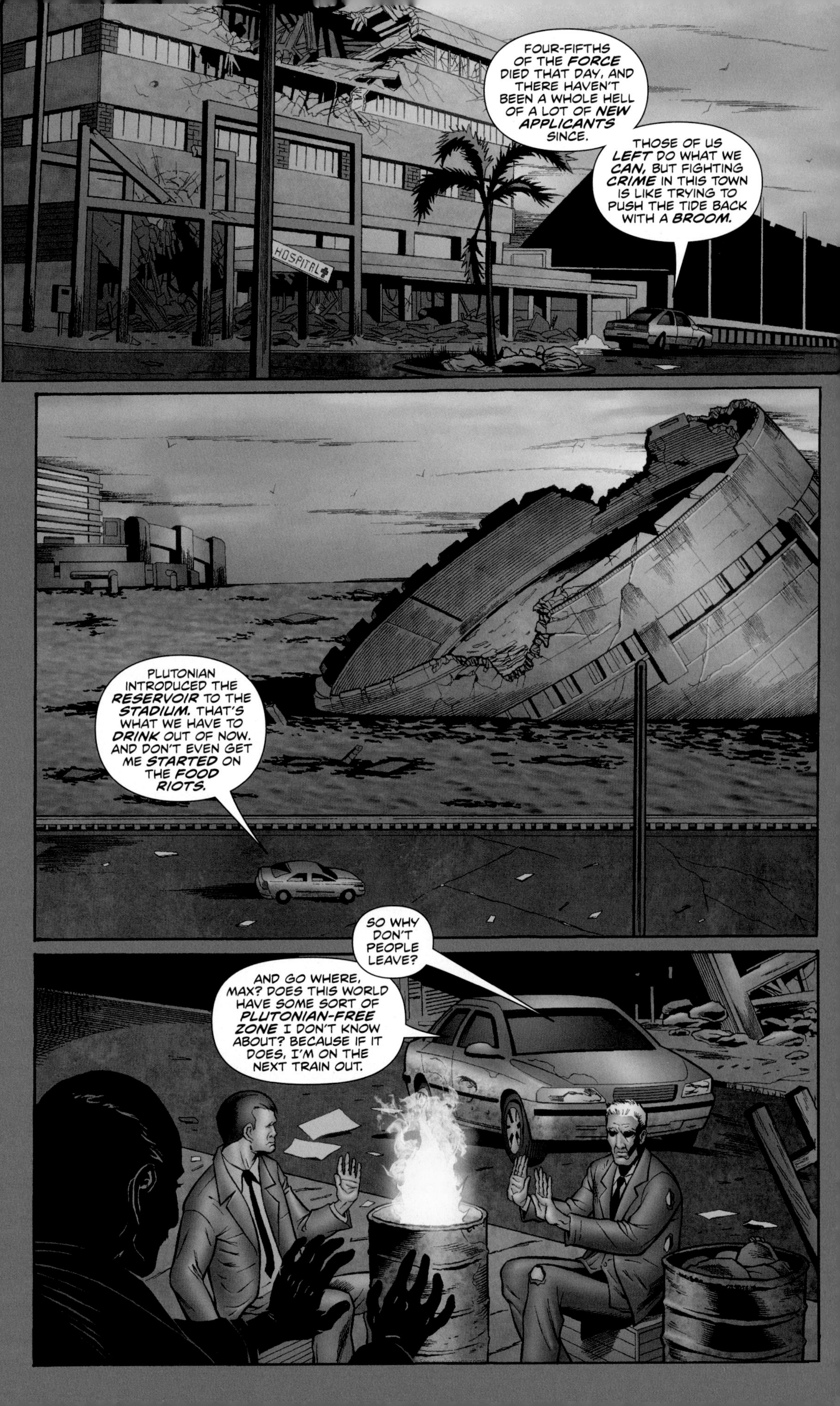
FOUR-FIFTHS OF THE FORCE DIED THAT DAY, AND THERE HAVEN'T BEEN A WHOLE HELL OF A LOT OF NEW APPLICANTS SINCE.
THOSE OF US LEFT DO WHAT WE CAN, BUT FIGHTING CRIME IN THIS TOWN IS LIKE TRYING TO PUSH THE TIDE BACK WITH A BROOM.
HOSPITAL
PLUTONIAN INTRODUCED THE RESERVOIR TO THE STADIUM. THAT'S WHAT WE HAVE TO DRINK OUT OF NOW. AND DON'T EVEN GET ME STARTED ON THE FOOD RIOTS.
SO WHY DON'T PEOPLE LEAVE?
AND GO WHERE, MAX? DOES THIS WORLD HAVE SOME SORT OF PLUTONIAN-FREE ZONE I DON'T KNOW ABOUT? BECAUSE IF IT DOES, I'M ON THE NEXT TRAIN OUT.

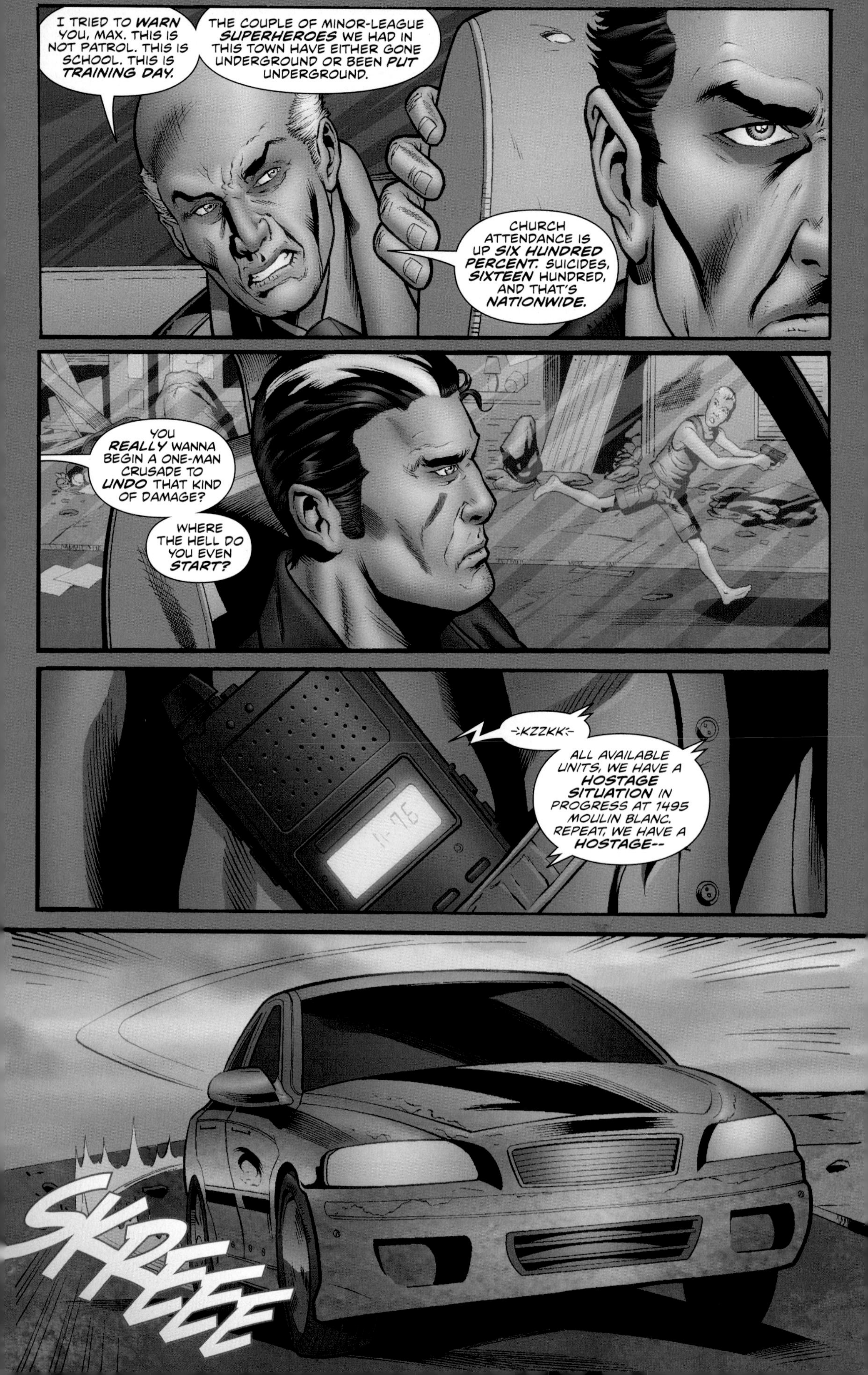
I TRIED TO WARN YOU, MAX. THIS IS NOT PATROL. THIS IS SCHOOL. THIS IS TRAINING DAY.
THE COUPLE OF MINOR-LEAGUE SUPERHEROES WE HAD IN THIS TOWN HAVE EITHER GONE UNDERGROUND OR BEEN PUT UNDERGROUND.
CHURCH ATTENDANCE IS UP SIX HUNDRED PERCENT. SUICIDES, SIXTEEN HUNDRED, AND THAT'S NATIONWIDE.
YOU REALLY WANNA BEGIN A ONE-MAN CRUSADE TO UNDO THAT KIND OF DAMAGE?
WHERE THE HELL DO YOU EVEN START?
-KZZKK-
ALL AVAILABLE UNITS, WE HAVE A HOSTAGE SITUATION IN PROGRESS AT 1495 MOULIN BLANC. REPEAT, WE HAVE A HOSTAGE--
SKREEEE

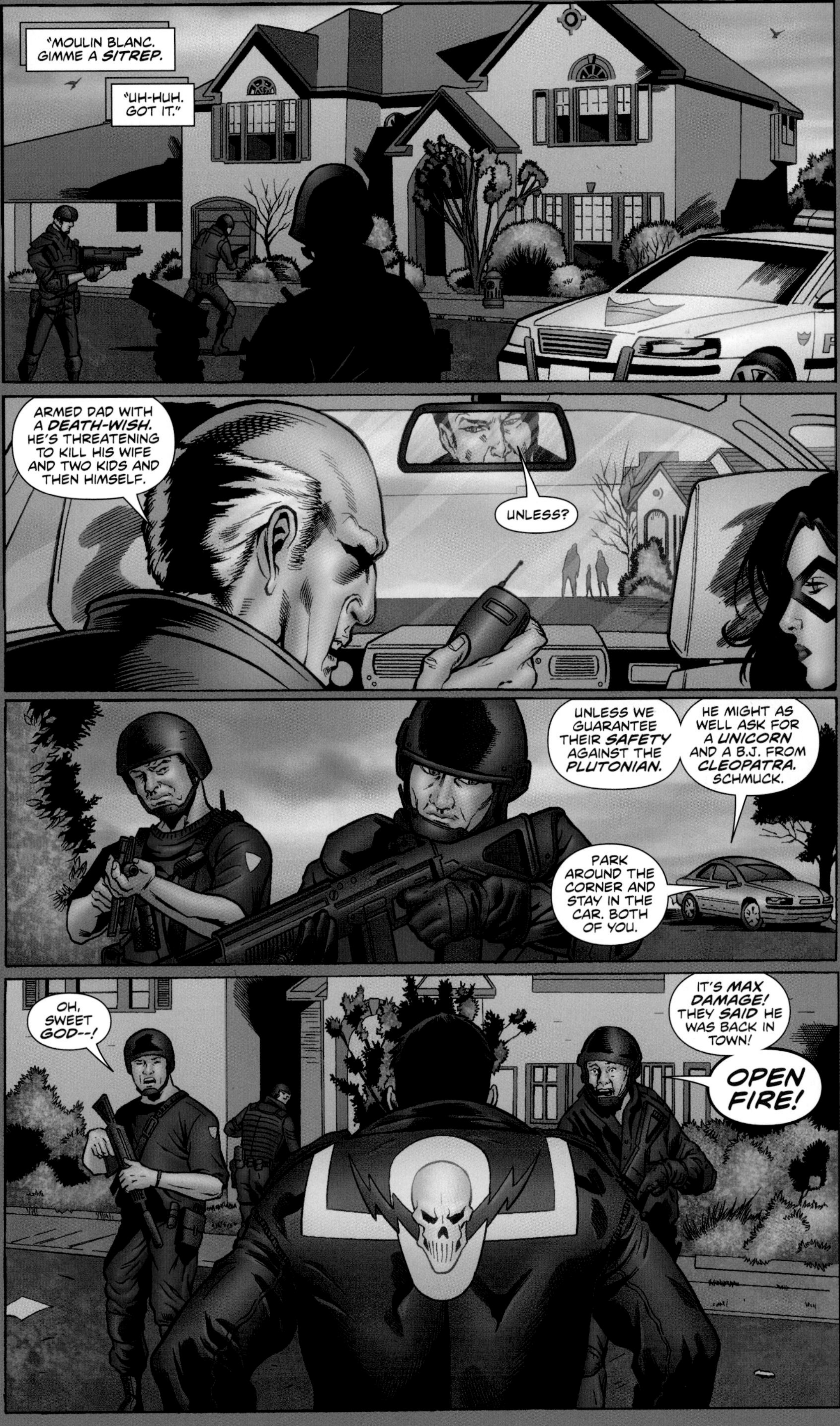
"MOULIN BLANC. GIMME A SITREP.
"UH-HUH. GOT IT."
ARMED DAD WITH A DEATH-WISH. HE'S THREATENING TO KILL HIS WIFE AND TWO KIDS AND THEN HIMSELF.
UNLESS?
UNLESS WE GUARANTEE THEIR SAFETY AGAINST THE PLUTONIAN.
HE MIGHT AS WELL ASK FOR A UNICORN AND A B.J. FROM CLEOPATRA. SCHMUCK.
PARK AROUND THE CORNER AND STAY IN THE CAR. BOTH OF YOU.
OH, SWEET GOD--!
IT'S MAX DAMAGE! THEY SAID HE WAS BACK IN TOWN!
OPEN FIRE!

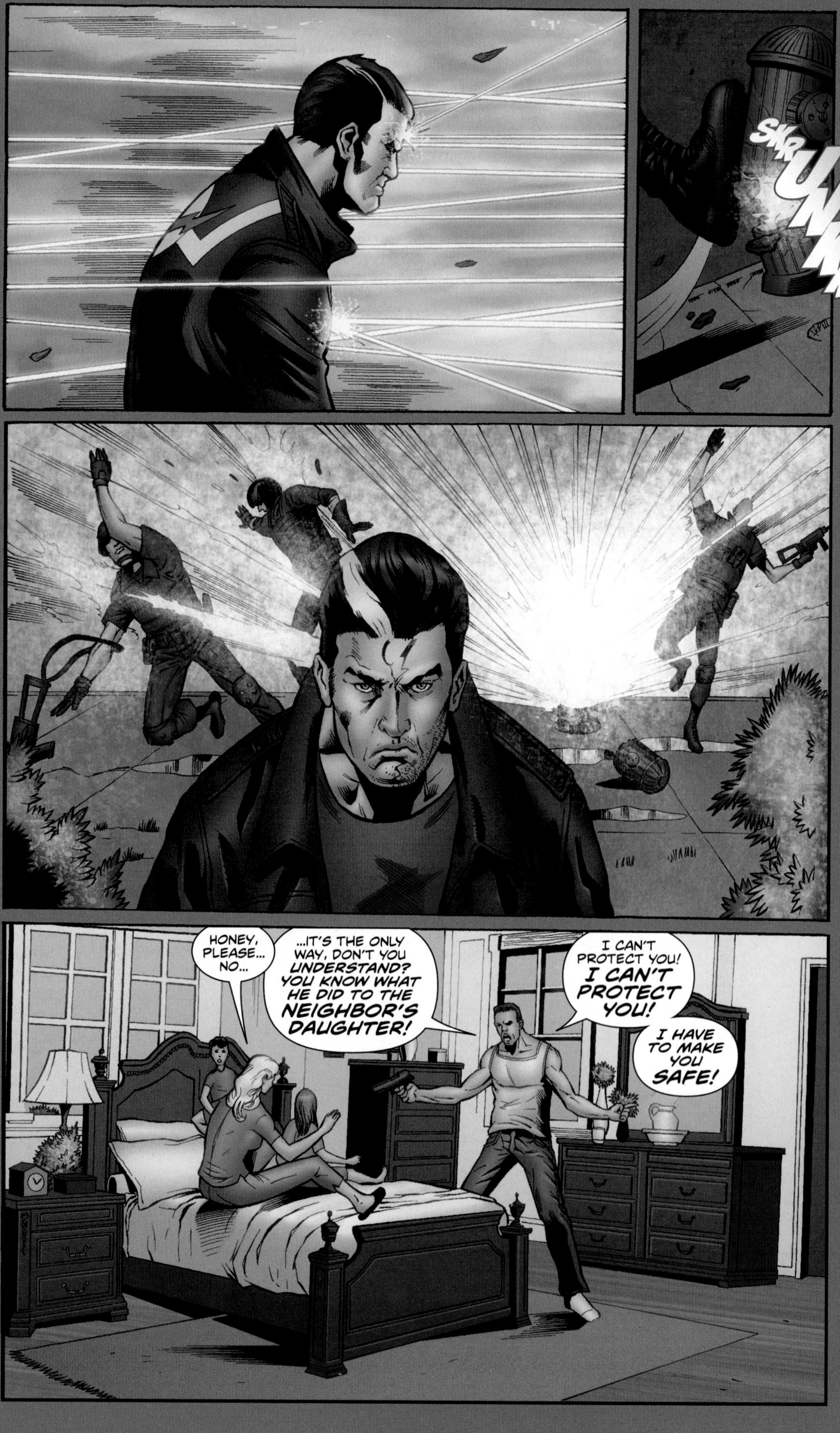
SKRUNKKK
HONEY, PLEASE... NO...
...IT'S THE ONLY WAY, DON'T YOU UNDERSTAND? YOU KNOW WHAT HE DID TO THE NEIGHBOR'S DAUGHTER!
I CAN'T PROTECT YOU! I CAN'T PROTECT YOU!
I HAVE TO MAKE YOU SAFE!

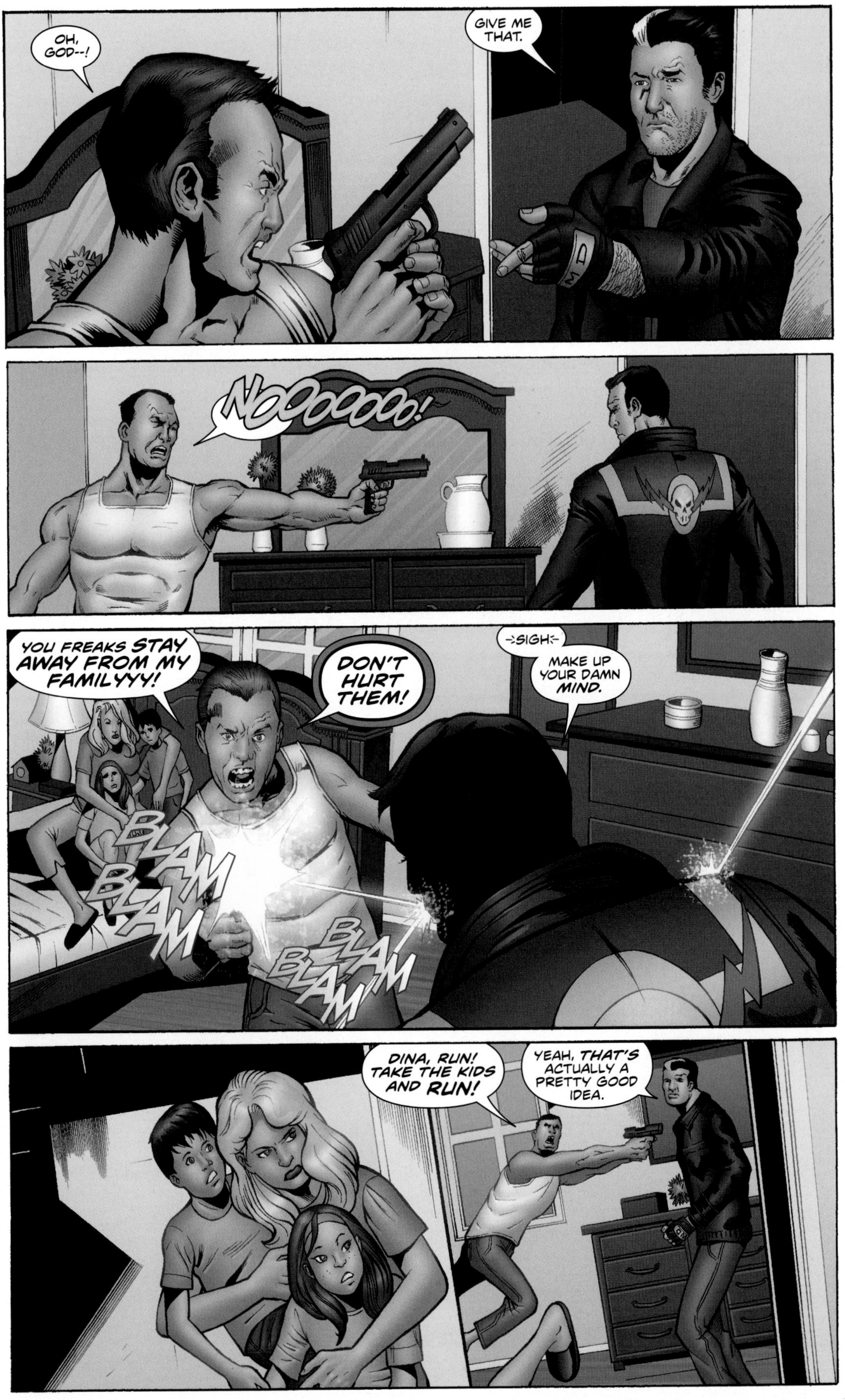
OH, GOD--!
GIVE ME THAT.
NOOOOOOO!
YOU FREAKS STAY AWAY FROM MY FAMILYYY!
DON'T HURT THEM!
-SIGH-
MAKE UP YOUR DAMN MIND.
BLAM
BLAM
BLAM
BLAM
BLAM
BLAM
DINA, RUN! TAKE THE KIDS AND RUN!
YEAH, THAT'S ACTUALLY A PRETTY GOOD IDEA.

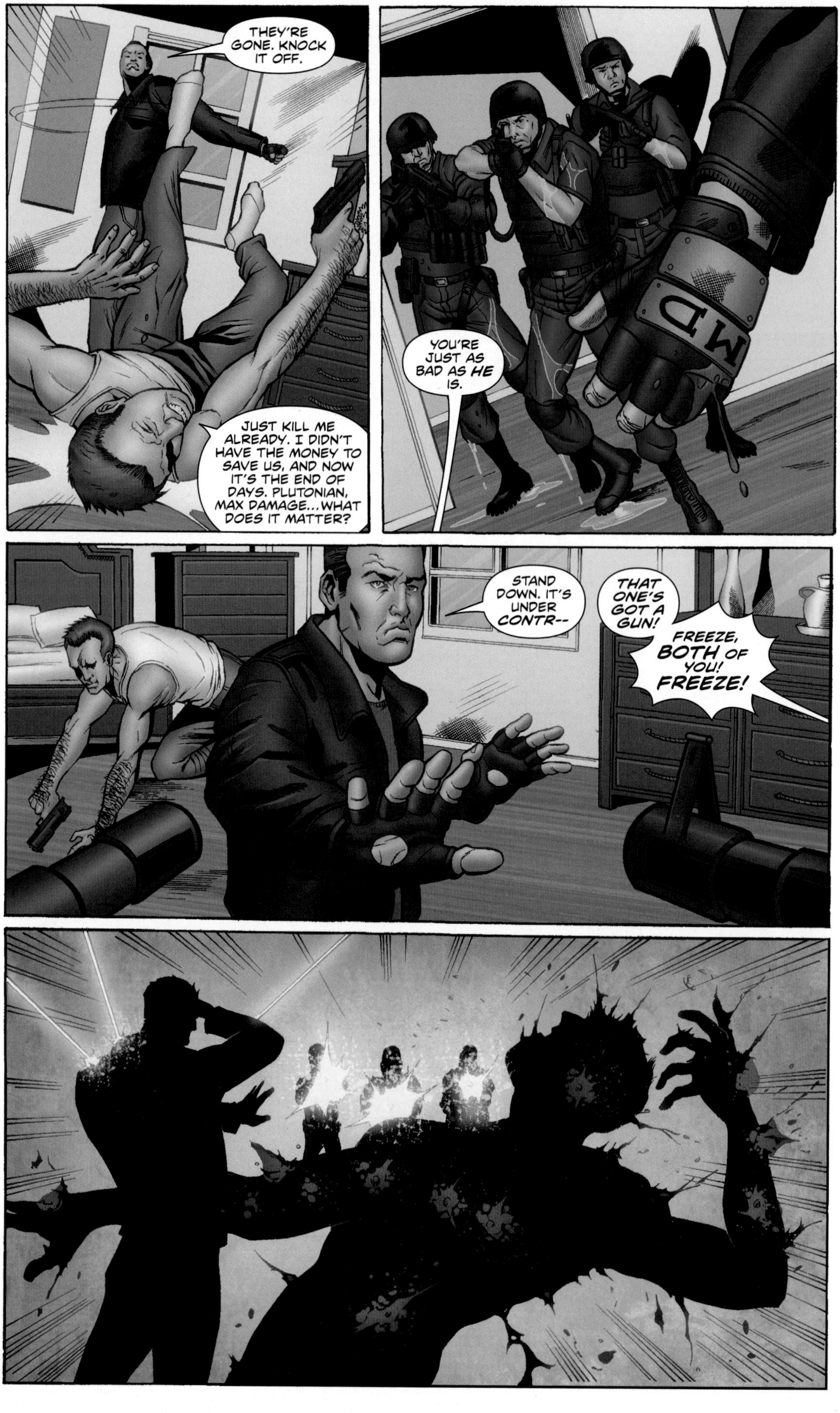
THEY'RE GONE. KNOCK IT OFF.
JUST KILL ME ALREADY. I DIDN'T HAVE THE MONEY TO SAVE US, AND NOW IT'S THE END OF DAYS. PLUTONIAN, MAX DAMAGE...WHAT DOES IT MATTER?
YOU'RE JUST AS BAD AS HE IS.
MD
STAND DOWN. IT'S UNDER CONTR--
THAT ONE'S GOT A GUN!
FREEZE, BOTH OF YOU! FREEZE!

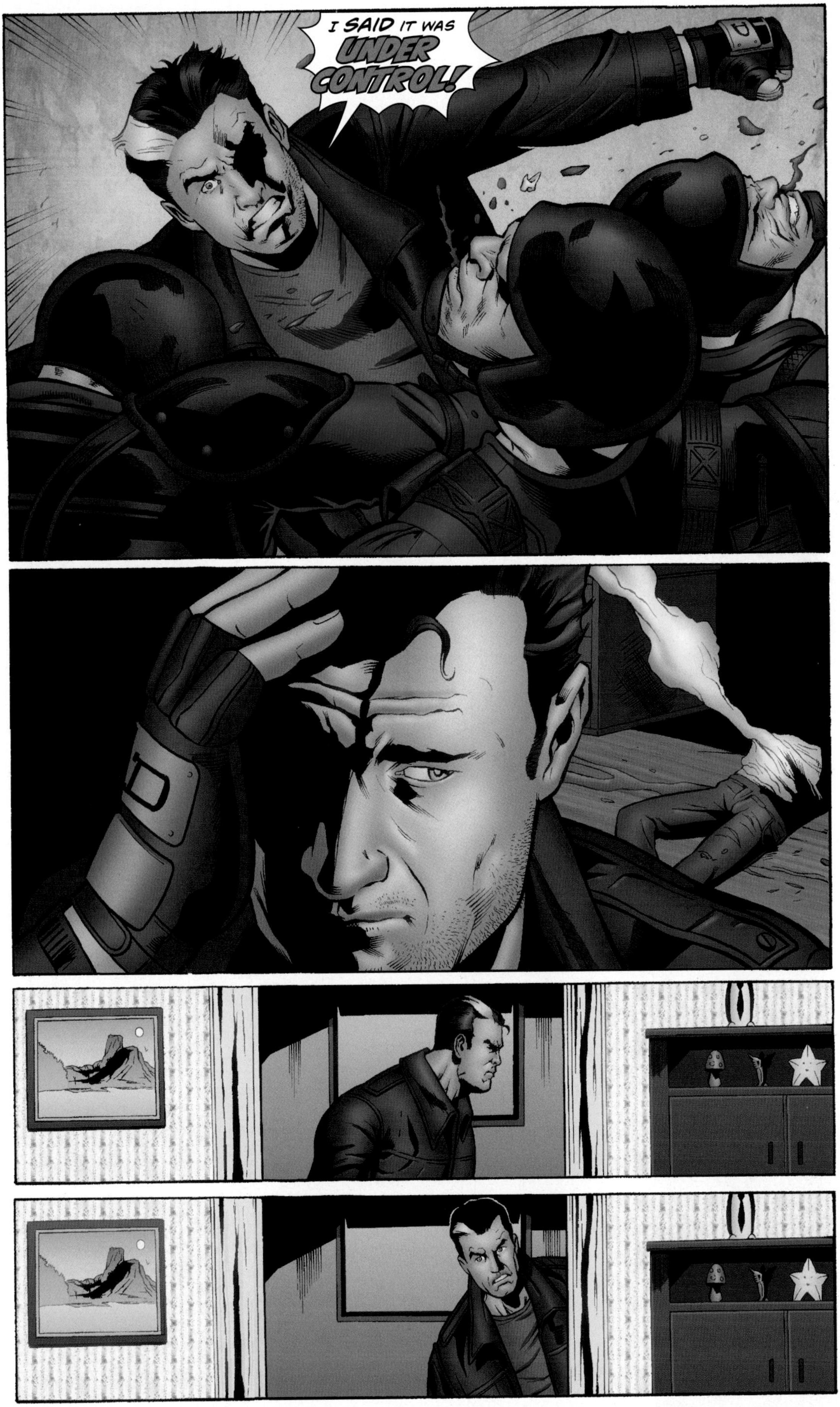
I SAID IT WAS UNDER CONTROL!

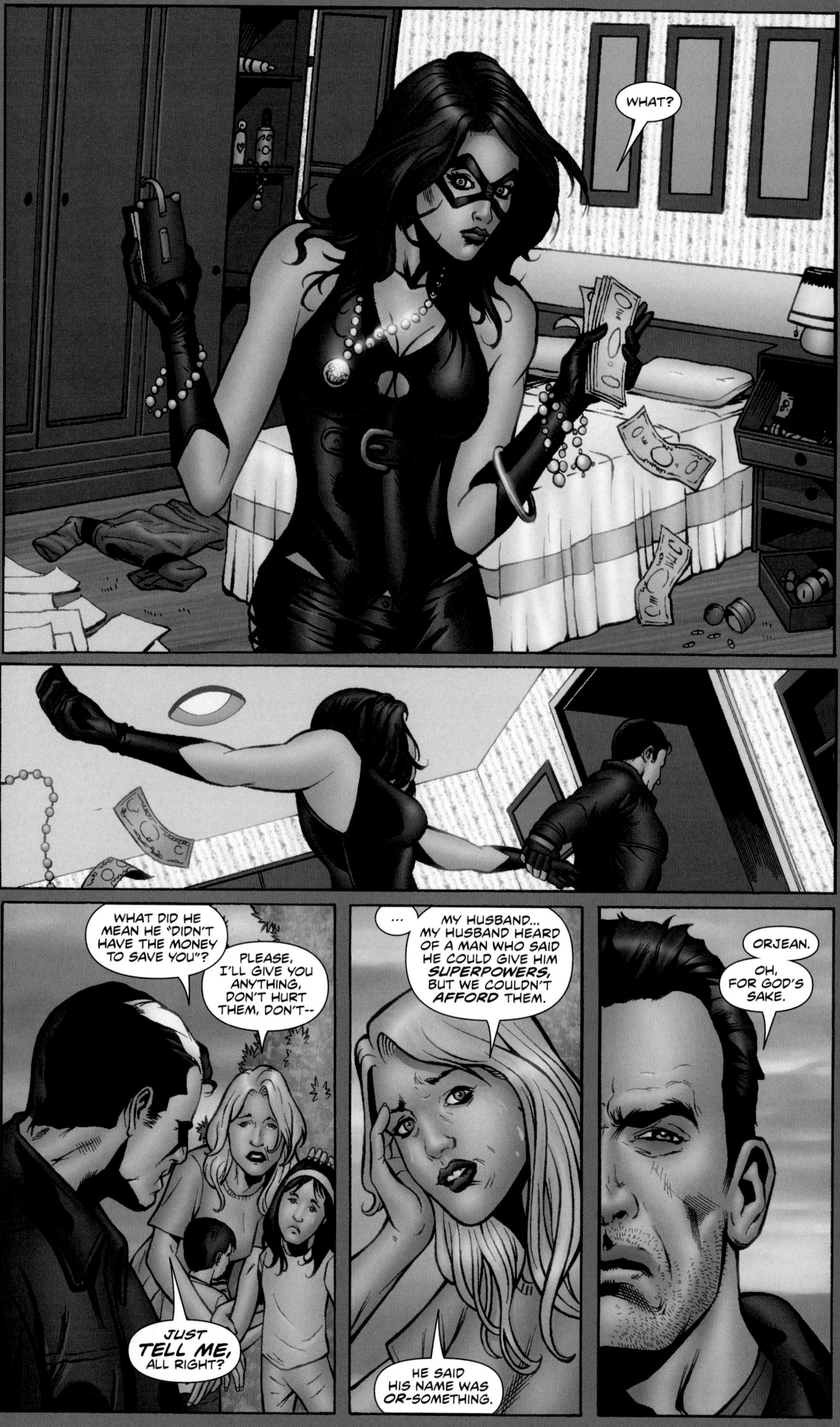
WHAT?
WHAT DID HE MEAN HE "DIDN'T HAVE THE MONEY TO SAVE YOU"?
PLEASE, I'LL GIVE YOU ANYTHING, DON'T HURT THEM, DON'T--
JUST TELL ME, ALL RIGHT?
...
MY HUSBAND... MY HUSBAND HEARD OF A MAN WHO SAID HE COULD GIVE HIM SUPERPOWERS, BUT WE COULDN'T AFFORD THEM.
HE SAID HIS NAME WAS OR-SOMETHING.
ORJEAN.
OH, FOR GOD'S SAKE.

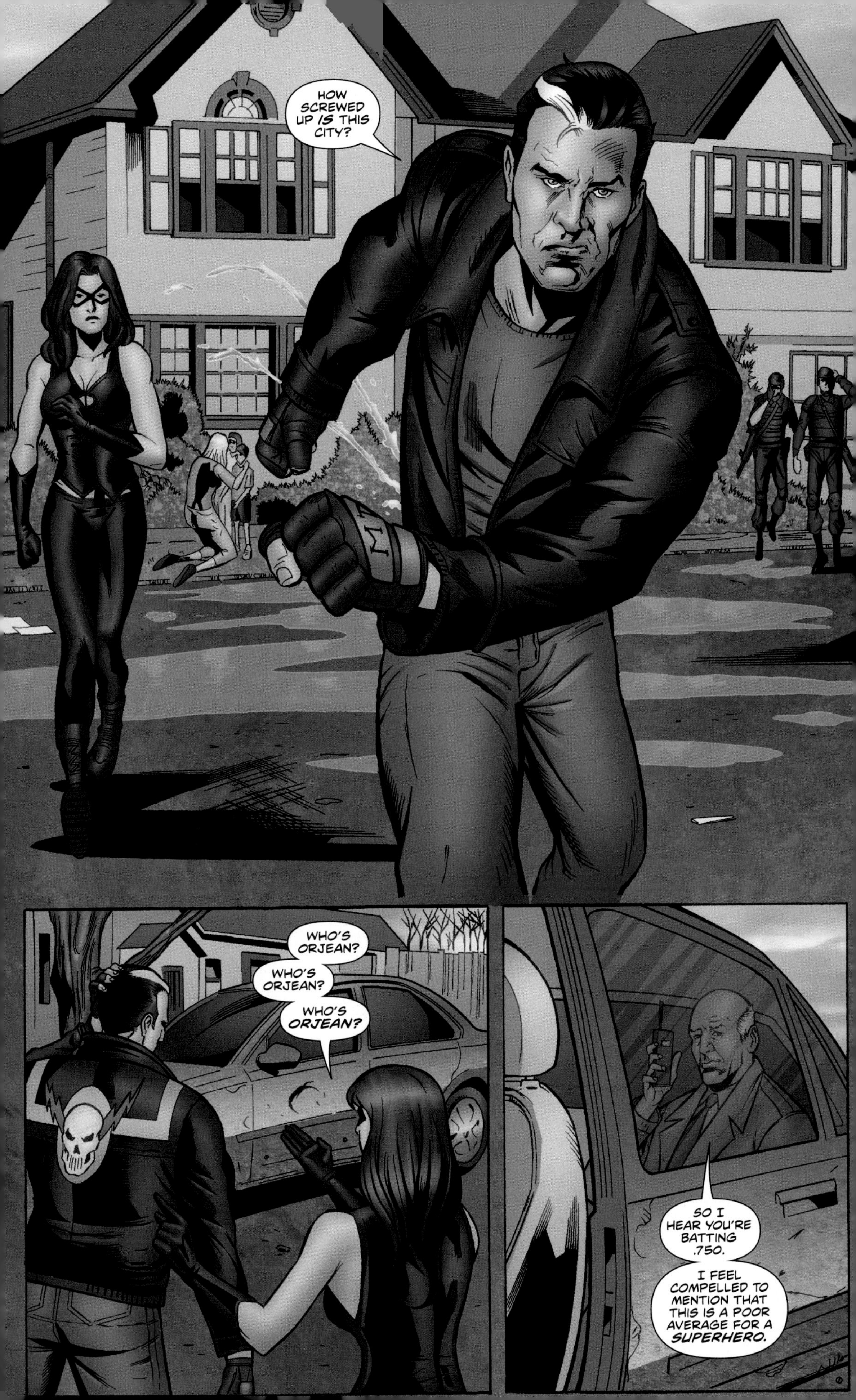
HOW SCREWED UP *IS* THIS CITY?
WHO'S ORJEAN?
WHO'S ORJEAN?
WHO'S *ORJEAN?*
SO I HEAR YOU'RE BATTING .750.
I FEEL COMPELLED TO MENTION THAT THIS IS A POOR AVERAGE FOR A *SUPERHERO.*

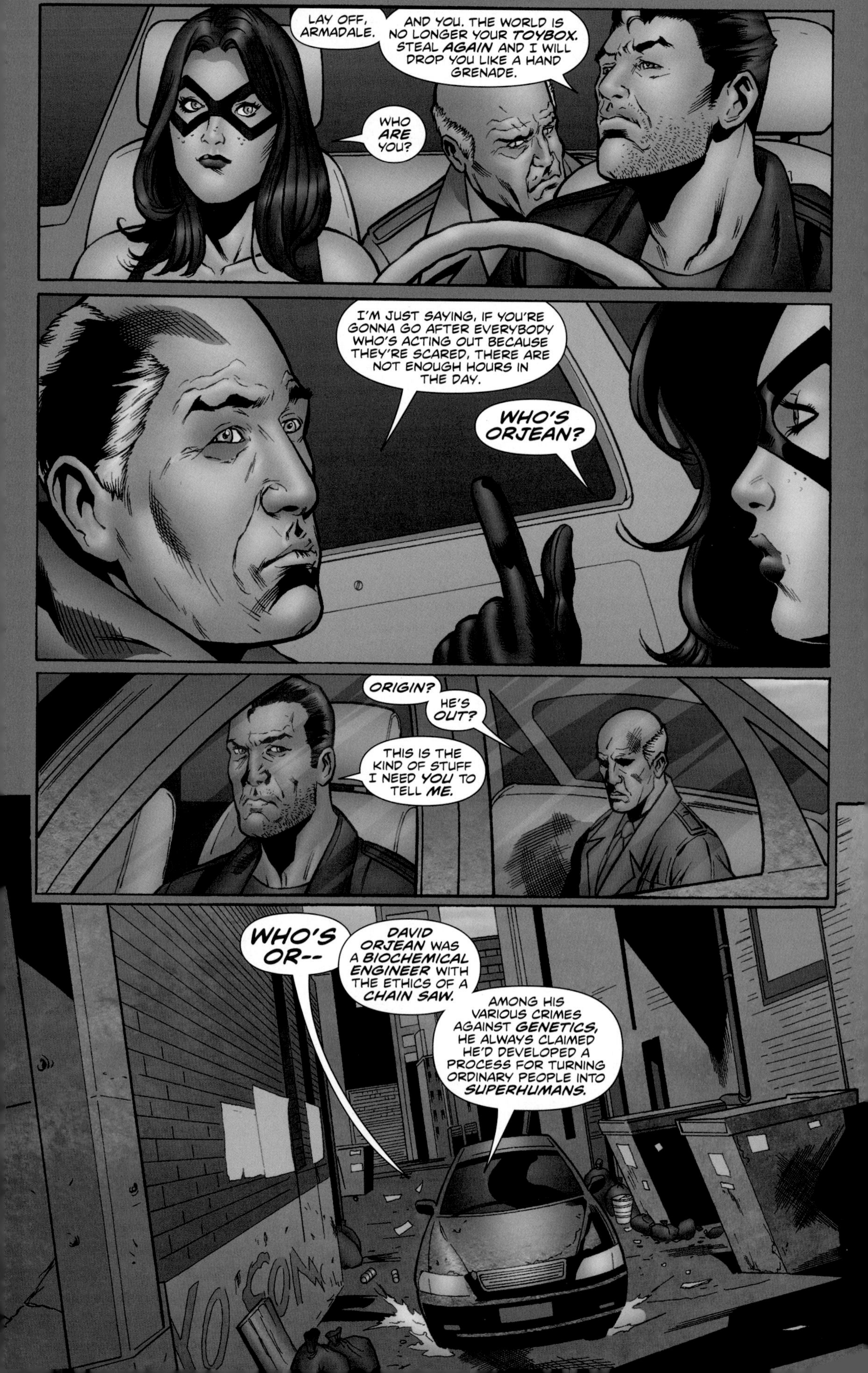
LAY OFF, ARMADALE.
AND YOU. THE WORLD IS NO LONGER YOUR TOYBOX. STEAL AGAIN AND I WILL DROP YOU LIKE A HAND GRENADE.
WHO ARE YOU?
I'M JUST SAYING, IF YOU'RE GONNA GO AFTER EVERYBODY WHO'S ACTING OUT BECAUSE THEY'RE SCARED, THERE ARE NOT ENOUGH HOURS IN THE DAY.
WHO'S ORJEAN?
ORIGIN?
HE'S OUT?
THIS IS THE KIND OF STUFF I NEED YOU TO TELL ME.
WHO'S OR--
DAVID ORJEAN WAS A BIOCHEMICAL ENGINEER WITH THE ETHICS OF A CHAIN SAW.
AMONG HIS VARIOUS CRIMES AGAINST GENETICS, HE ALWAYS CLAIMED HE'D DEVELOPED A PROCESS FOR TURNING ORDINARY PEOPLE INTO SUPERHUMANS.

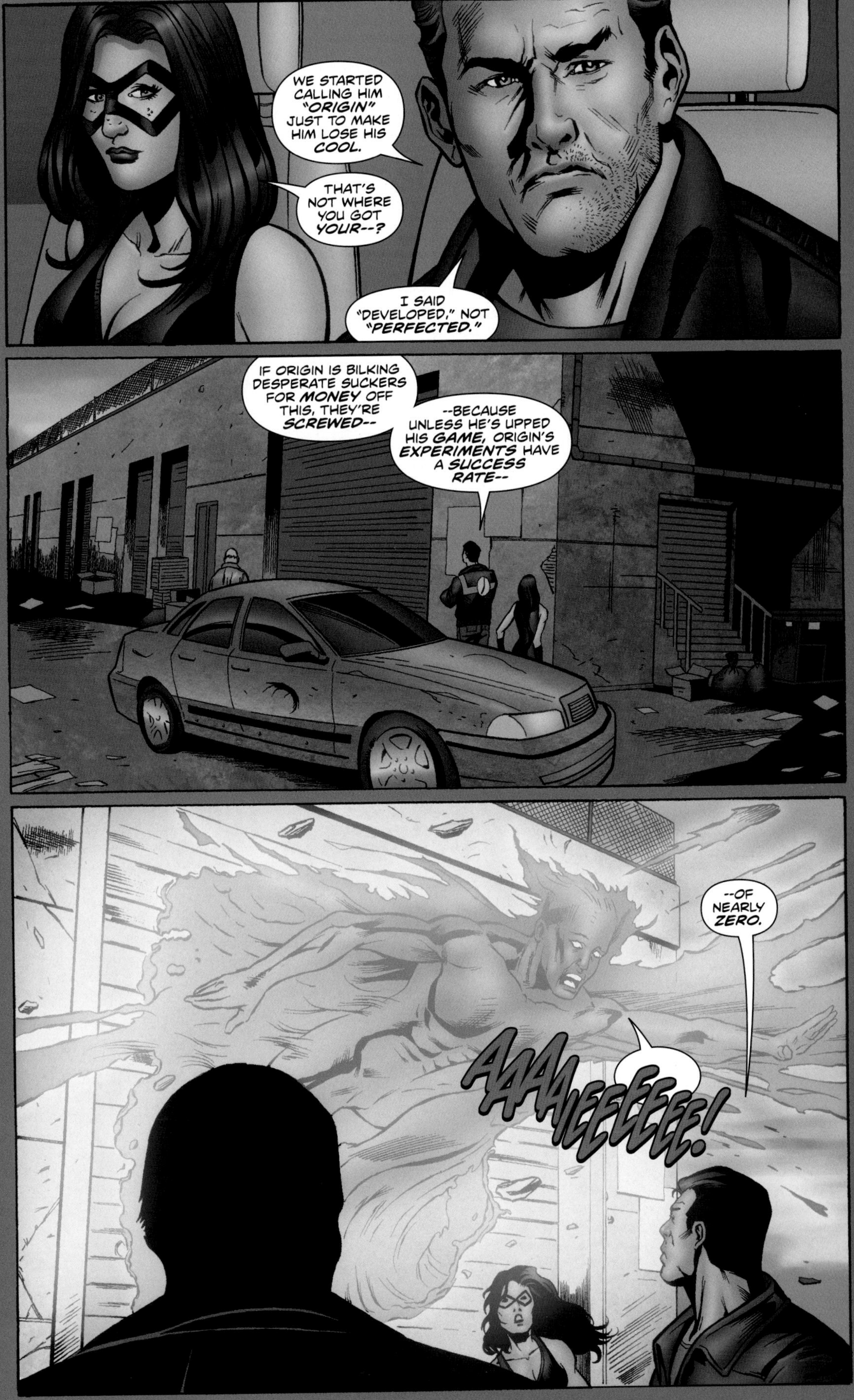
WE STARTED CALLING HIM "ORIGIN" JUST TO MAKE HIM LOSE HIS COOL.
THAT'S NOT WHERE YOU GOT YOUR--?
I SAID "DEVELOPED," NOT "PERFECTED."
IF ORIGIN IS BILKING DESPERATE SUCKERS FOR MONEY OFF THIS, THEY'RE SCREWED--
--BECAUSE UNLESS HE'S UPPED HIS GAME, ORIGIN'S EXPERIMENTS HAVE A SUCCESS RATE--
--OF NEARLY ZERO.
AAAAIEEEEEEE!

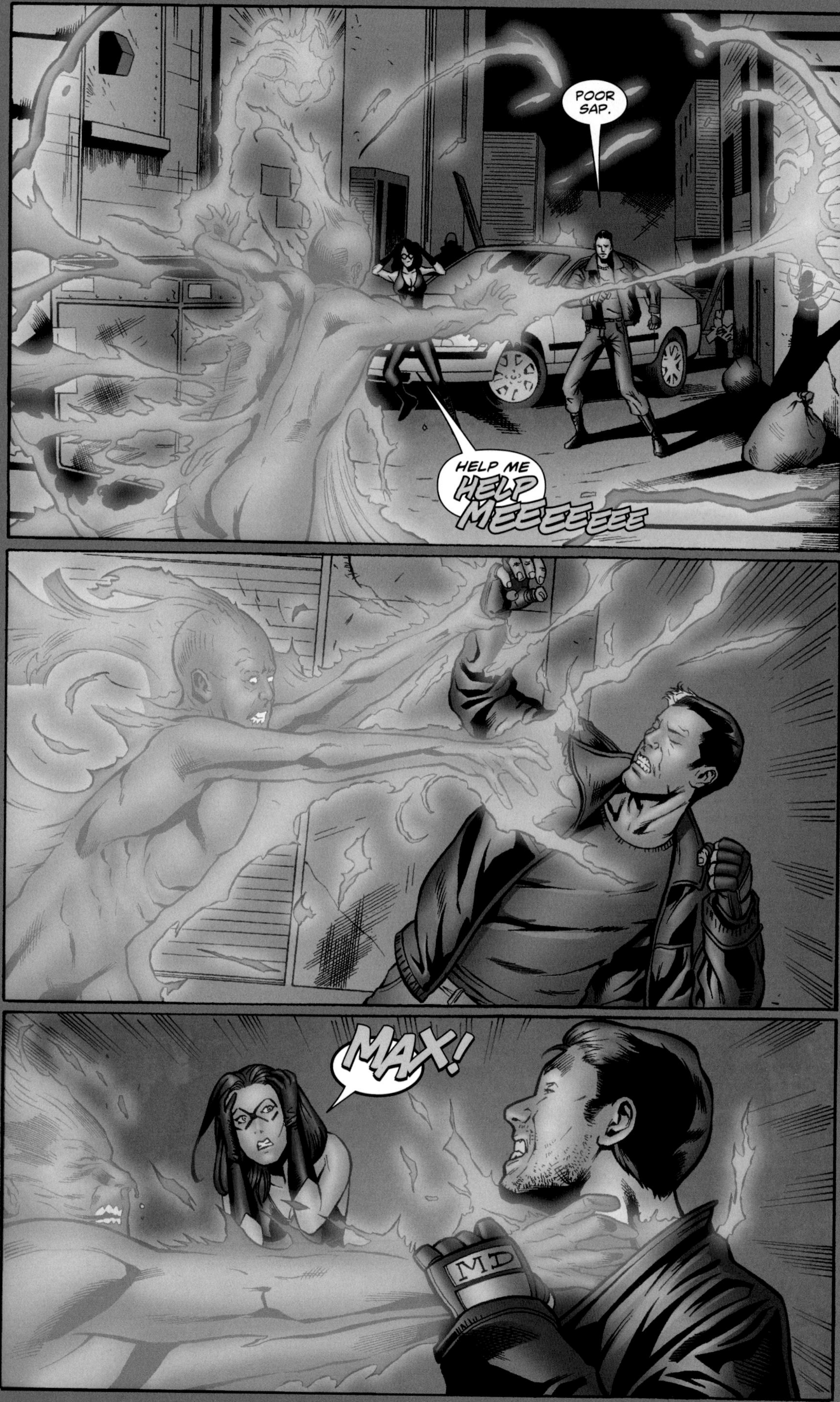
POOR SAP.
HELP ME HELP MEEEEEEE
MAX!

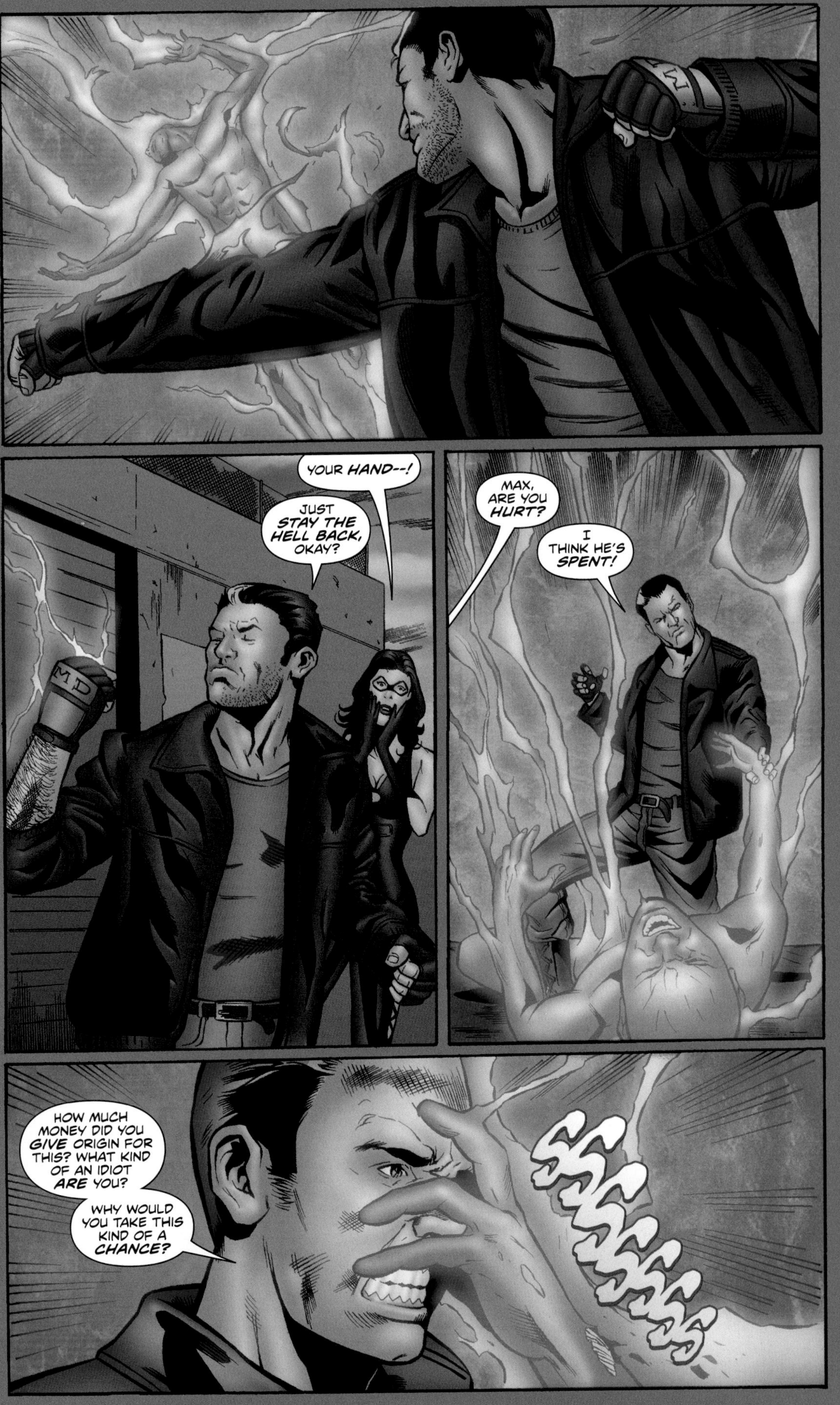
YOUR *HAND*--!
JUST *STAY THE HELL BACK,* OKAY?
MAX, ARE YOU *HURT?*
I THINK HE'S *SPENT!*
HOW MUCH MONEY DID YOU *GIVE* ORIGIN FOR THIS? WHAT KIND OF AN IDIOT *ARE* YOU?
WHY WOULD YOU TAKE THIS KIND OF A *CHANCE?*

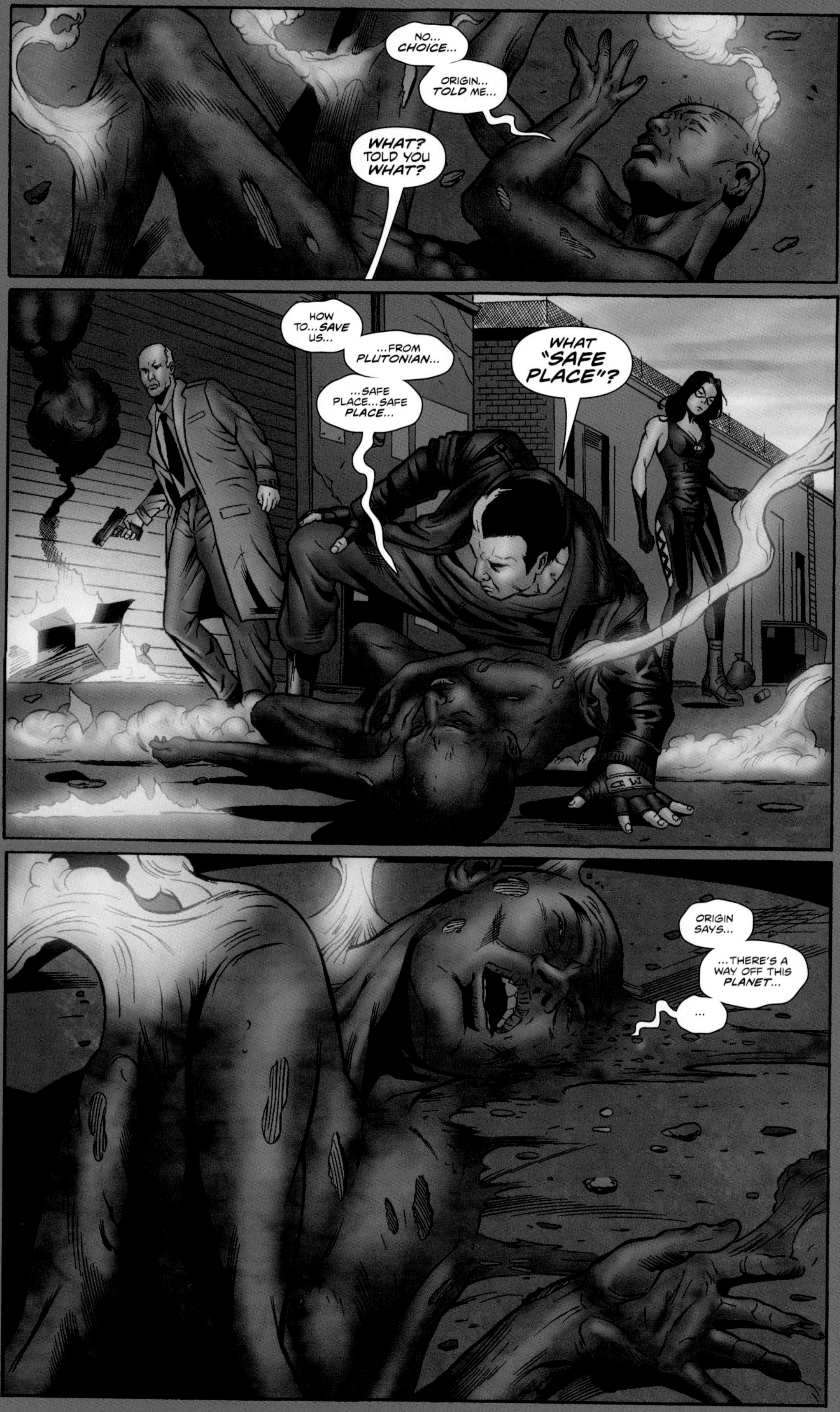
NO... CHOICE...
ORIGIN... TOLD ME...
WHAT? TOLD YOU WHAT?
HOW TO... SAVE US...
...FROM PLUTONIAN...
...SAFE PLACE... SAFE PLACE...
WHAT "SAFE PLACE"?
ORIGIN SAYS...
...THERE'S A WAY OFF THIS PLANET...
...

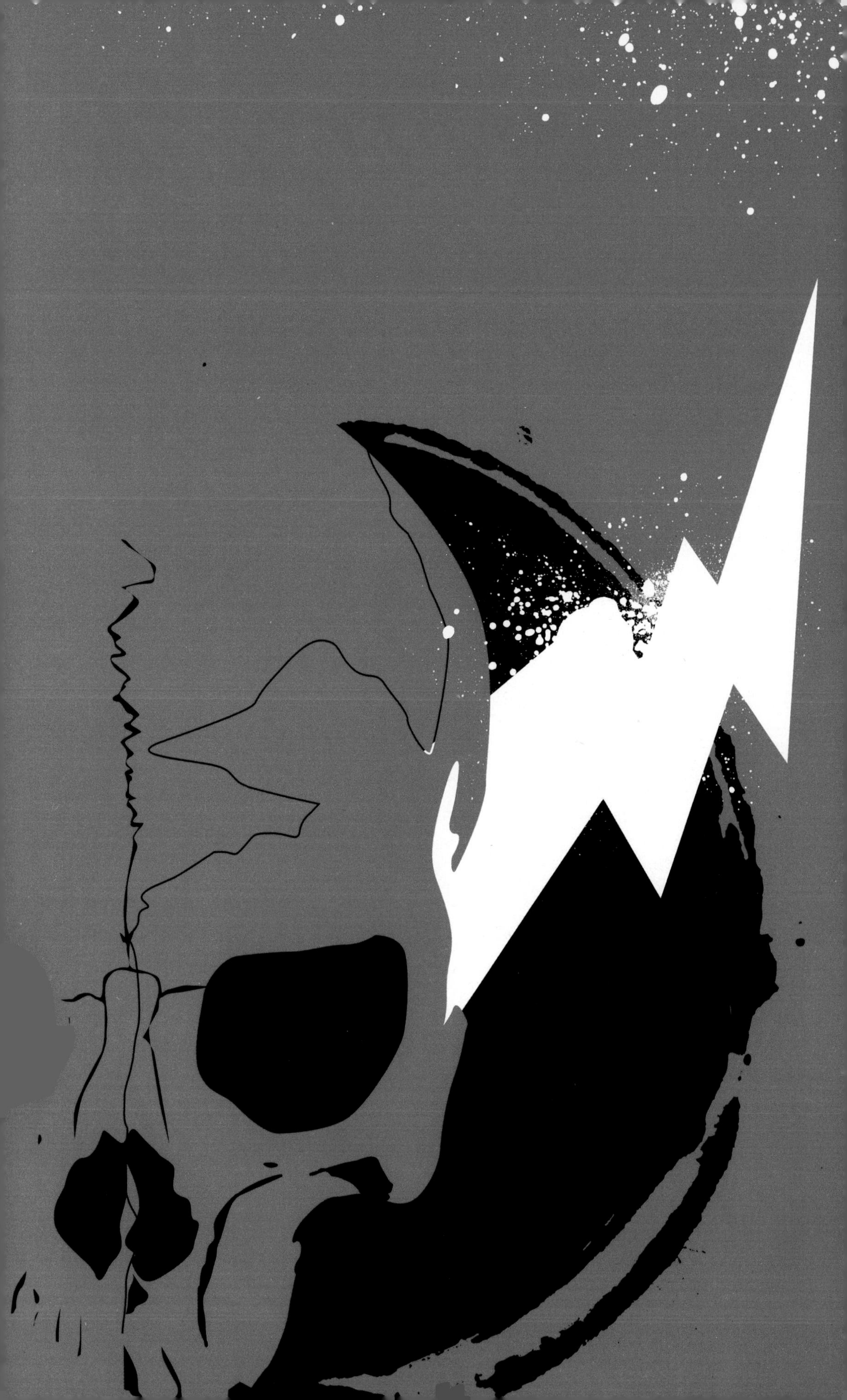

CHAPTER 3

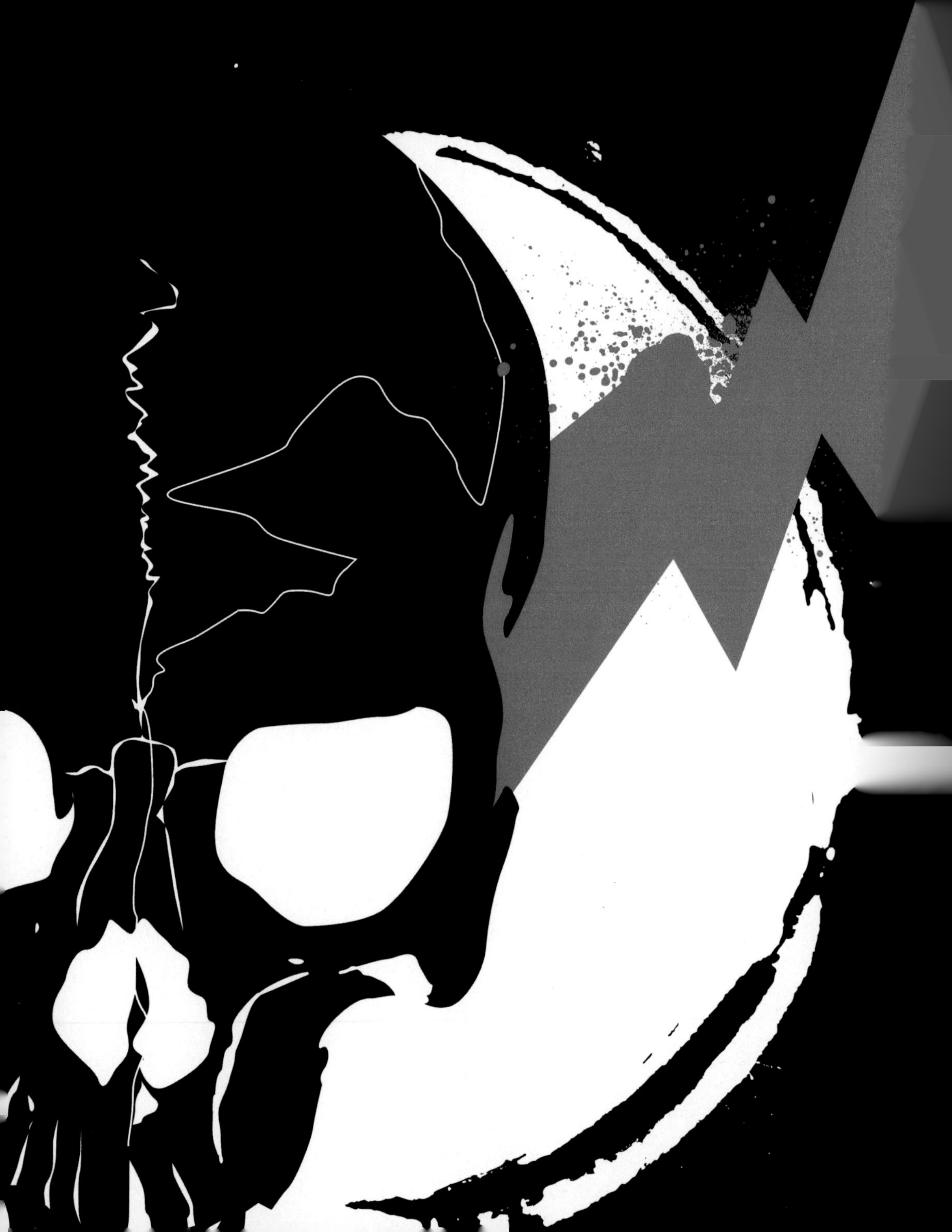

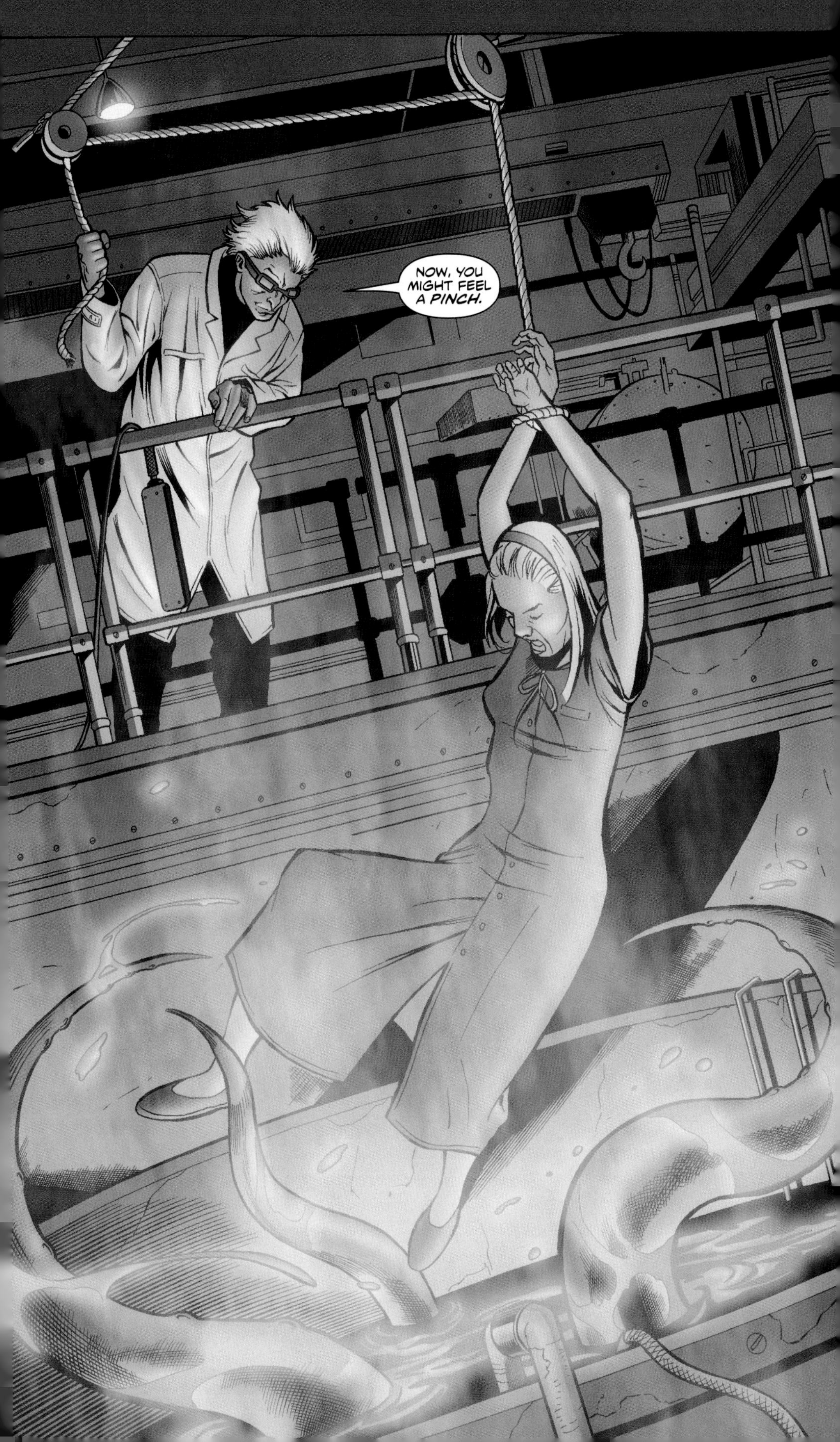
NOW, YOU MIGHT FEEL A PINCH.

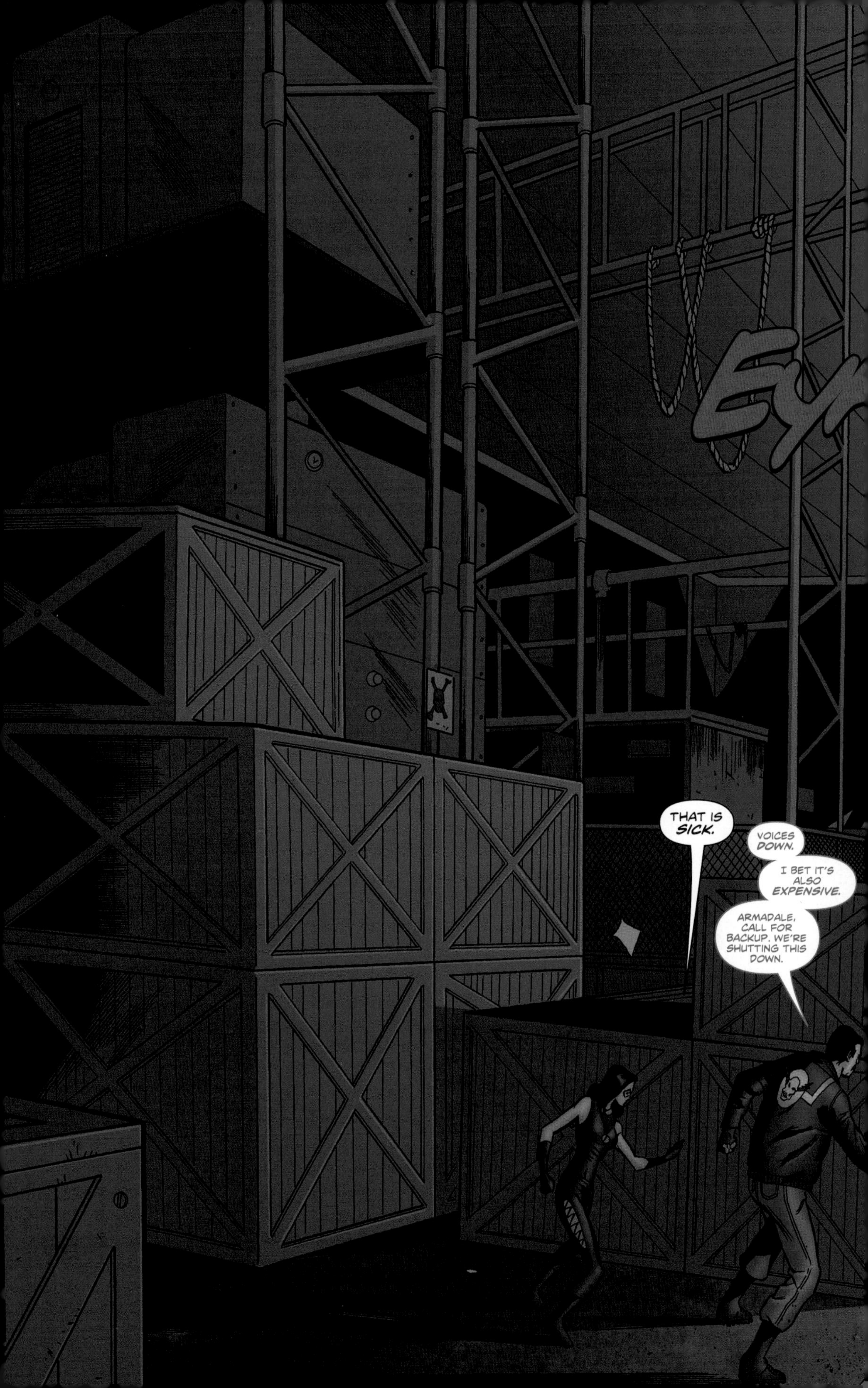

THAT IS SICK.
VOICES DOWN.
I BET IT'S ALSO EXPENSIVE.
ARMADALE, CALL FOR BACKUP. WE'RE SHUTTING THIS DOWN.

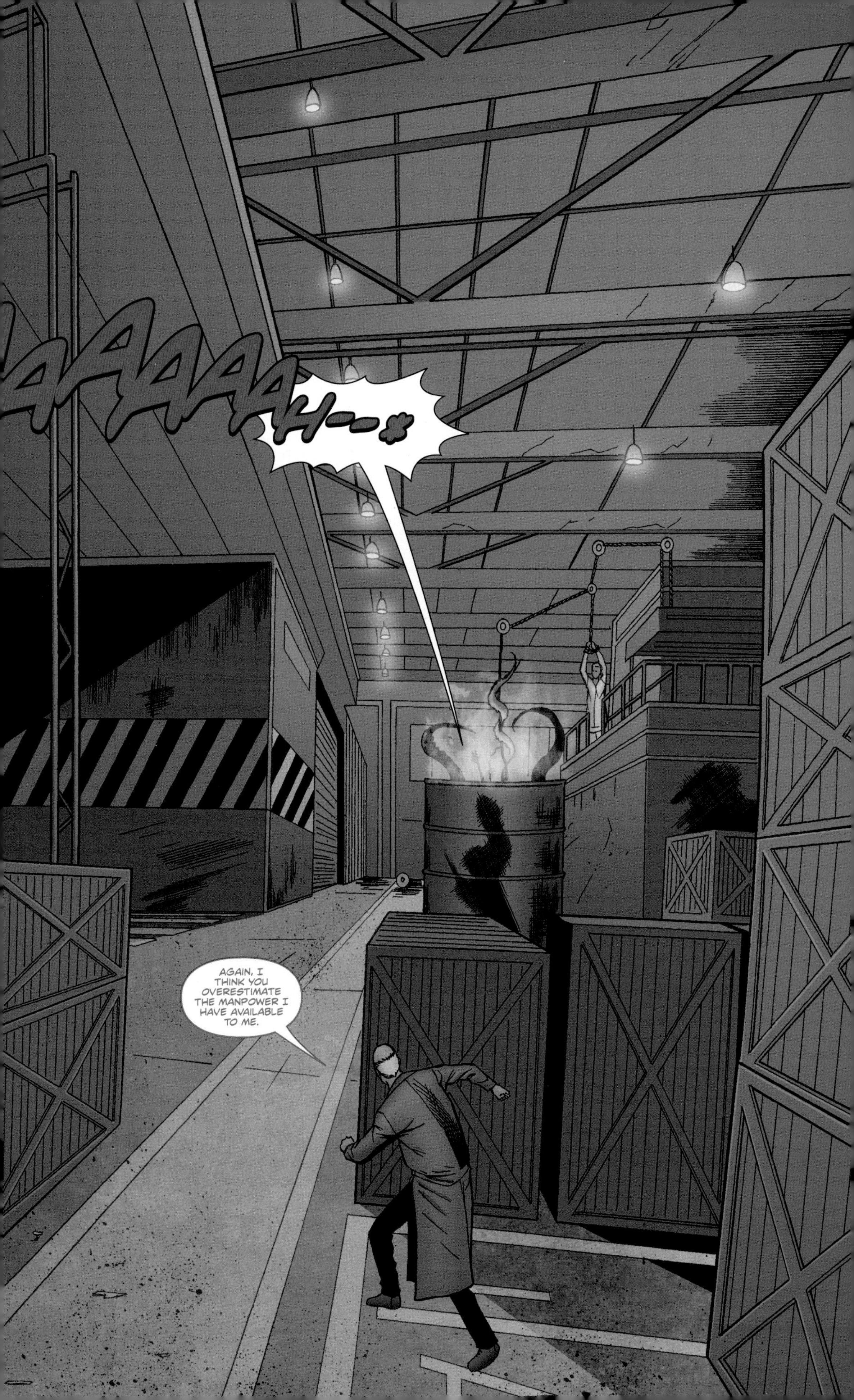

AAAAAAAH--!!
AGAIN, I THINK YOU OVERESTIMATE THE MANPOWER I HAVE AVAILABLE TO ME.

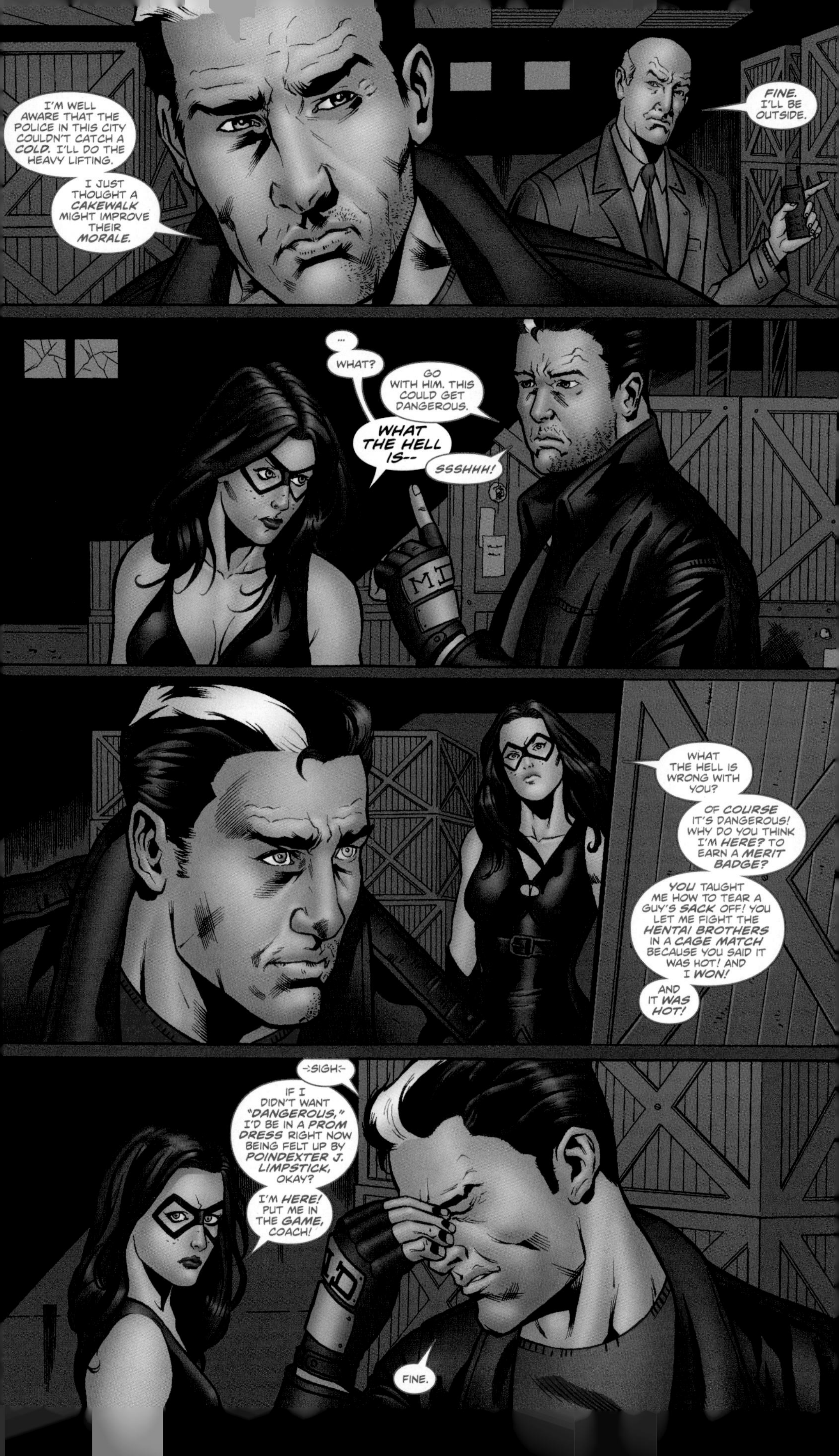
I'M WELL AWARE THAT THE POLICE IN THIS CITY COULDN'T CATCH A COLD. I'LL DO THE HEAVY LIFTING.
I JUST THOUGHT A CAKEWALK MIGHT IMPROVE THEIR MORALE.
FINE. I'LL BE OUTSIDE.
...
WHAT?
GO WITH HIM. THIS COULD GET DANGEROUS.
WHAT THE HELL IS--
SSSHHH!
WHAT THE HELL IS WRONG WITH YOU?
OF COURSE IT'S DANGEROUS! WHY DO YOU THINK I'M HERE? TO EARN A MERIT BADGE?
YOU TAUGHT ME HOW TO TEAR A GUY'S SACK OFF! YOU LET ME FIGHT THE HENTAI BROTHERS IN A CAGE MATCH BECAUSE YOU SAID IT WAS HOT! AND I WON!
AND IT WAS HOT!
-SIGH-
IF I DIDN'T WANT "DANGEROUS," I'D BE IN A PROM DRESS RIGHT NOW BEING FELT UP BY POINDEXTER J. LIMPSTICK, OKAY?
I'M HERE! PUT ME IN THE GAME, COACH!
FINE.

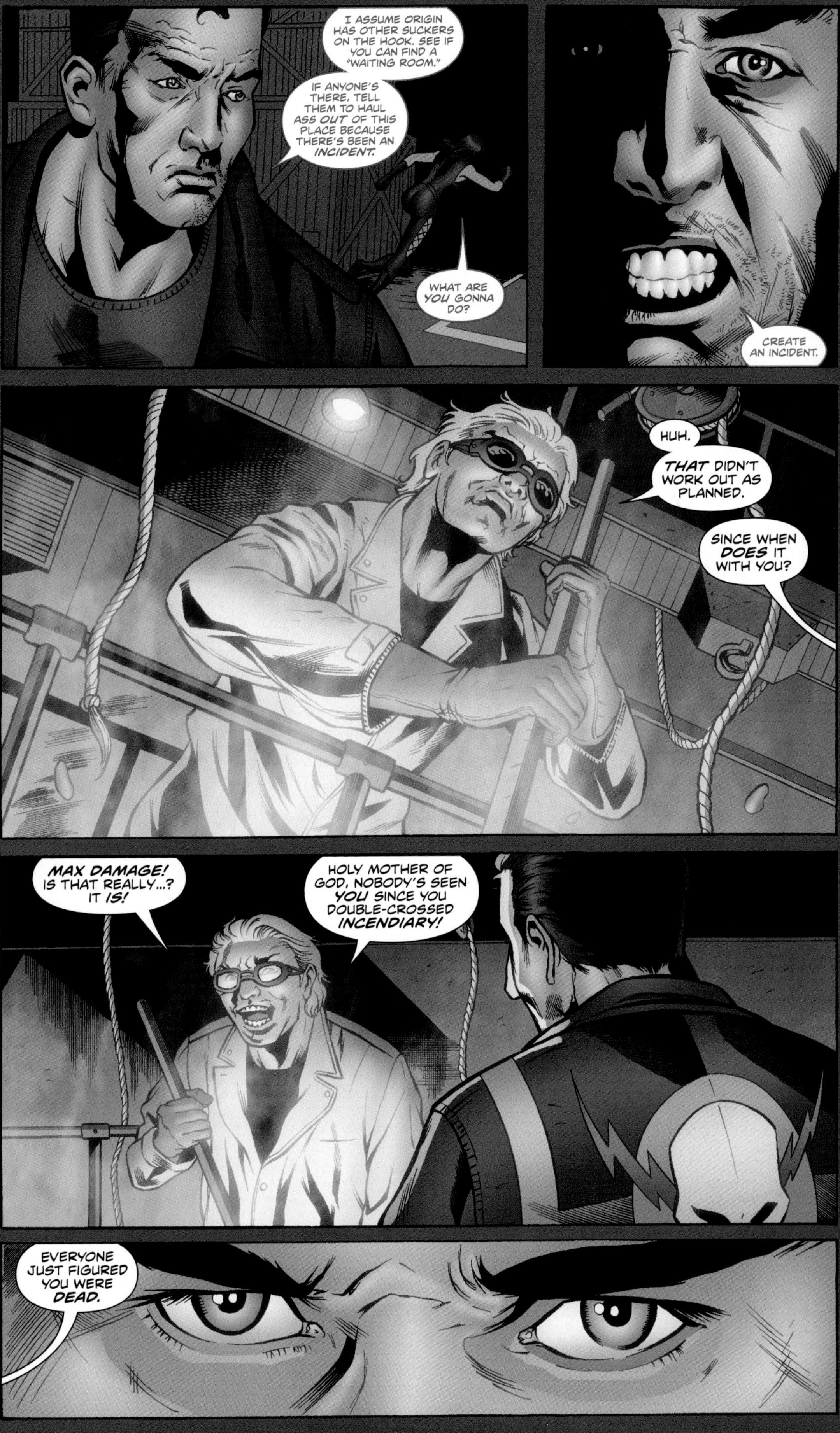
I ASSUME ORIGIN HAS OTHER SUCKERS ON THE HOOK. SEE IF YOU CAN FIND A "WAITING ROOM."
IF ANYONE'S THERE, TELL THEM TO HAUL ASS *OUT* OF THIS PLACE BECAUSE THERE'S BEEN AN *INCIDENT.*
WHAT ARE *YOU* GONNA DO?
CREATE AN INCIDENT.
HUH.
THAT DIDN'T WORK OUT AS PLANNED.
SINCE WHEN *DOES* IT WITH YOU?
MAX DAMAGE! IS THAT REALLY...? IT *IS!*
HOLY MOTHER OF GOD, NOBODY'S SEEN *YOU* SINCE YOU DOUBLE-CROSSED *INCENDIARY!*
EVERYONE JUST FIGURED YOU WERE *DEAD.*

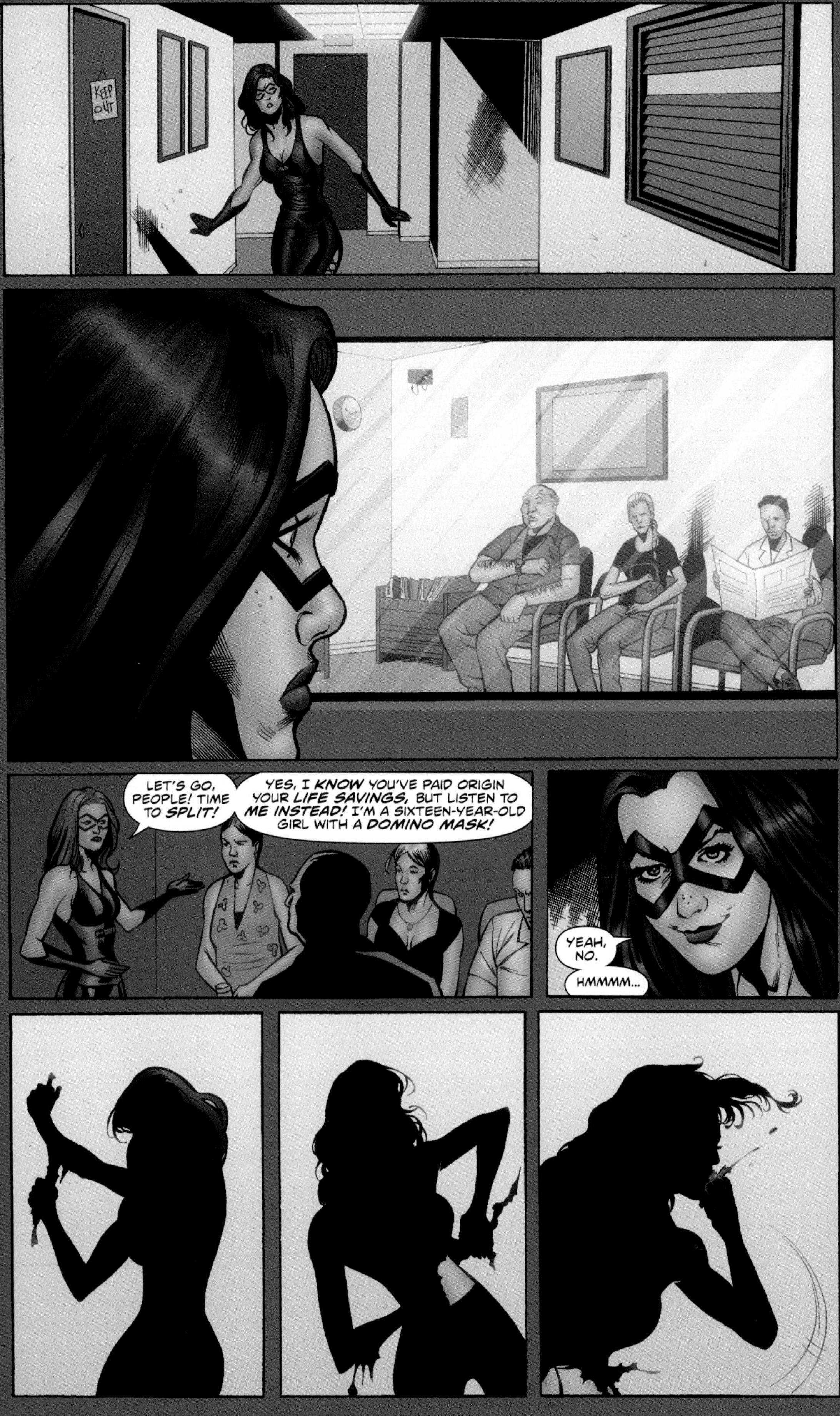
KEEP OUT
LET'S GO, PEOPLE! TIME TO SPLIT!
YES, I KNOW YOU'VE PAID ORIGIN YOUR LIFE SAVINGS, BUT LISTEN TO ME INSTEAD! I'M A SIXTEEN-YEAR-OLD GIRL WITH A DOMINO MASK!
YEAH, NO.
HMMMM...

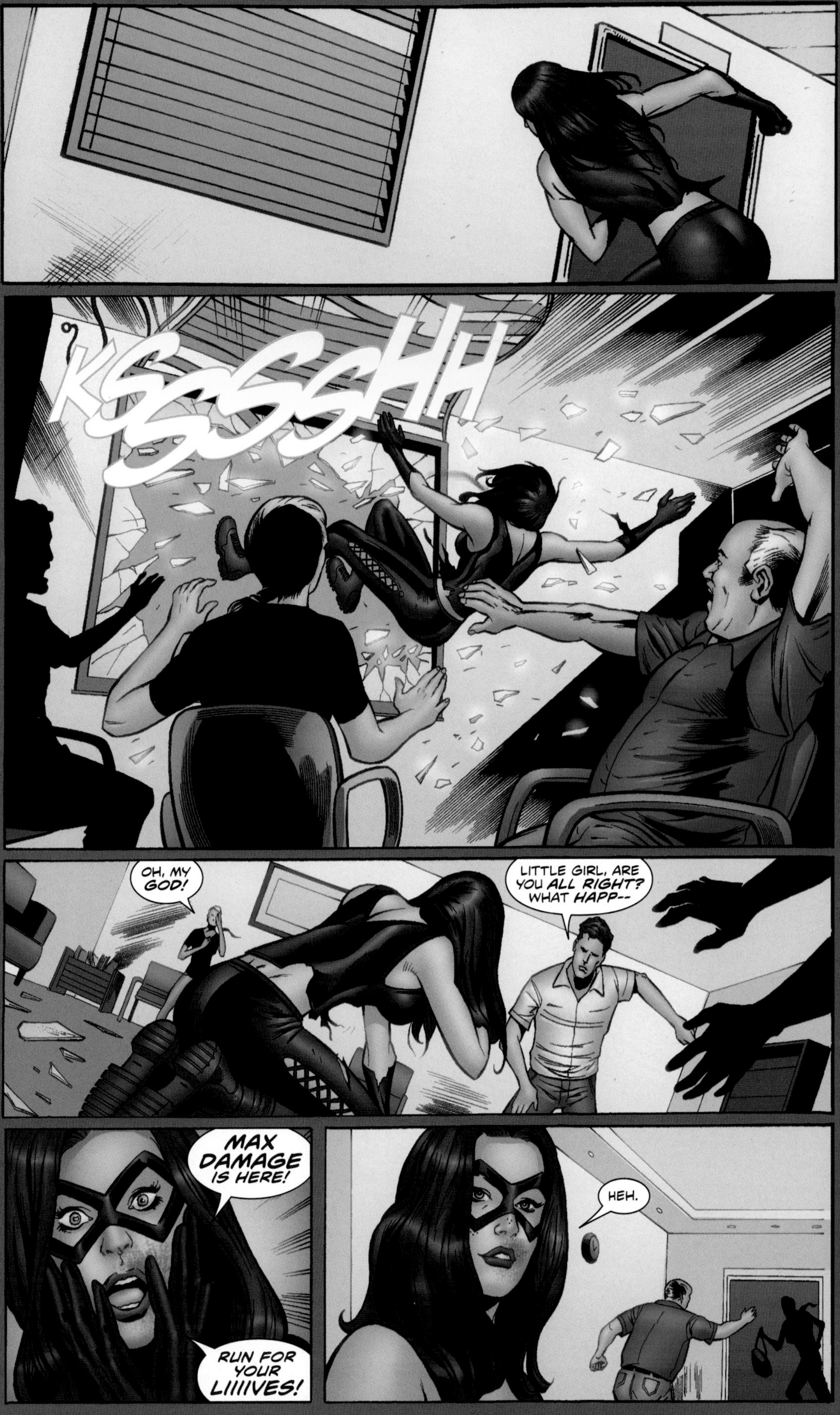
KSSSHH
OH, MY GOD!
LITTLE GIRL, ARE YOU ALL RIGHT? WHAT HAPP--
MAX DAMAGE IS HERE!
RUN FOR YOUR LIIIIVES!
HEH.

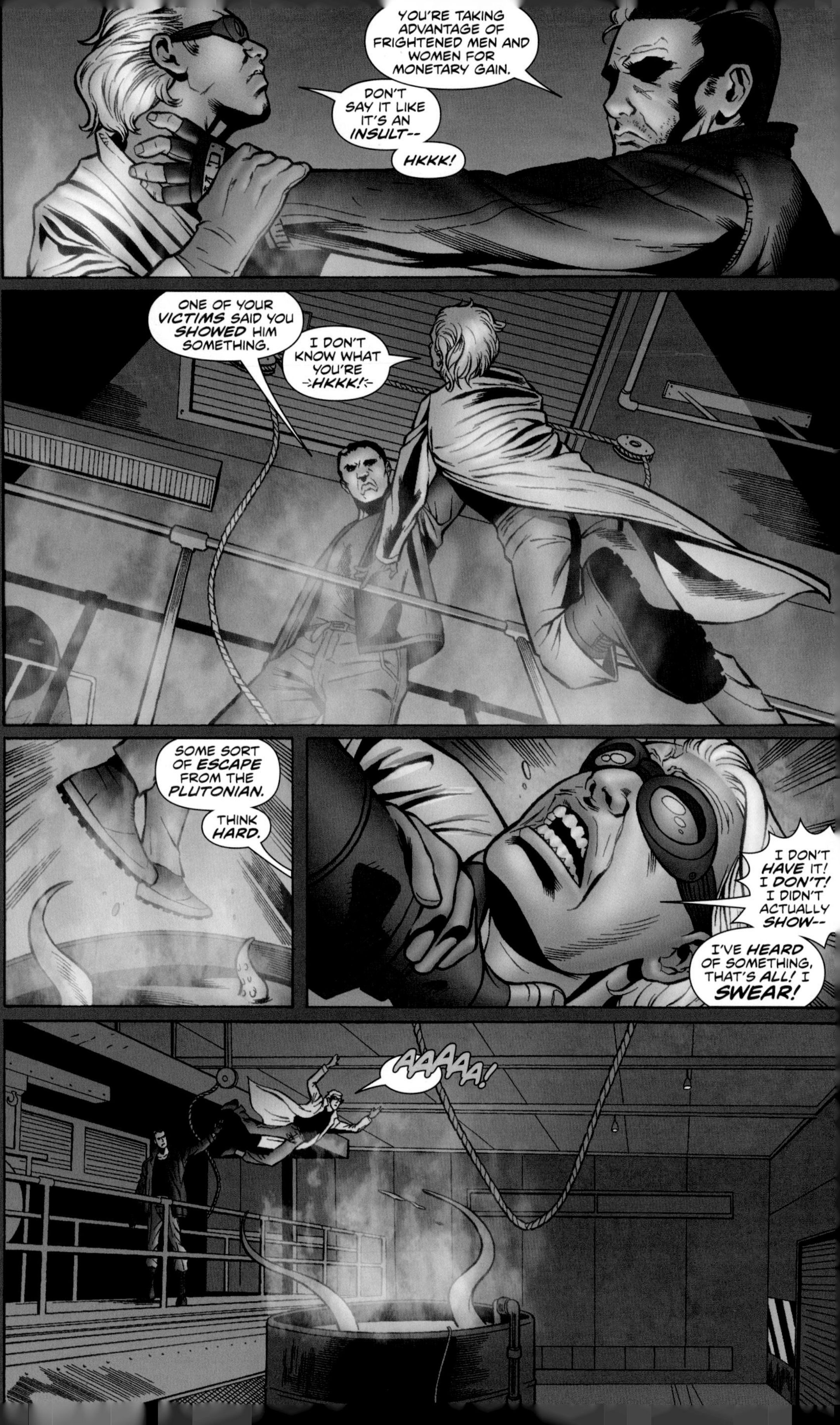
YOU'RE TAKING ADVANTAGE OF FRIGHTENED MEN AND WOMEN FOR MONETARY GAIN.
DON'T SAY IT LIKE IT'S AN INSULT--
HKKK!
ONE OF YOUR VICTIMS SAID YOU SHOWED HIM SOMETHING.
I DON'T KNOW WHAT YOU'RE -HKKK!-
SOME SORT OF ESCAPE FROM THE PLUTONIAN.
THINK HARD.
I DON'T HAVE IT! I DON'T! I DIDN'T ACTUALLY SHOW--
I'VE HEARD OF SOMETHING, THAT'S ALL! I SWEAR!
AAAAA!

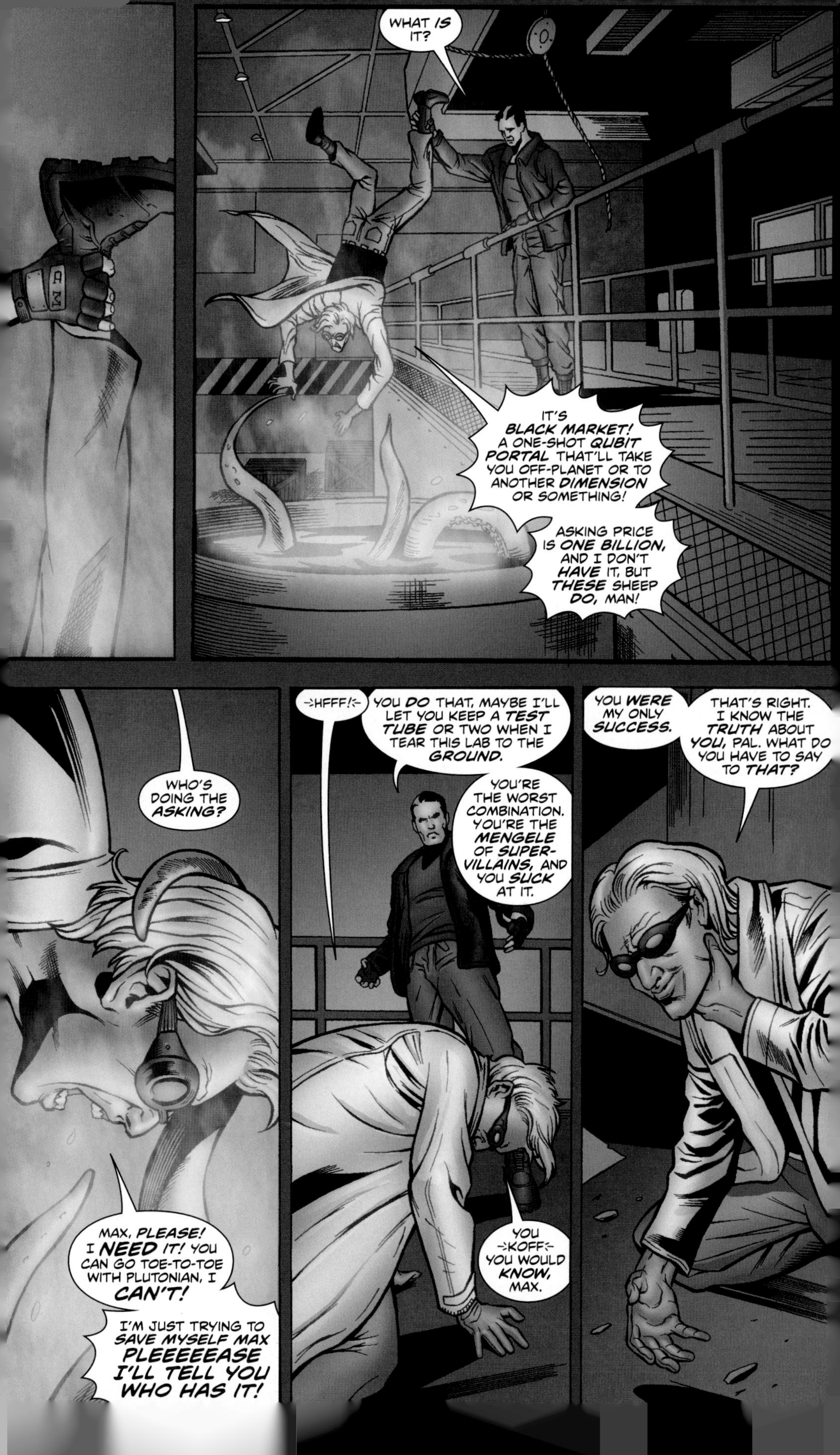

WHAT IS IT?
IT'S BLACK MARKET! A ONE-SHOT QUBIT PORTAL THAT'LL TAKE YOU OFF-PLANET OR TO ANOTHER DIMENSION OR SOMETHING!
ASKING PRICE IS ONE BILLION, AND I DON'T HAVE IT, BUT THESE SHEEP DO, MAN!
WHO'S DOING THE ASKING?
MAX, PLEASE! I NEED IT! YOU CAN GO TOE-TO-TOE WITH PLUTONIAN, I CAN'T!
I'M JUST TRYING TO SAVE MYSELF MAX PLEEEEEASE I'LL TELL YOU WHO HAS IT!
-HFFF!-
YOU DO THAT, MAYBE I'LL LET YOU KEEP A TEST TUBE OR TWO WHEN I TEAR THIS LAB TO THE GROUND.
YOU'RE THE WORST COMBINATION. YOU'RE THE MENGELE OF SUPER-VILLAINS, AND YOU SUCK AT IT.
YOU -KOFF- YOU WOULD KNOW, MAX.
YOU WERE MY ONLY SUCCESS.
THAT'S RIGHT. I KNOW THE TRUTH ABOUT YOU, PAL. WHAT DO YOU HAVE TO SAY TO THAT?

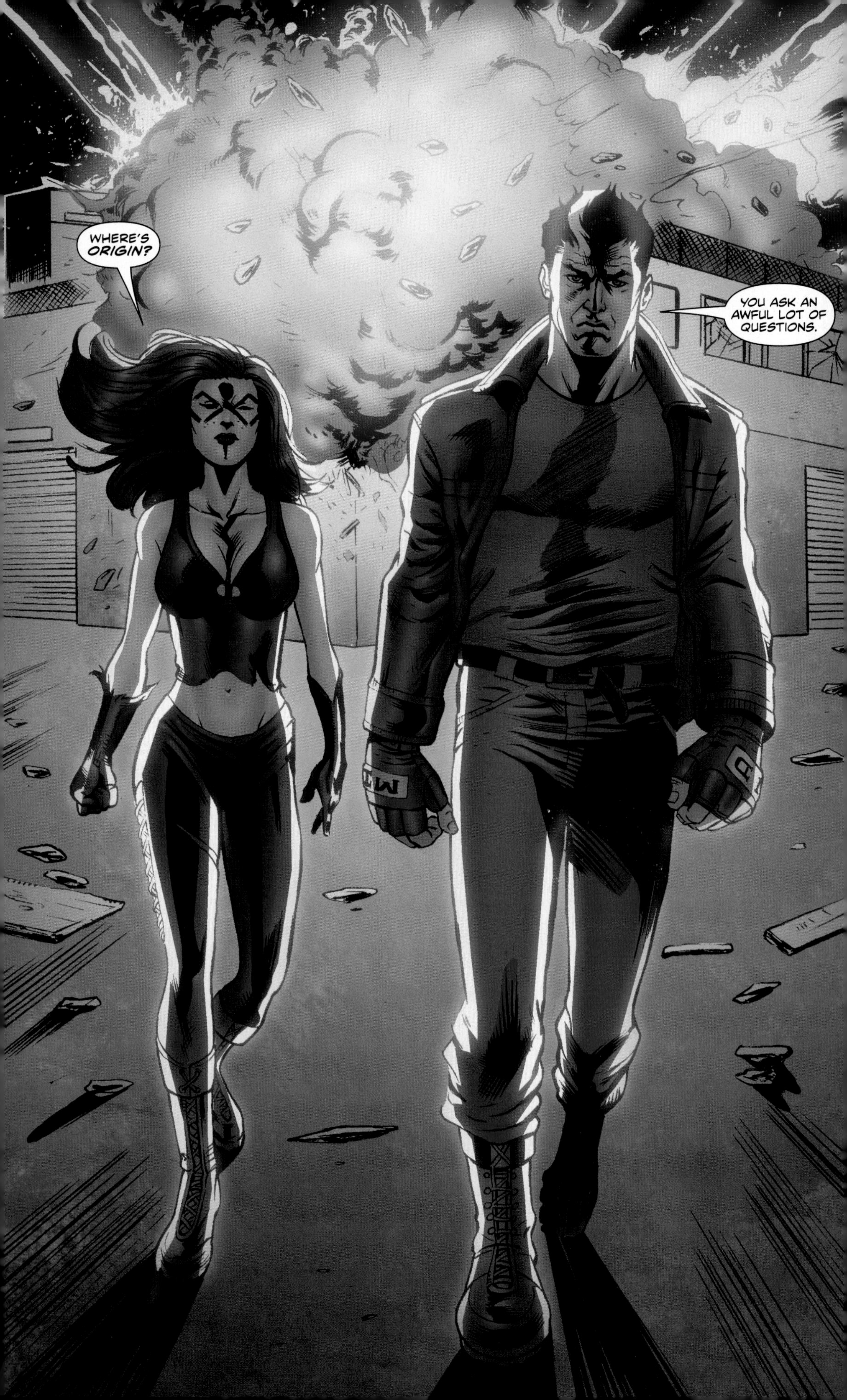
WHERE'S ORIGIN?
YOU ASK AN AWFUL LOT OF QUESTIONS.

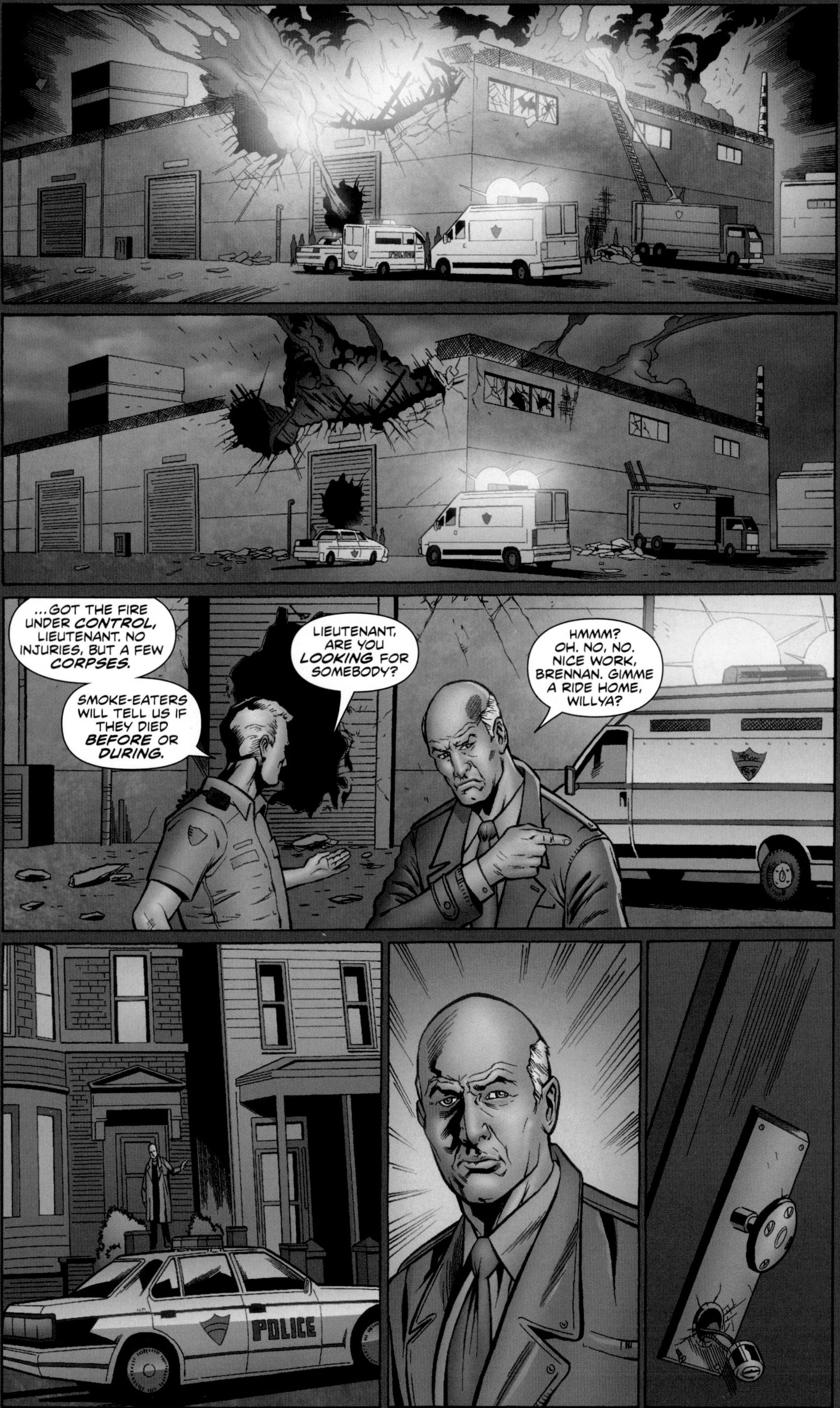
POLICE
...GOT THE FIRE UNDER CONTROL, LIEUTENANT. NO INJURIES, BUT A FEW CORPSES.
SMOKE-EATERS WILL TELL US IF THEY DIED BEFORE OR DURING.
LIEUTENANT, ARE YOU LOOKING FOR SOMEBODY?
HMMM? OH. NO, NO. NICE WORK, BRENNAN. GIMME A RIDE HOME, WILLYA?
POLICE

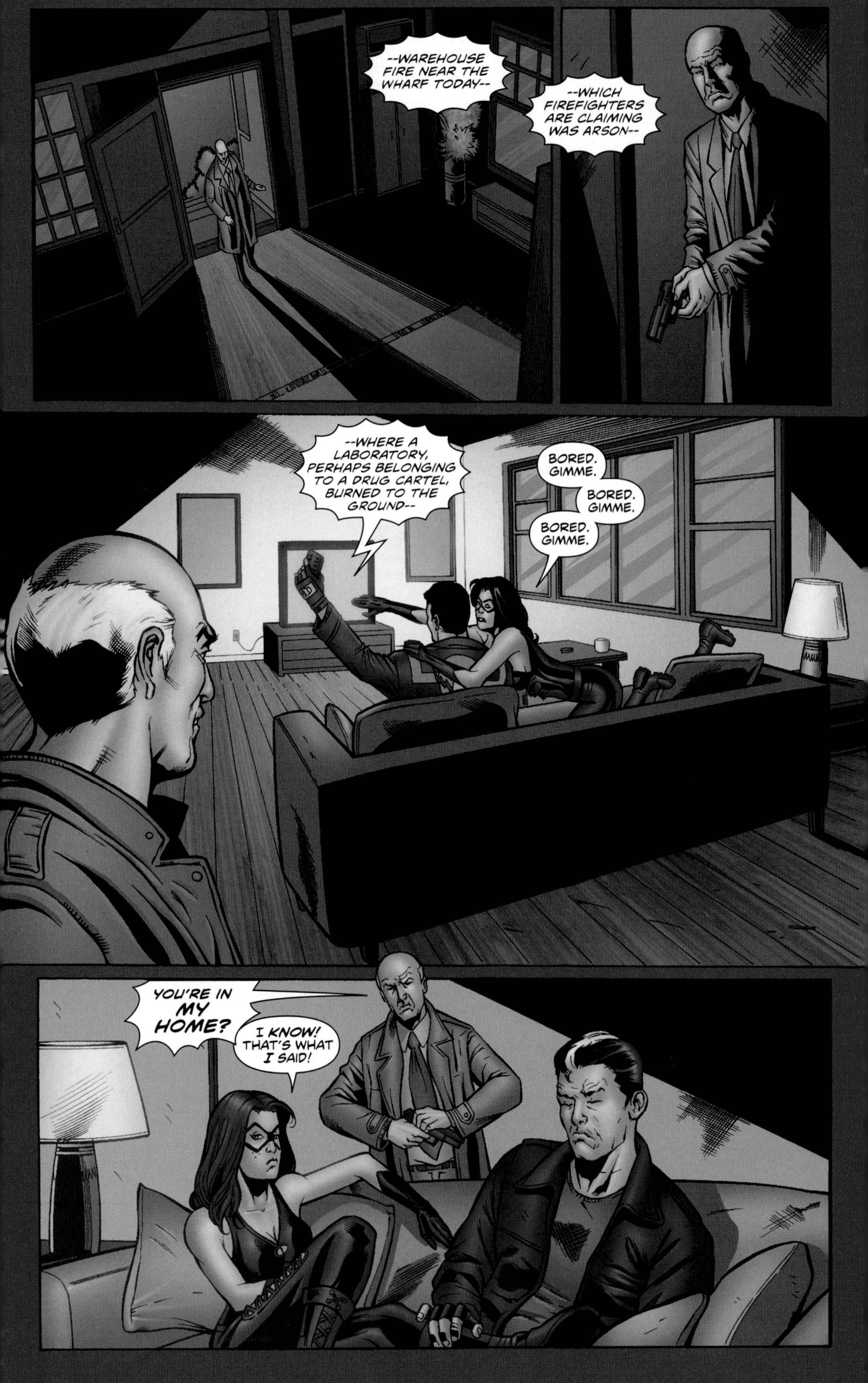
--WAREHOUSE FIRE NEAR THE WHARF TODAY--
--WHICH FIREFIGHTERS ARE CLAIMING WAS ARSON--
--WHERE A LABORATORY, PERHAPS BELONGING TO A DRUG CARTEL, BURNED TO THE GROUND--
BORED. GIMME.
BORED. GIMME.
BORED. GIMME.
YOU'RE IN MY HOME?
I KNOW! THAT'S WHAT I SAID!

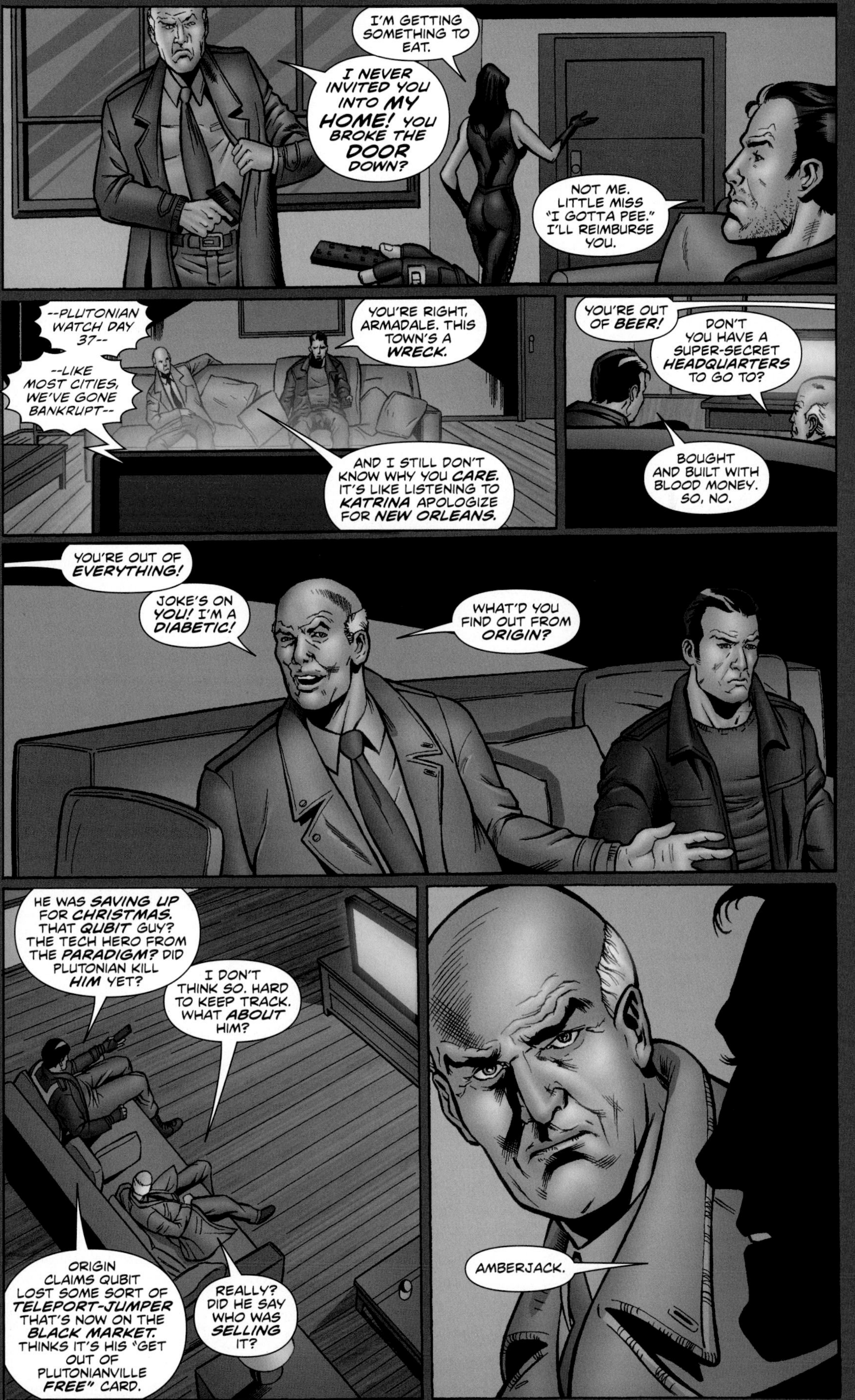
I'M GETTING SOMETHING TO EAT.
I NEVER INVITED YOU INTO MY HOME! YOU BROKE THE DOOR DOWN?
NOT ME. LITTLE MISS "I GOTTA PEE." I'LL REIMBURSE YOU.
--PLUTONIAN WATCH DAY 37--
--LIKE MOST CITIES, WE'VE GONE BANKRUPT--
YOU'RE RIGHT, ARMADALE. THIS TOWN'S A WRECK.
AND I STILL DON'T KNOW WHY YOU CARE. IT'S LIKE LISTENING TO KATRINA APOLOGIZE FOR NEW ORLEANS.
YOU'RE OUT OF BEER!
DON'T YOU HAVE A SUPER-SECRET HEADQUARTERS TO GO TO?
BOUGHT AND BUILT WITH BLOOD MONEY. SO, NO.
YOU'RE OUT OF EVERYTHING!
JOKE'S ON YOU! I'M A DIABETIC!
WHAT'D YOU FIND OUT FROM ORIGIN?
HE WAS SAVING UP FOR CHRISTMAS. THAT QUBIT GUY? THE TECH HERO FROM THE PARADIGM? DID PLUTONIAN KILL HIM YET?
I DON'T THINK SO. HARD TO KEEP TRACK. WHAT ABOUT HIM?
ORIGIN CLAIMS QUBIT LOST SOME SORT OF TELEPORT-JUMPER THAT'S NOW ON THE BLACK MARKET. THINKS IT'S HIS "GET OUT OF PLUTONIANVILLE FREE" CARD.
REALLY? DID HE SAY WHO WAS SELLING IT?
AMBERJACK.

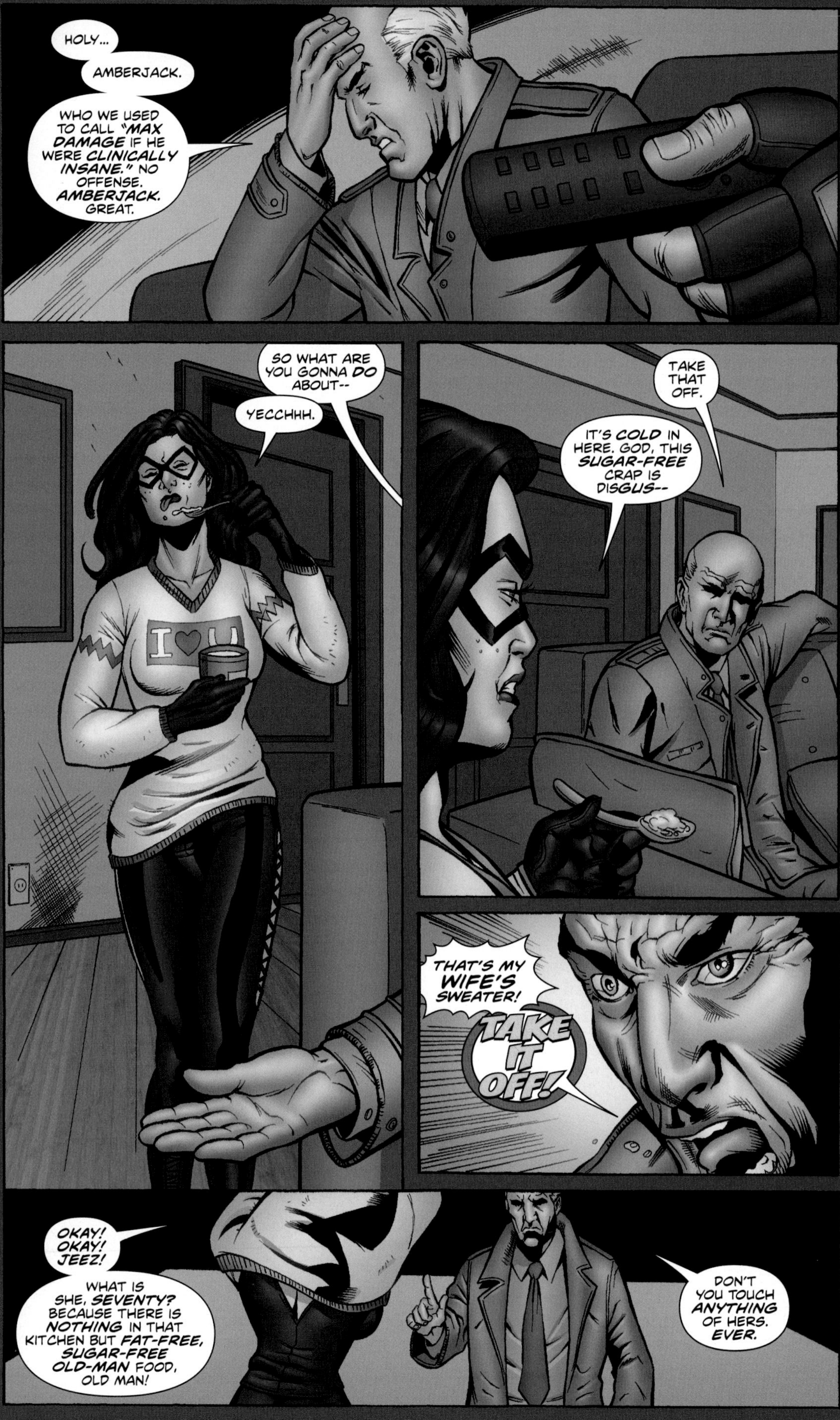
HOLY...
AMBERJACK.
WHO WE USED TO CALL "MAX DAMAGE IF HE WERE CLINICALLY INSANE." NO OFFENSE. AMBERJACK. GREAT.
SO WHAT ARE YOU GONNA DO ABOUT--
YECCHHH.
TAKE THAT OFF.
IT'S COLD IN HERE. GOD, THIS SUGAR-FREE CRAP IS DISGUS--
THAT'S MY WIFE'S SWEATER!
TAKE IT OFF!
OKAY! OKAY! JEEZ!
WHAT IS SHE, SEVENTY? BECAUSE THERE IS NOTHING IN THAT KITCHEN BUT FAT-FREE, SUGAR-FREE OLD-MAN FOOD, OLD MAN!
DON'T YOU TOUCH ANYTHING OF HERS. EVER.

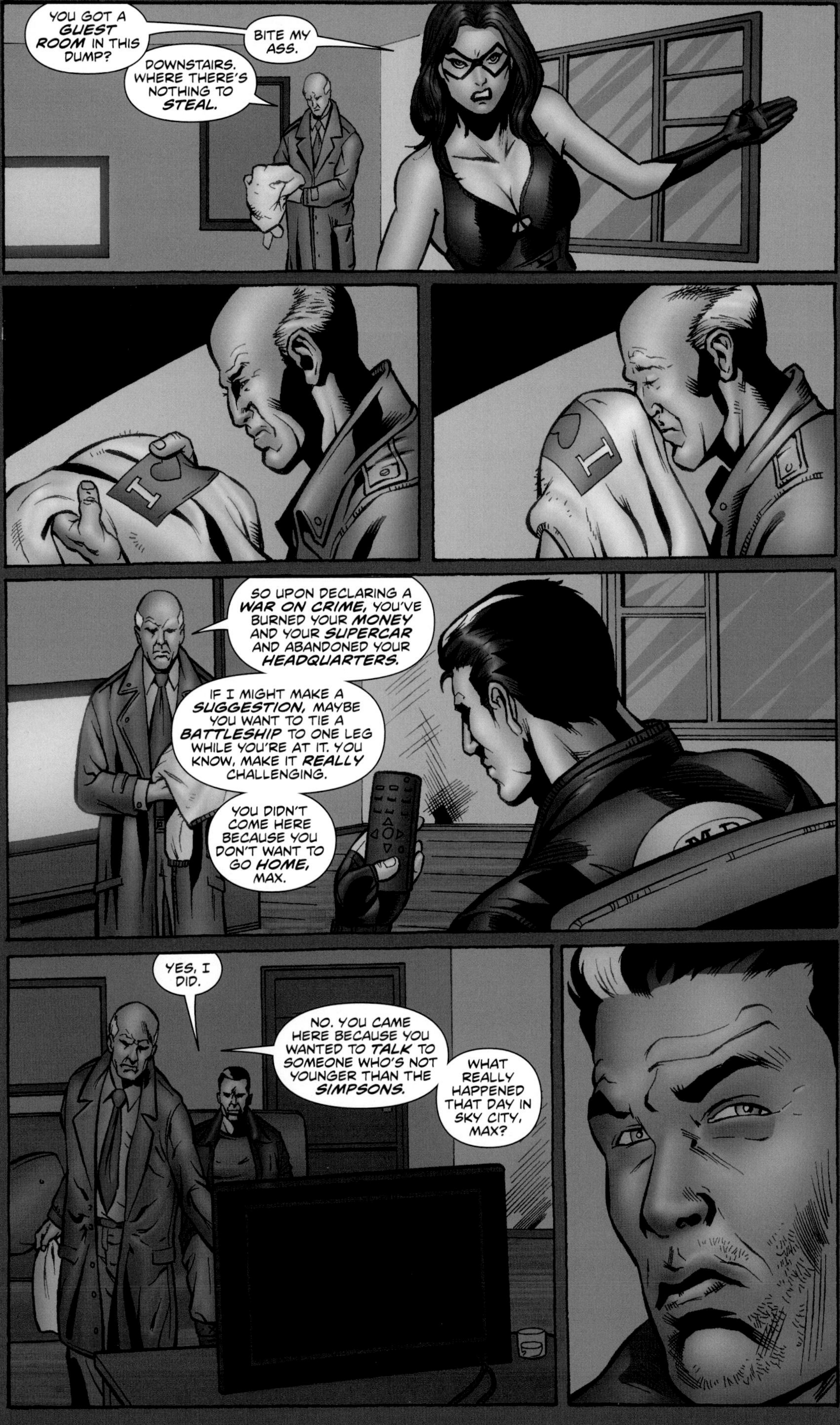
YOU GOT A GUEST ROOM IN THIS DUMP?
BITE MY ASS.
DOWNSTAIRS. WHERE THERE'S NOTHING TO STEAL.
SO UPON DECLARING A WAR ON CRIME, YOU'VE BURNED YOUR MONEY AND YOUR SUPERCAR AND ABANDONED YOUR HEADQUARTERS.
IF I MIGHT MAKE A SUGGESTION, MAYBE YOU WANT TO TIE A BATTLESHIP TO ONE LEG WHILE YOU'RE AT IT. YOU KNOW, MAKE IT REALLY CHALLENGING.
YOU DIDN'T COME HERE BECAUSE YOU DON'T WANT TO GO HOME, MAX.
YES, I DID.
NO. YOU CAME HERE BECAUSE YOU WANTED TO TALK TO SOMEONE WHO'S NOT YOUNGER THAN THE SIMPSONS.
WHAT REALLY HAPPENED THAT DAY IN SKY CITY, MAX?

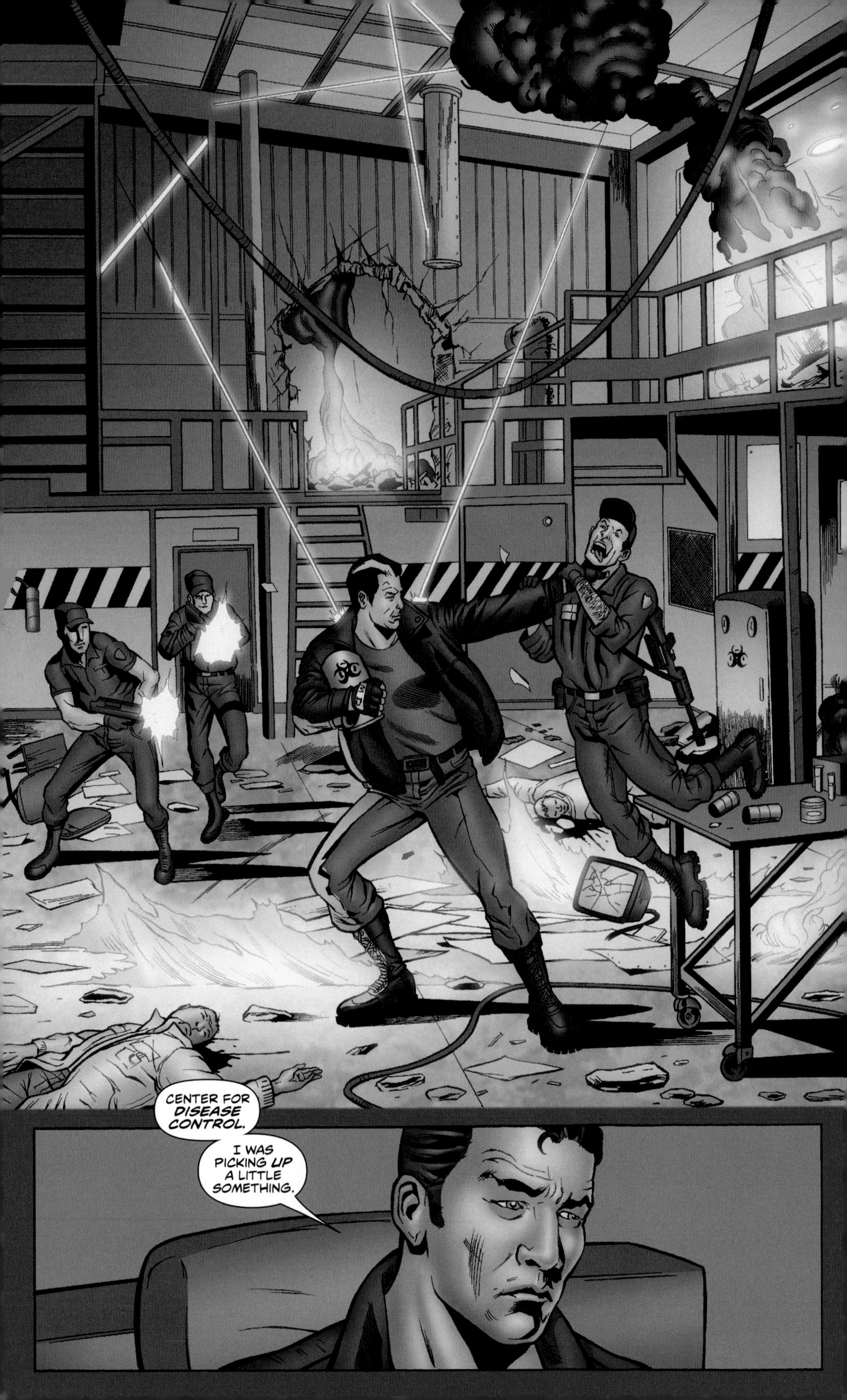
CENTER FOR DISEASE CONTROL.
I WAS PICKING UP A LITTLE SOMETHING.

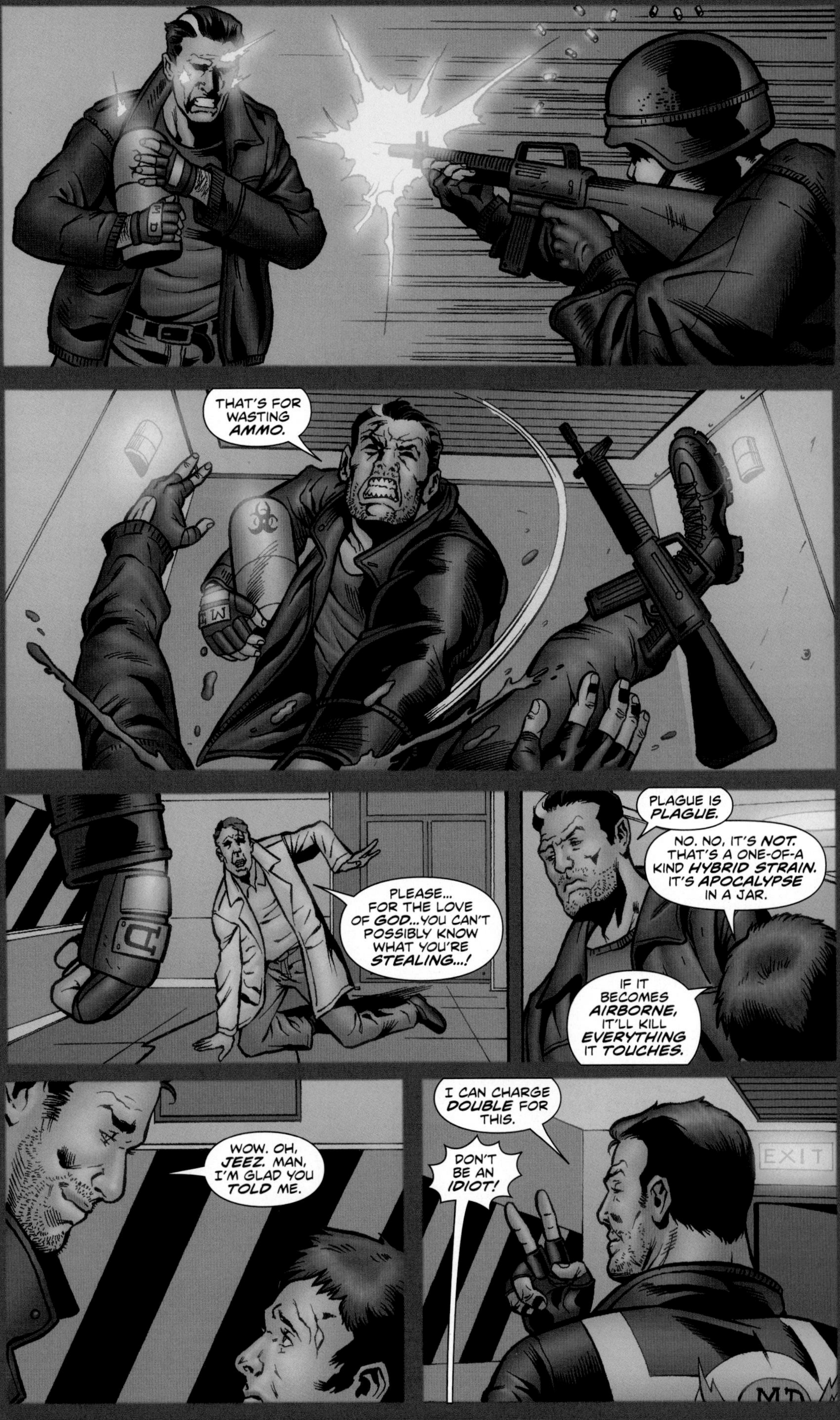
THAT'S FOR WASTING AMMO.
PLEASE... FOR THE LOVE OF GOD...YOU CAN'T POSSIBLY KNOW WHAT YOU'RE STEALING...!
PLAGUE IS PLAGUE.
NO. NO, IT'S NOT. THAT'S A ONE-OF-A KIND HYBRID STRAIN. IT'S APOCALYPSE IN A JAR.
IF IT BECOMES AIRBORNE, IT'LL KILL EVERYTHING IT TOUCHES.
WOW. OH, JEEZ. MAN, I'M GLAD YOU TOLD ME.
I CAN CHARGE DOUBLE FOR THIS.
DON'T BE AN IDIOT!
EXIT

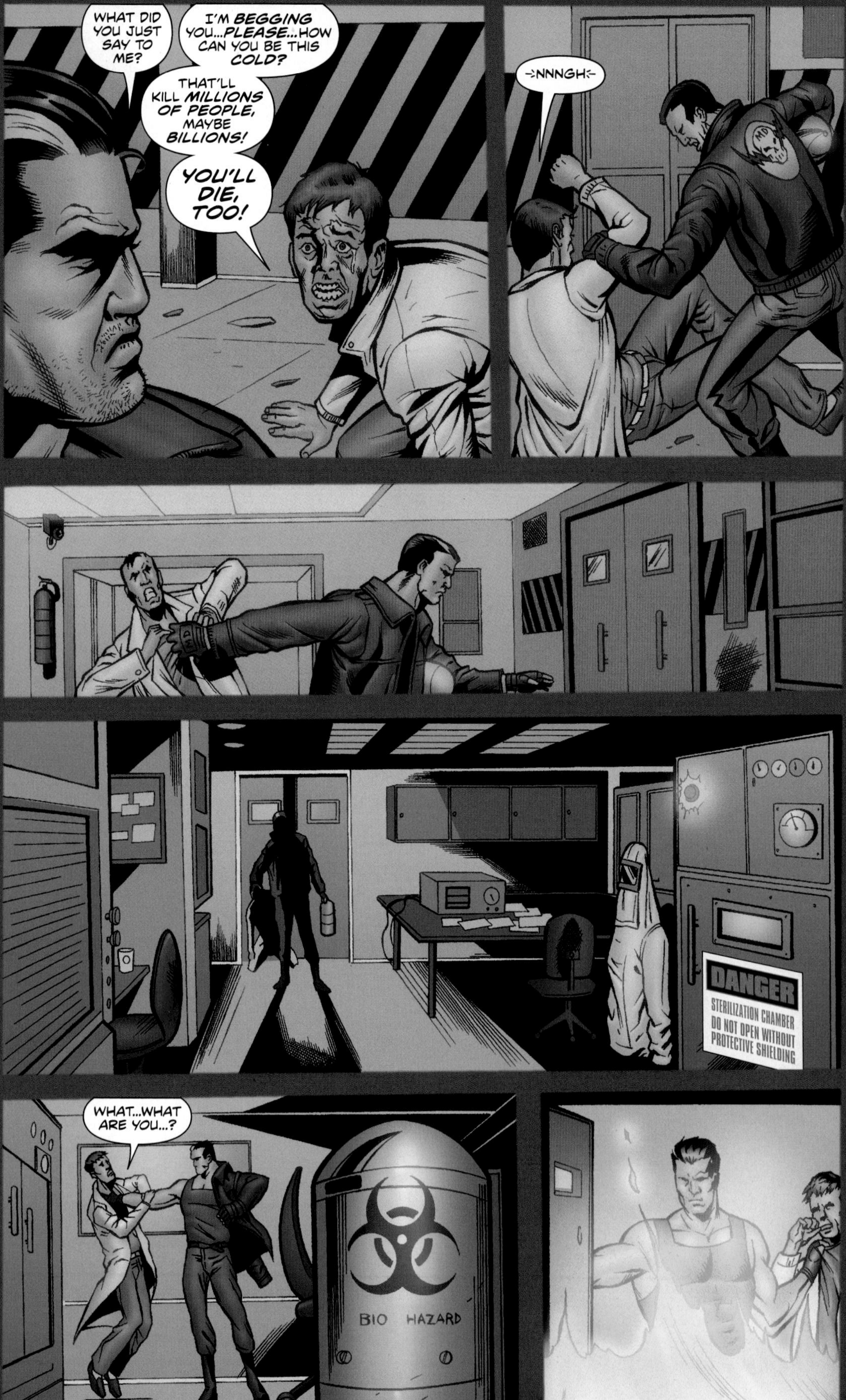
WHAT DID YOU JUST SAY TO ME?
I'M BEGGING YOU...PLEASE...HOW CAN YOU BE THIS COLD?
THAT'LL KILL MILLIONS OF PEOPLE, MAYBE BILLIONS!
YOU'LL DIE, TOO!
-NNNGH-
DANGER
STERILIZATION CHAMBER
DO NOT OPEN WITHOUT
PROTECTIVE SHIELDING
WHAT...WHAT ARE YOU...?
BIO HAZARD

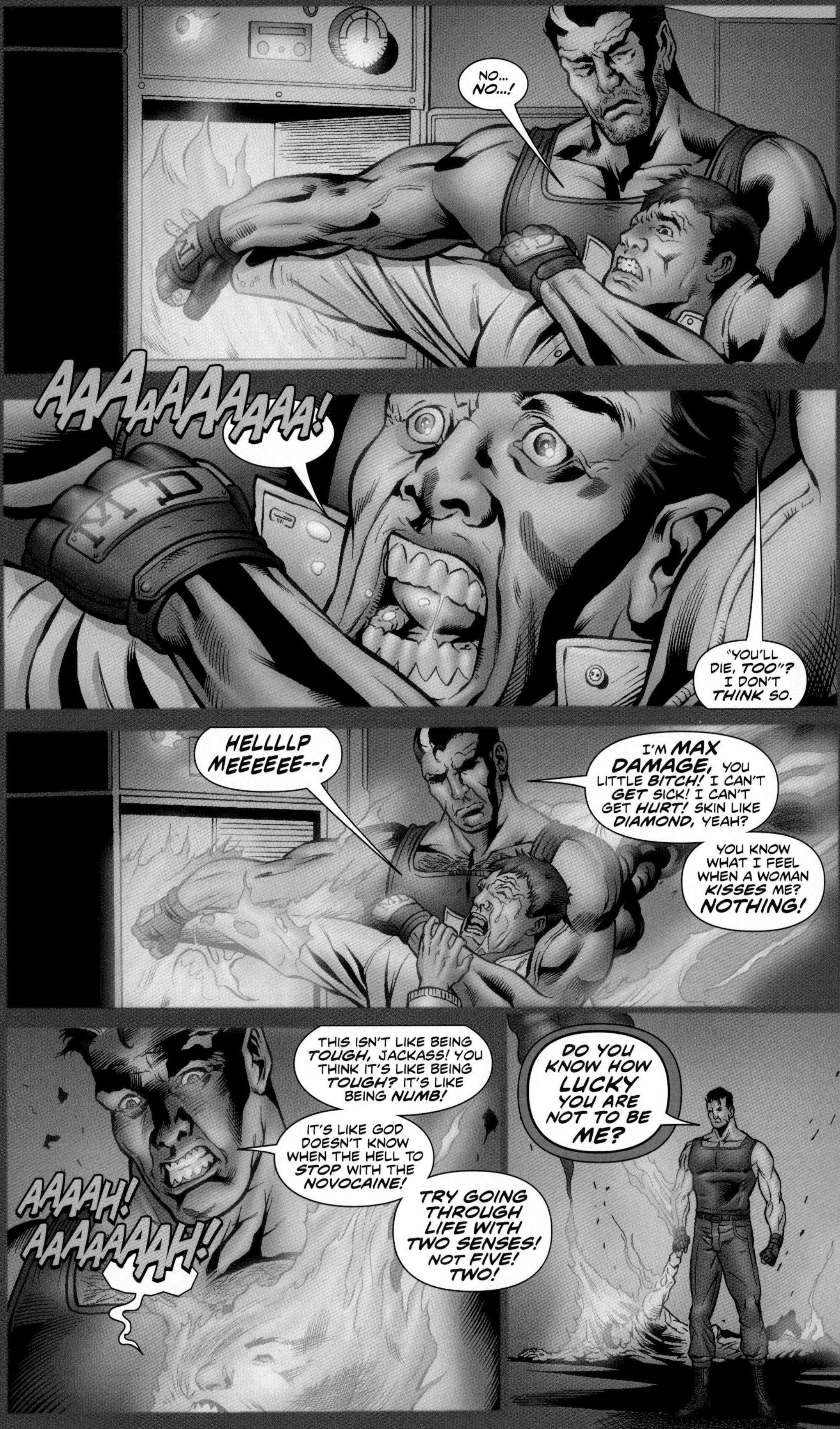
NO... NO...!
AAAAAAAAAAA!
"YOU'LL DIE, TOO"? I DON'T THINK SO.
HELLLLP MEEEEEE--!
I'M MAX DAMAGE, YOU LITTLE BITCH! I CAN'T GET SICK! I CAN'T GET HURT! SKIN LIKE DIAMOND, YEAH?
YOU KNOW WHAT I FEEL WHEN A WOMAN KISSES ME? NOTHING!
THIS ISN'T LIKE BEING TOUGH, JACKASS! YOU THINK IT'S LIKE BEING TOUGH? IT'S LIKE BEING NUMB!
IT'S LIKE GOD DOESN'T KNOW WHEN THE HELL TO STOP WITH THE NOVOCAINE!
AAAAH! AAAAAAAH!
TRY GOING THROUGH LIFE WITH TWO SENSES! NOT FIVE! TWO!
DO YOU KNOW HOW LUCKY YOU ARE NOT TO BE ME?

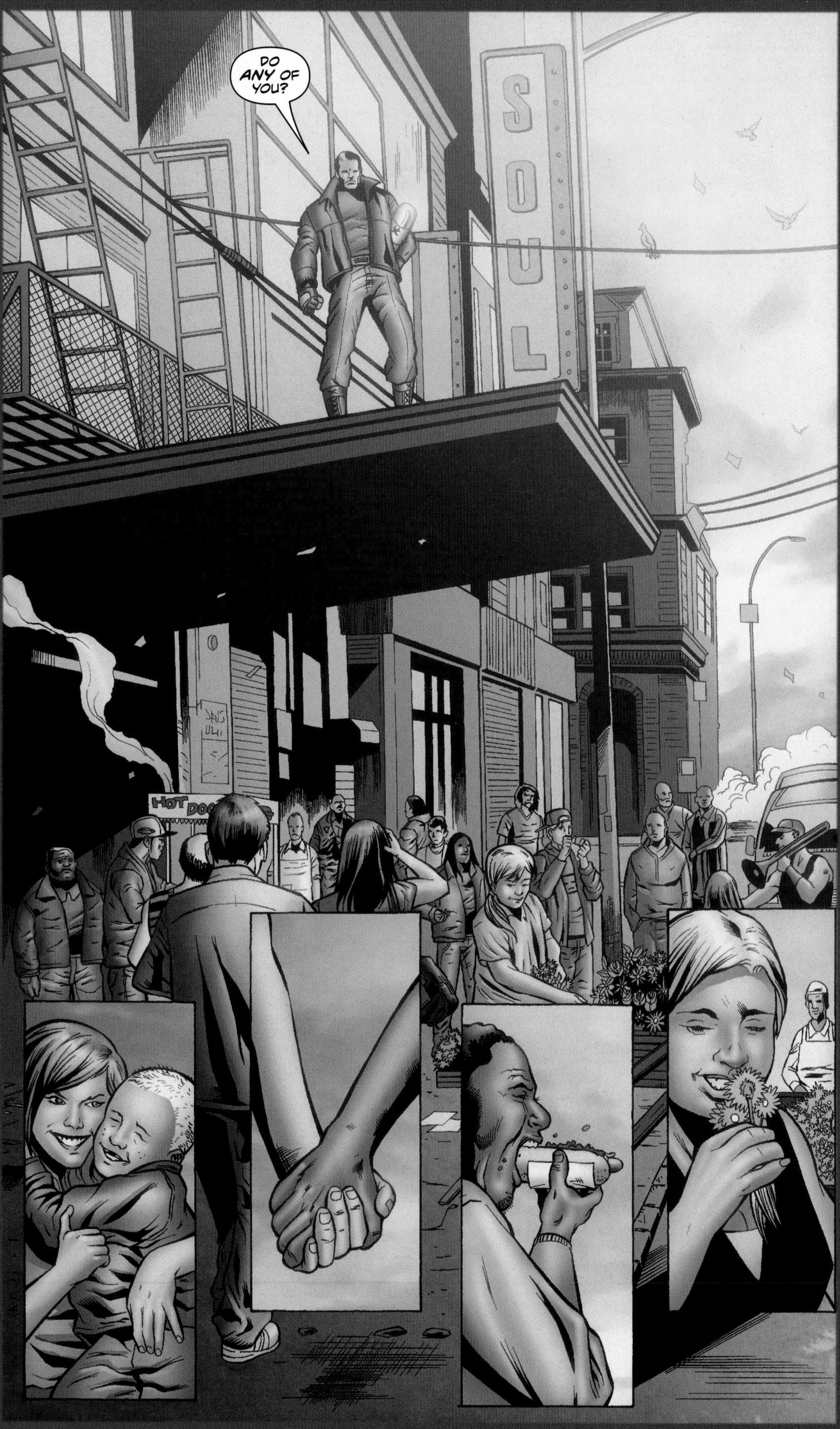
DO ANY OF YOU?
SOUL
HOT DOG

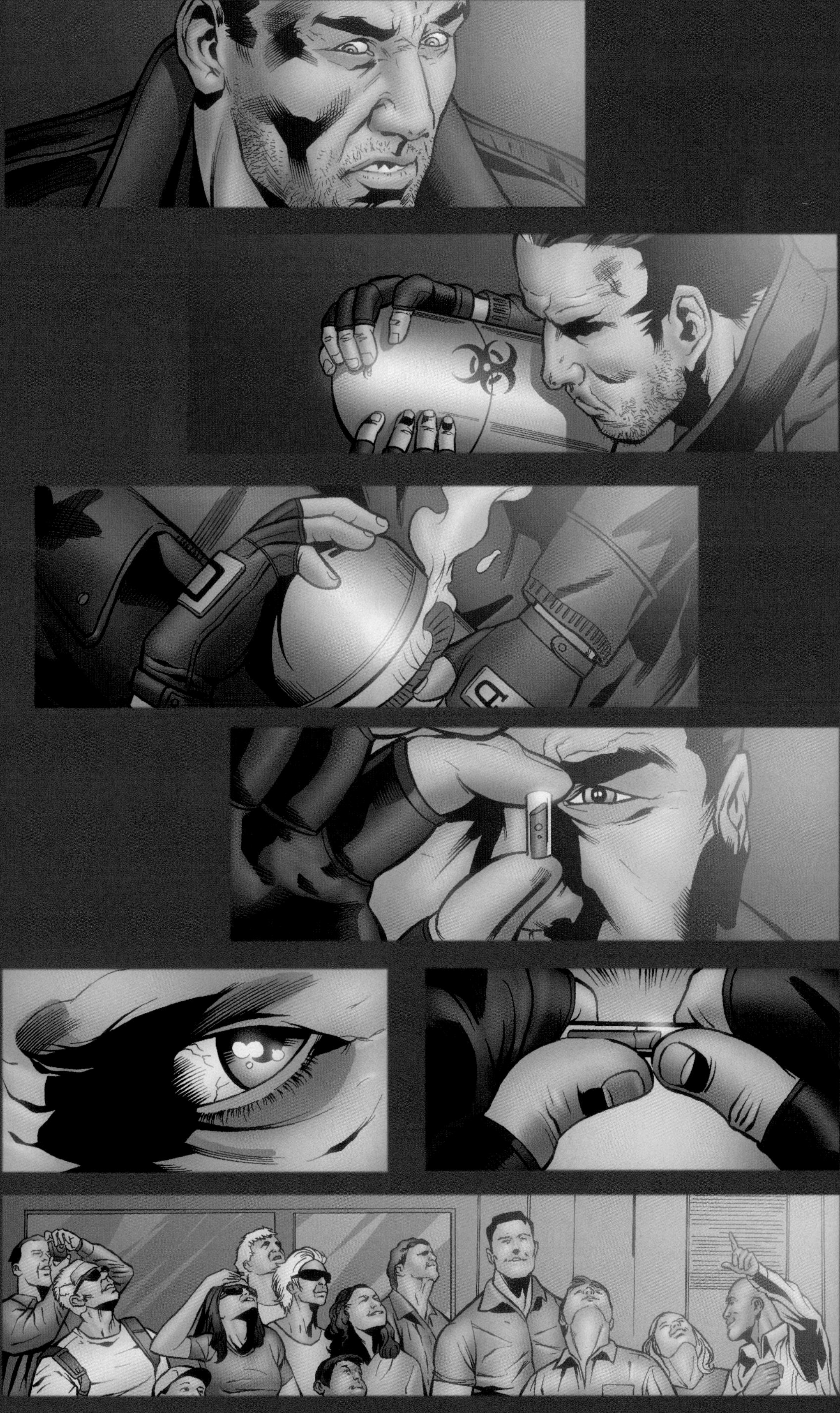

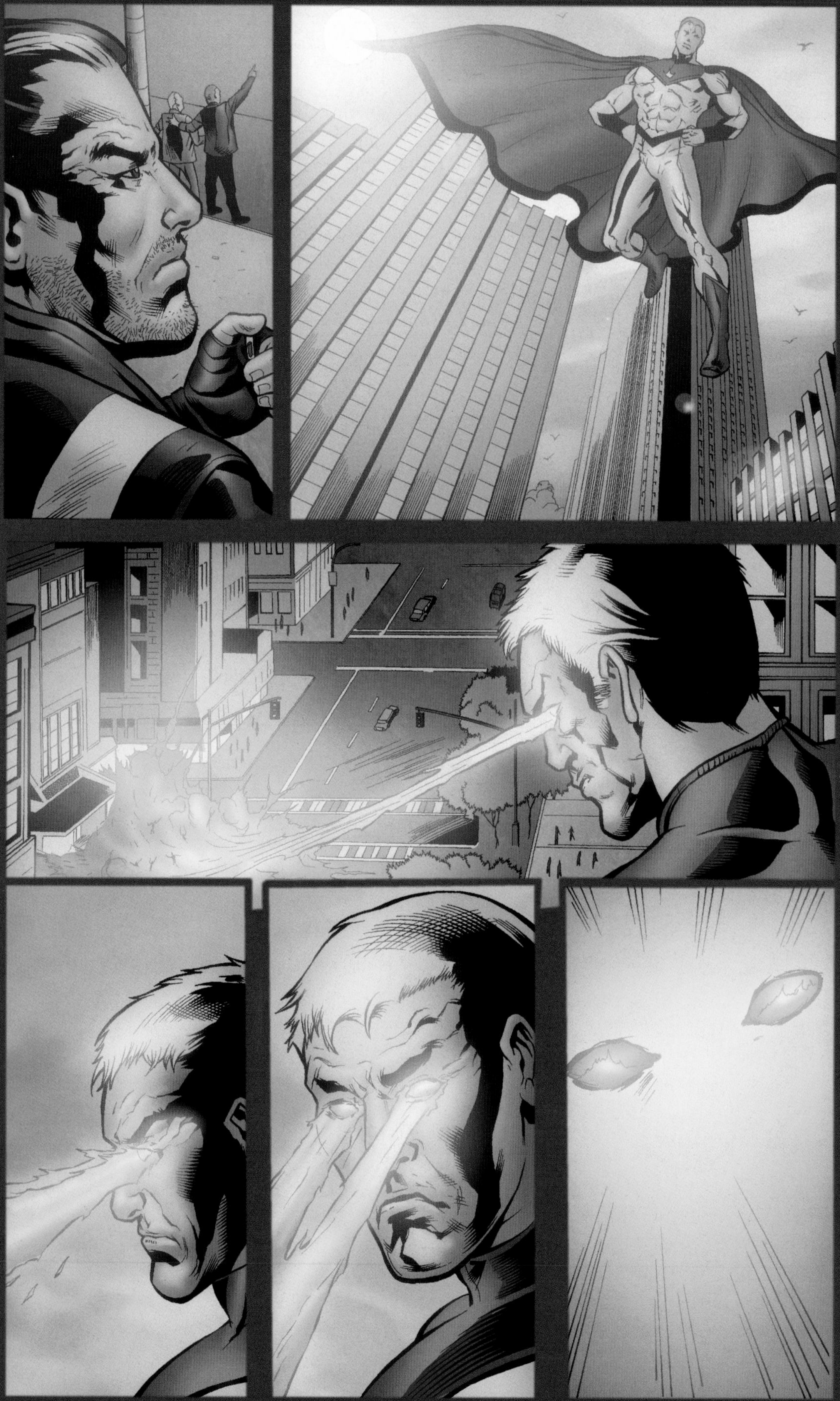

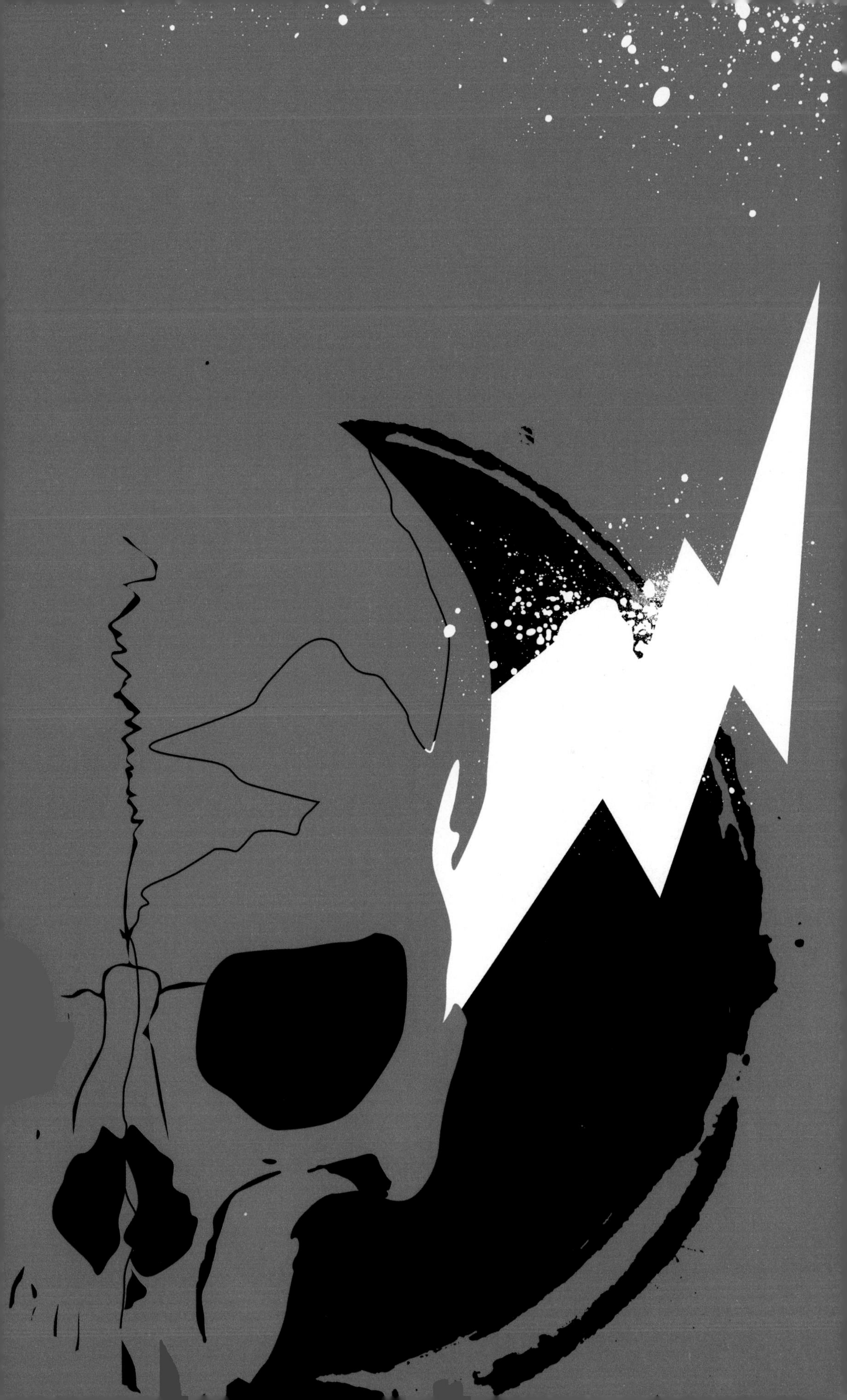

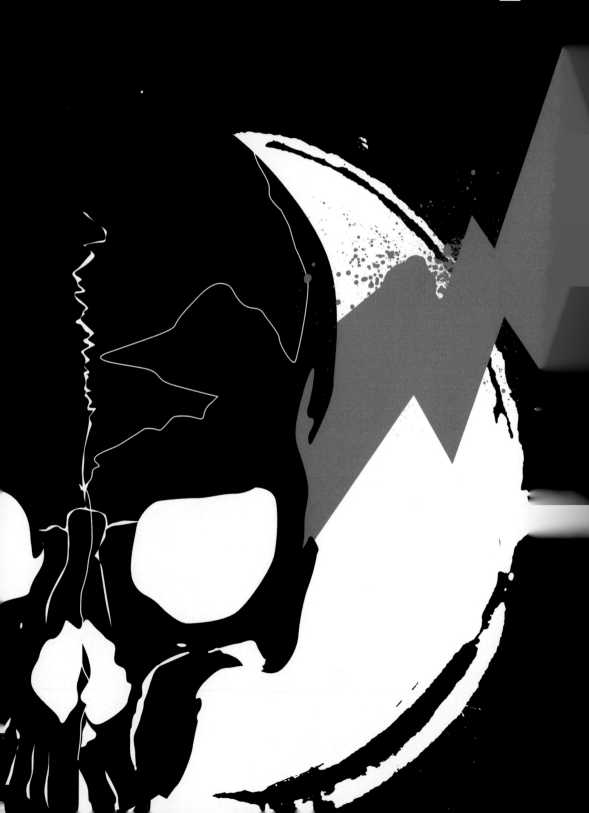

CHAPTER 4

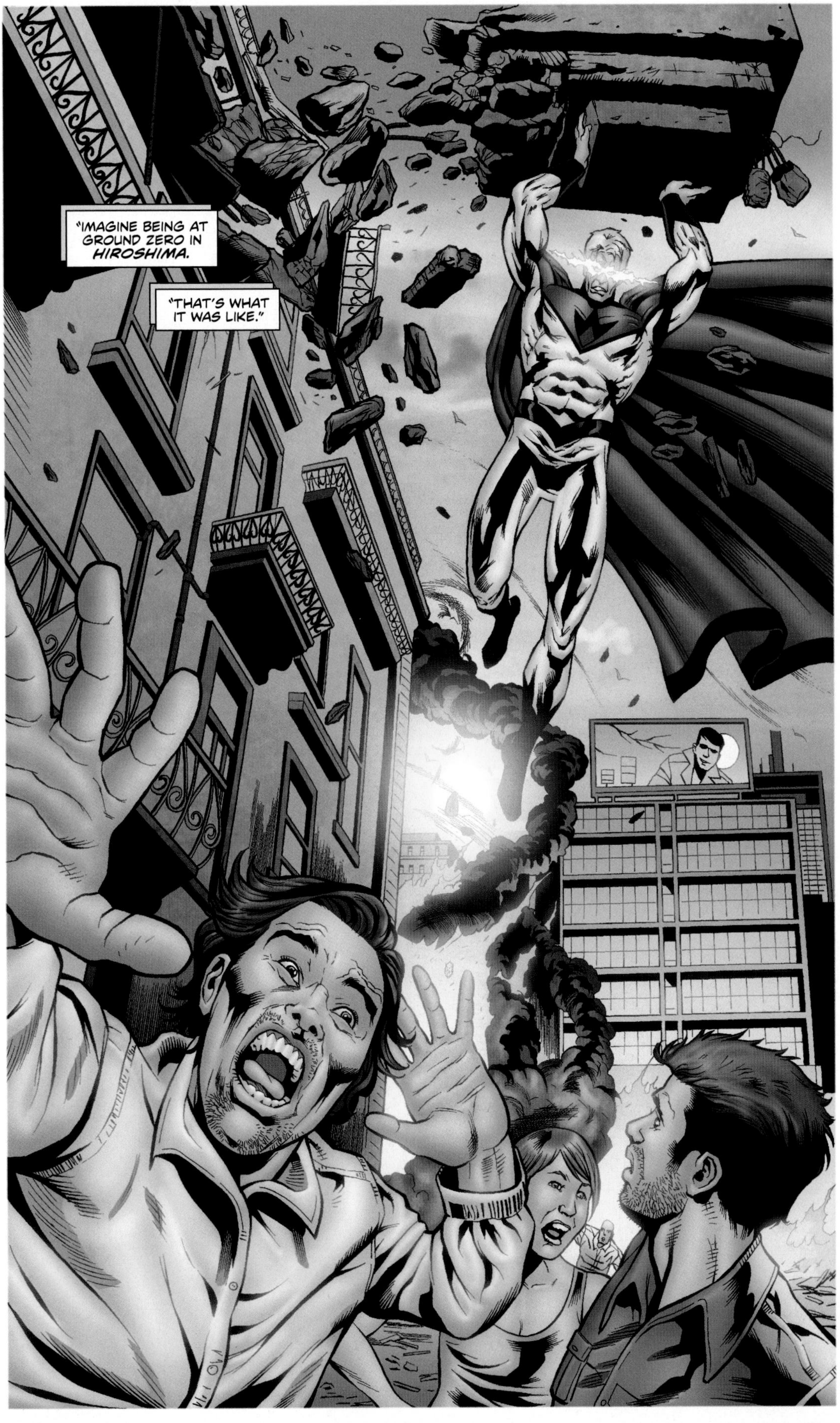
"IMAGINE BEING AT GROUND ZERO IN HIROSHIMA.
"THAT'S WHAT IT WAS LIKE."

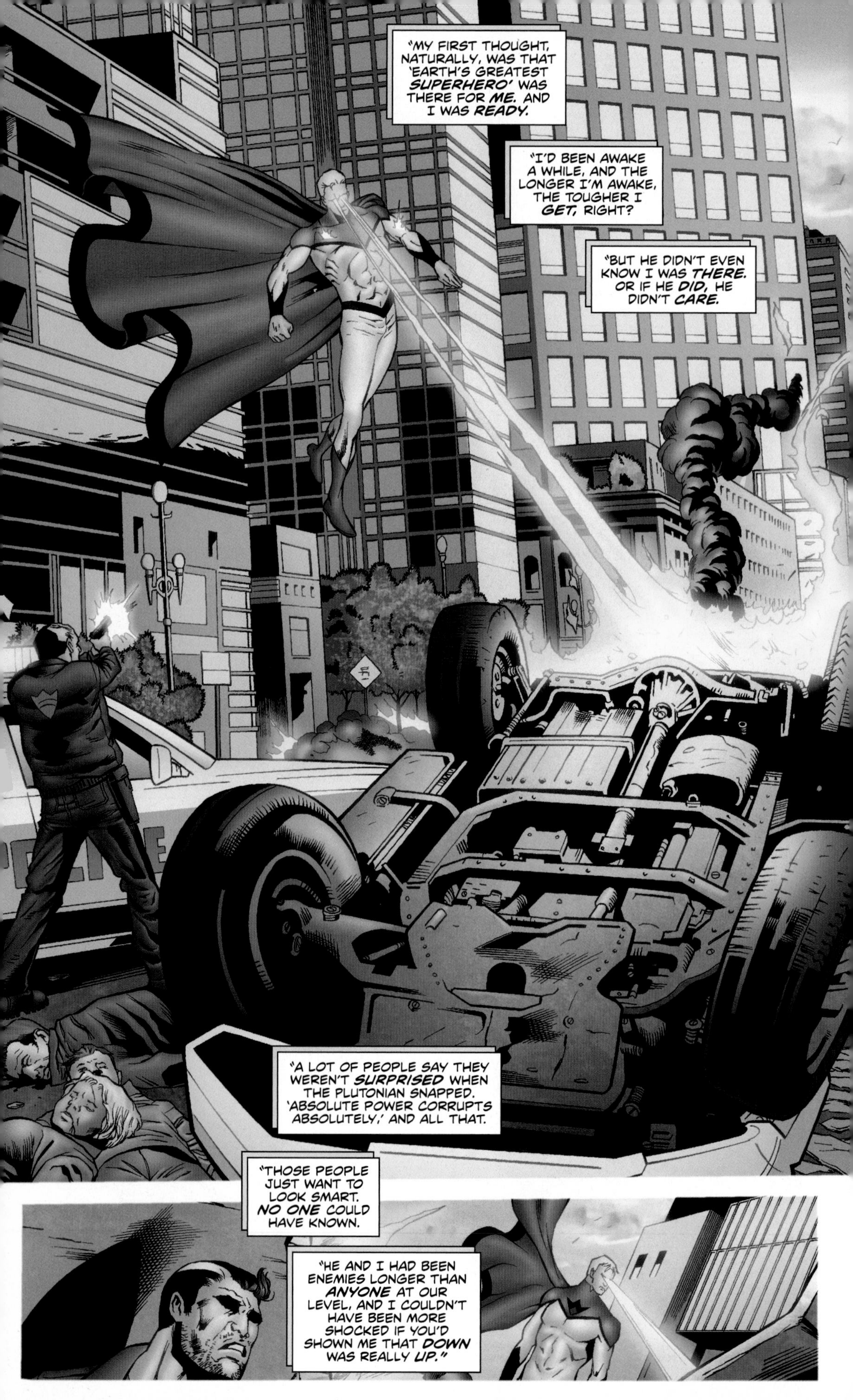
"MY FIRST THOUGHT, NATURALLY, WAS THAT 'EARTH'S GREATEST SUPERHERO' WAS THERE FOR ME. AND I WAS READY.
"I'D BEEN AWAKE A WHILE, AND THE LONGER I'M AWAKE, THE TOUGHER I GET, RIGHT?
"BUT HE DIDN'T EVEN KNOW I WAS THERE. OR IF HE DID, HE DIDN'T CARE.
"A LOT OF PEOPLE SAY THEY WEREN'T SURPRISED WHEN THE PLUTONIAN SNAPPED. 'ABSOLUTE POWER CORRUPTS ABSOLUTELY,' AND ALL THAT.
"THOSE PEOPLE JUST WANT TO LOOK SMART. NO ONE COULD HAVE KNOWN.
"HE AND I HAD BEEN ENEMIES LONGER THAN ANYONE AT OUR LEVEL, AND I COULDN'T HAVE BEEN MORE SHOCKED IF YOU'D SHOWN ME THAT DOWN WAS REALLY UP."

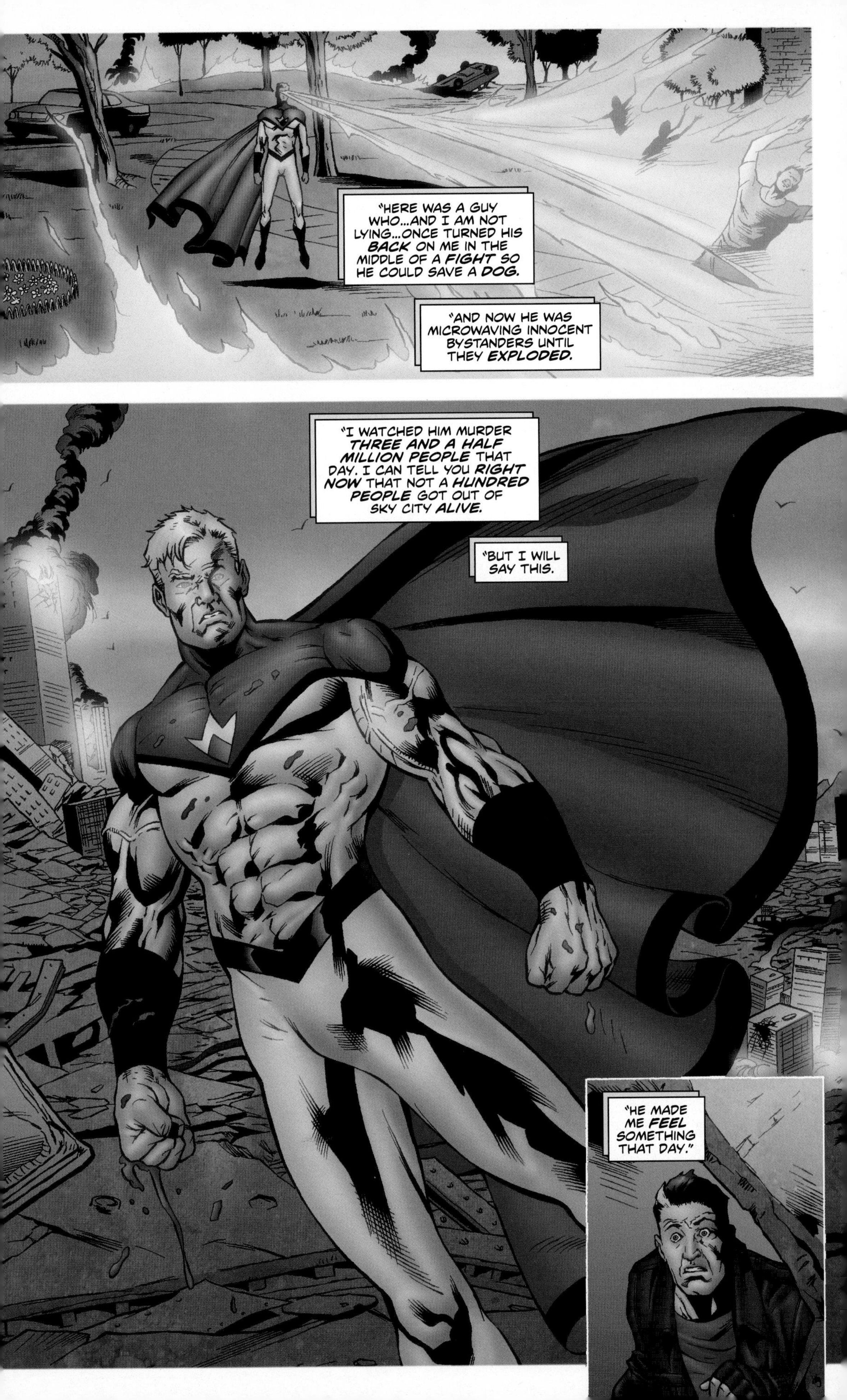
"HERE WAS A GUY WHO...AND I AM NOT LYING...ONCE TURNED HIS BACK ON ME IN THE MIDDLE OF A FIGHT SO HE COULD SAVE A DOG.
"AND NOW HE WAS MICROWAVING INNOCENT BYSTANDERS UNTIL THEY EXPLODED.
"I WATCHED HIM MURDER THREE AND A HALF MILLION PEOPLE THAT DAY. I CAN TELL YOU RIGHT NOW THAT NOT A HUNDRED PEOPLE GOT OUT OF SKY CITY ALIVE.
"BUT I WILL SAY THIS.
"HE MADE ME FEEL SOMETHING THAT DAY."

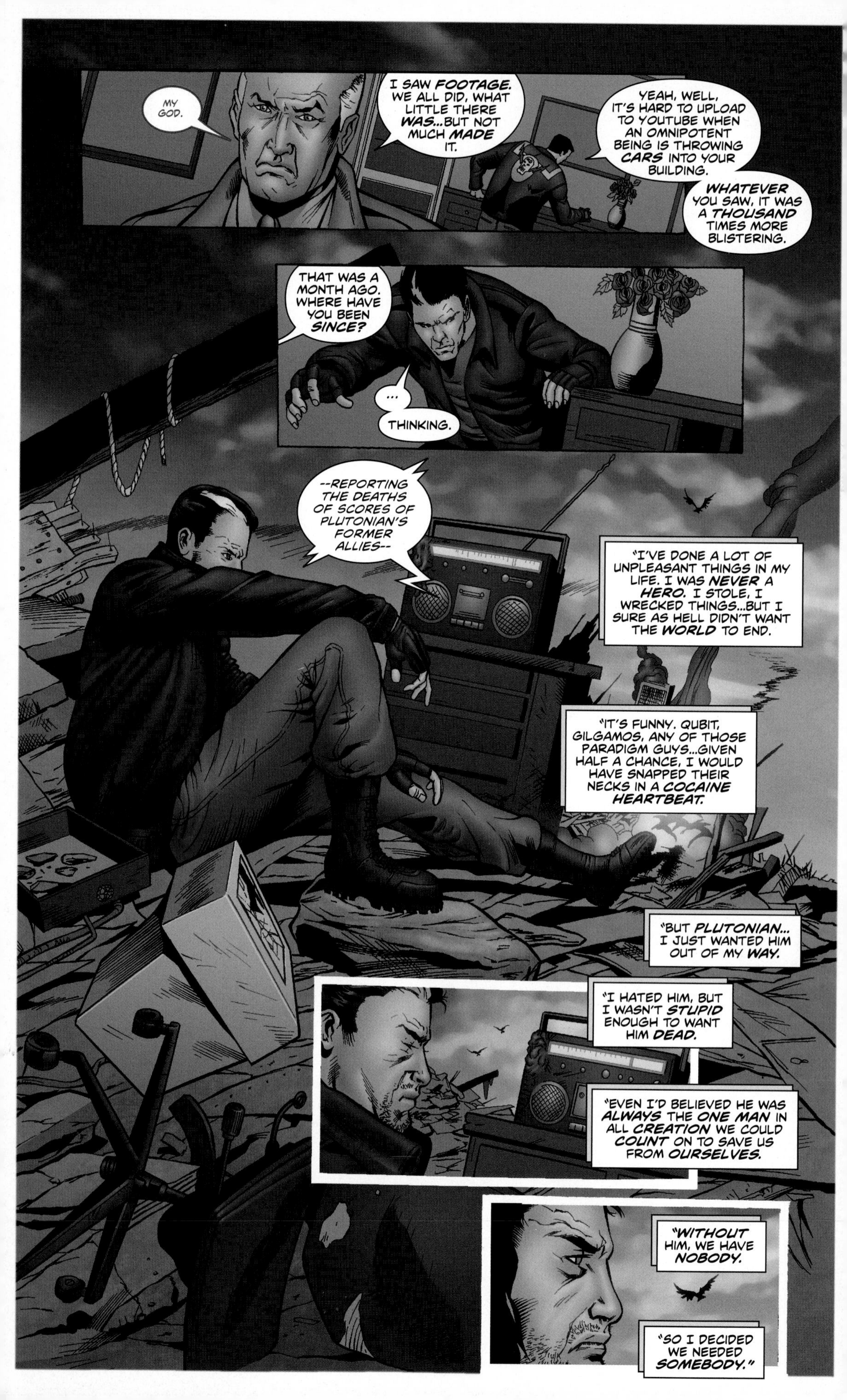

MY GOD.
I SAW FOOTAGE. WE ALL DID, WHAT LITTLE THERE WAS...BUT NOT MUCH MADE IT.
YEAH, WELL, IT'S HARD TO UPLOAD TO YOUTUBE WHEN AN OMNIPOTENT BEING IS THROWING CARS INTO YOUR BUILDING.
WHATEVER YOU SAW, IT WAS A THOUSAND TIMES MORE BLISTERING.
THAT WAS A MONTH AGO. WHERE HAVE YOU BEEN SINCE?
...
THINKING.
--REPORTING THE DEATHS OF SCORES OF PLUTONIAN'S FORMER ALLIES--
"I'VE DONE A LOT OF UNPLEASANT THINGS IN MY LIFE. I WAS NEVER A HERO. I STOLE, I WRECKED THINGS...BUT I SURE AS HELL DIDN'T WANT THE WORLD TO END.
"IT'S FUNNY. QUBIT, GILGAMOS, ANY OF THOSE PARADIGM GUYS...GIVEN HALF A CHANCE, I WOULD HAVE SNAPPED THEIR NECKS IN A COCAINE HEARTBEAT.
"BUT PLUTONIAN... I JUST WANTED HIM OUT OF MY WAY.
"I HATED HIM, BUT I WASN'T STUPID ENOUGH TO WANT HIM DEAD.
"EVEN I'D BELIEVED HE WAS ALWAYS THE ONE MAN IN ALL CREATION WE COULD COUNT ON TO SAVE US FROM OURSELVES.
"WITHOUT HIM, WE HAVE NOBODY.
"SO I DECIDED WE NEEDED SOMEBODY."

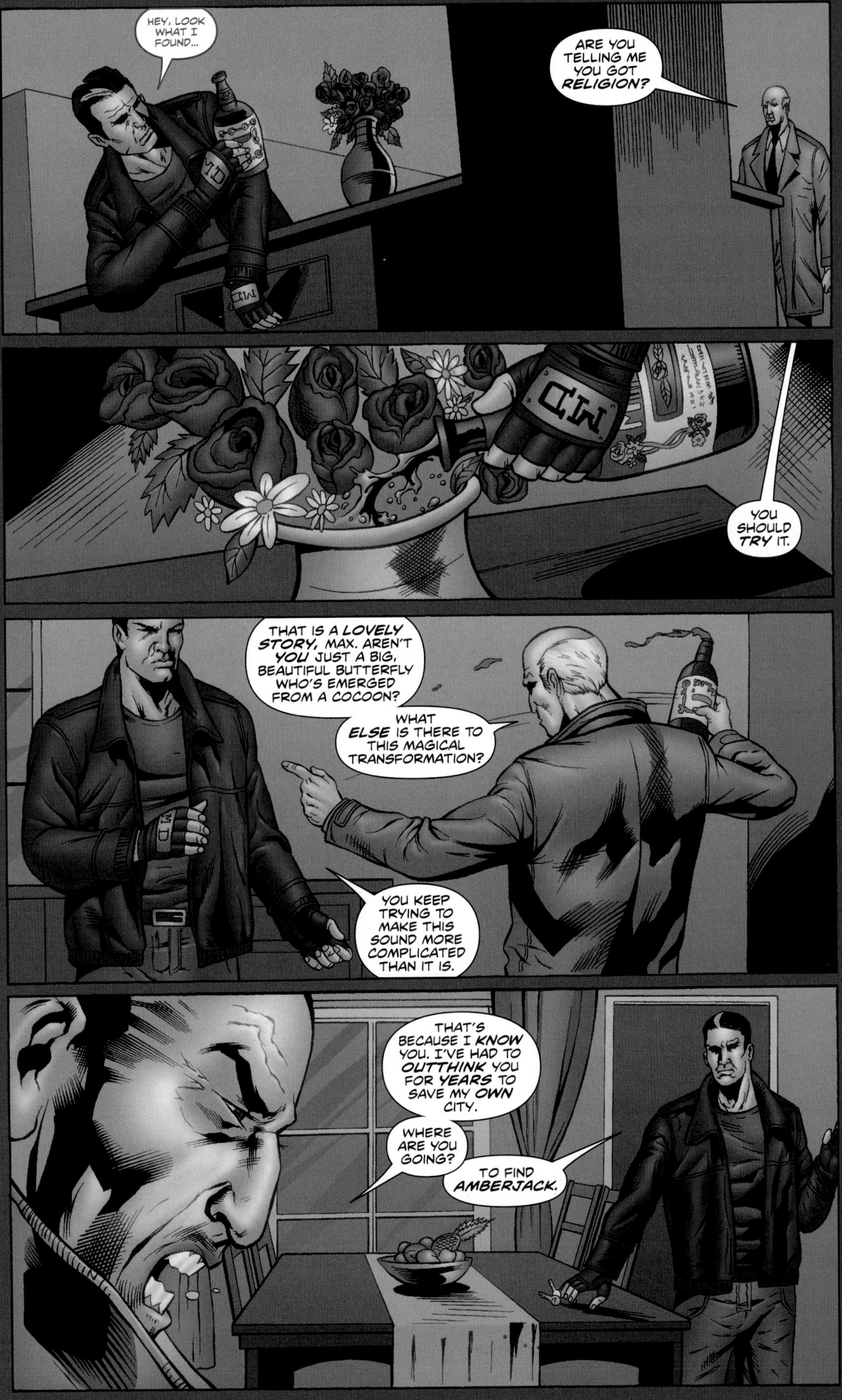

HEY, LOOK WHAT I FOUND...
ARE YOU TELLING ME YOU GOT RELIGION?
YOU SHOULD TRY IT.
THAT IS A LOVELY STORY, MAX. AREN'T YOU JUST A BIG, BEAUTIFUL BUTTERFLY WHO'S EMERGED FROM A COCOON?
WHAT ELSE IS THERE TO THIS MAGICAL TRANSFORMATION?
YOU KEEP TRYING TO MAKE THIS SOUND MORE COMPLICATED THAN IT IS.
THAT'S BECAUSE I KNOW YOU. I'VE HAD TO OUTTHINK YOU FOR YEARS TO SAVE MY OWN CITY.
WHERE ARE YOU GOING?
TO FIND AMBERJACK.

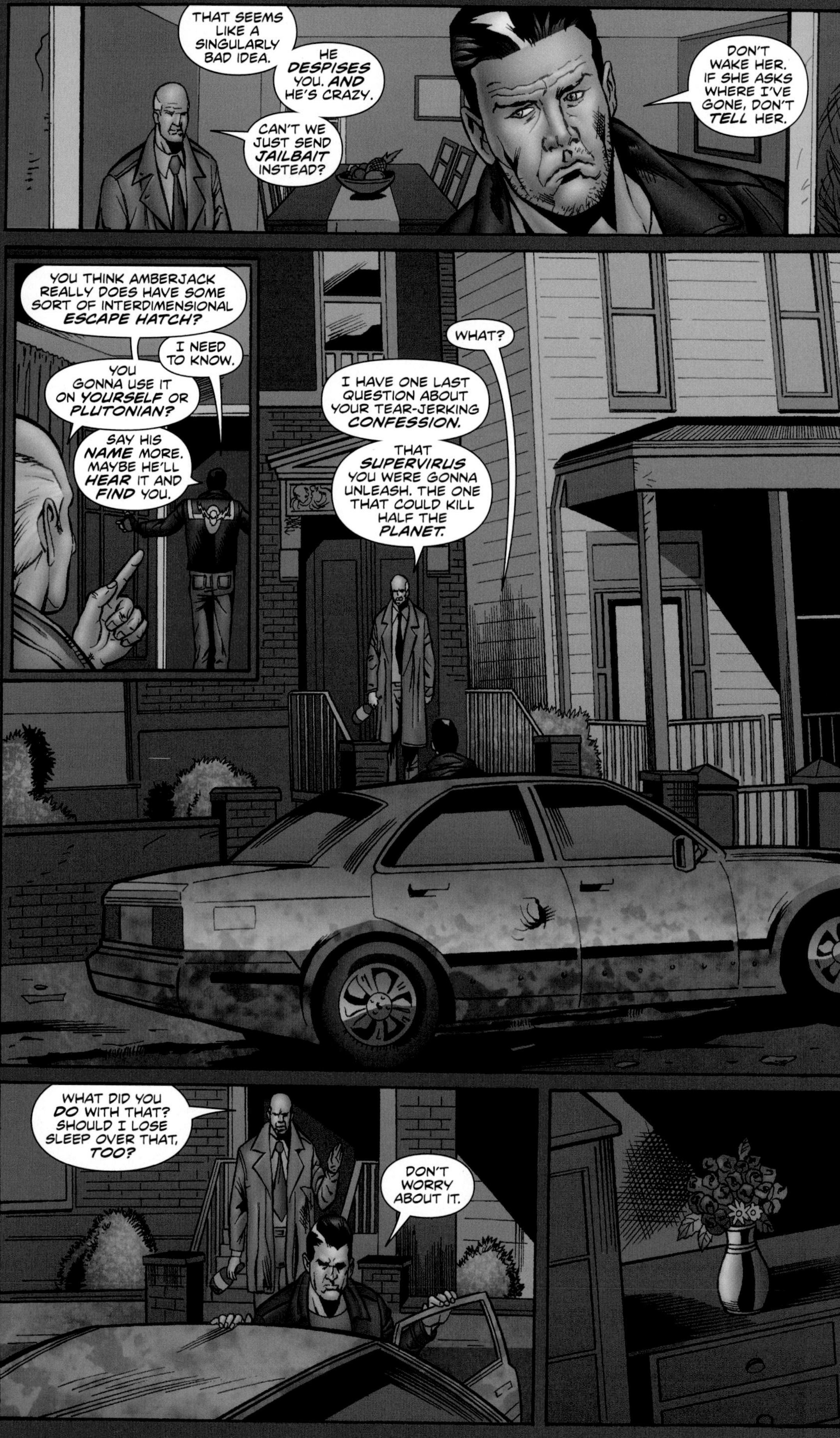
THAT SEEMS LIKE A SINGULARLY BAD IDEA.
HE DESPISES YOU. AND HE'S CRAZY.
CAN'T WE JUST SEND JAILBAIT INSTEAD?
DON'T WAKE HER. IF SHE ASKS WHERE I'VE GONE, DON'T TELL HER.
YOU THINK AMBERJACK REALLY DOES HAVE SOME SORT OF INTERDIMENSIONAL ESCAPE HATCH?
I NEED TO KNOW.
YOU GONNA USE IT ON YOURSELF OR PLUTONIAN?
SAY HIS NAME MORE. MAYBE HE'LL HEAR IT AND FIND YOU.
I HAVE ONE LAST QUESTION ABOUT YOUR TEAR-JERKING CONFESSION.
THAT SUPERVIRUS YOU WERE GONNA UNLEASH. THE ONE THAT COULD KILL HALF THE PLANET.
WHAT?
WHAT DID YOU DO WITH THAT? SHOULD I LOSE SLEEP OVER THAT, TOO?
DON'T WORRY ABOUT IT.

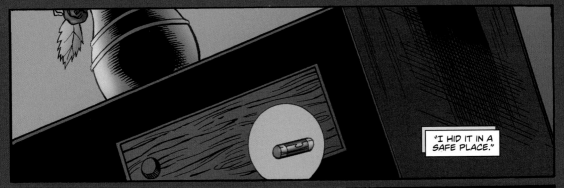

"I HID IT IN A SAFE PLACE."

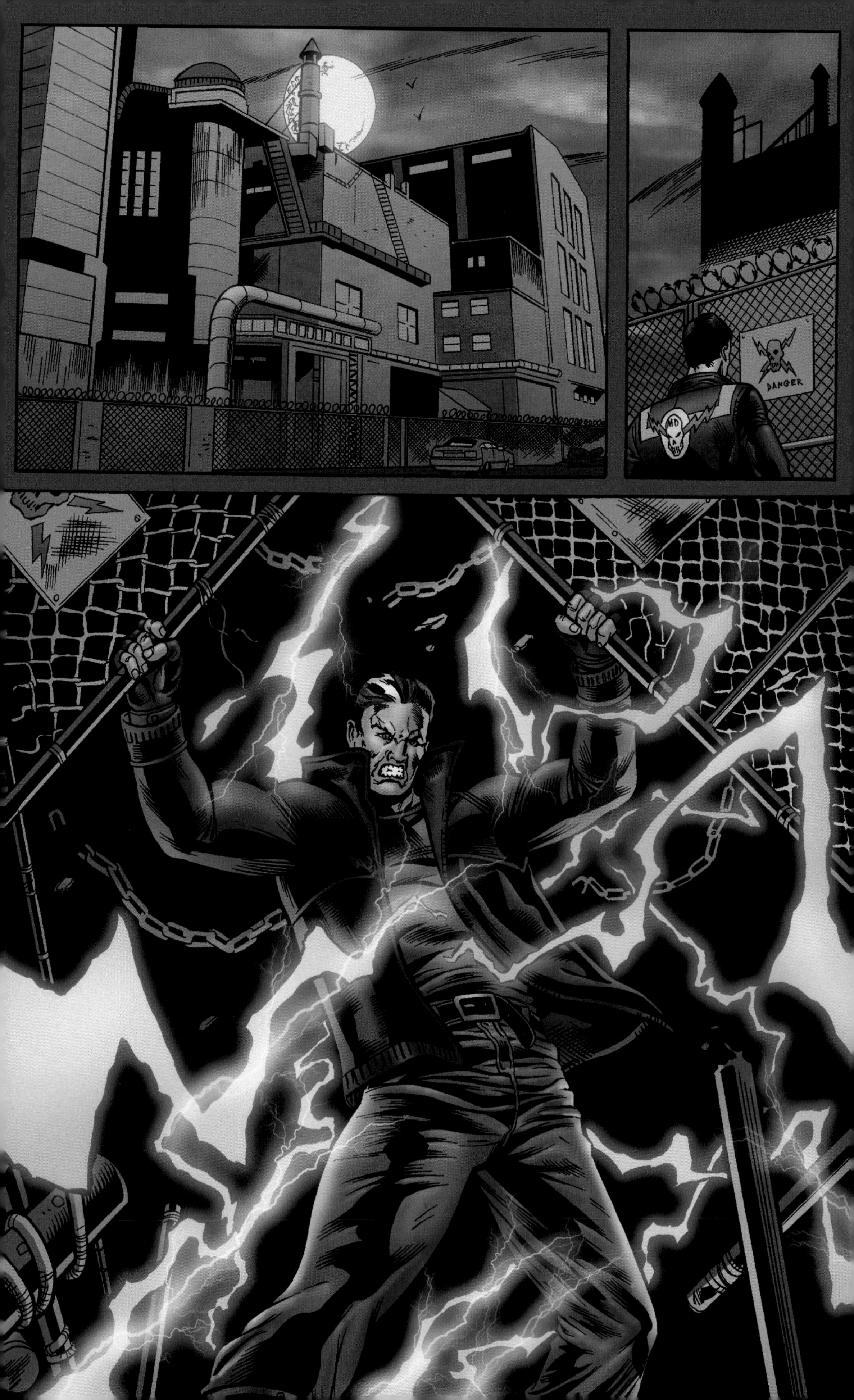
DANGER

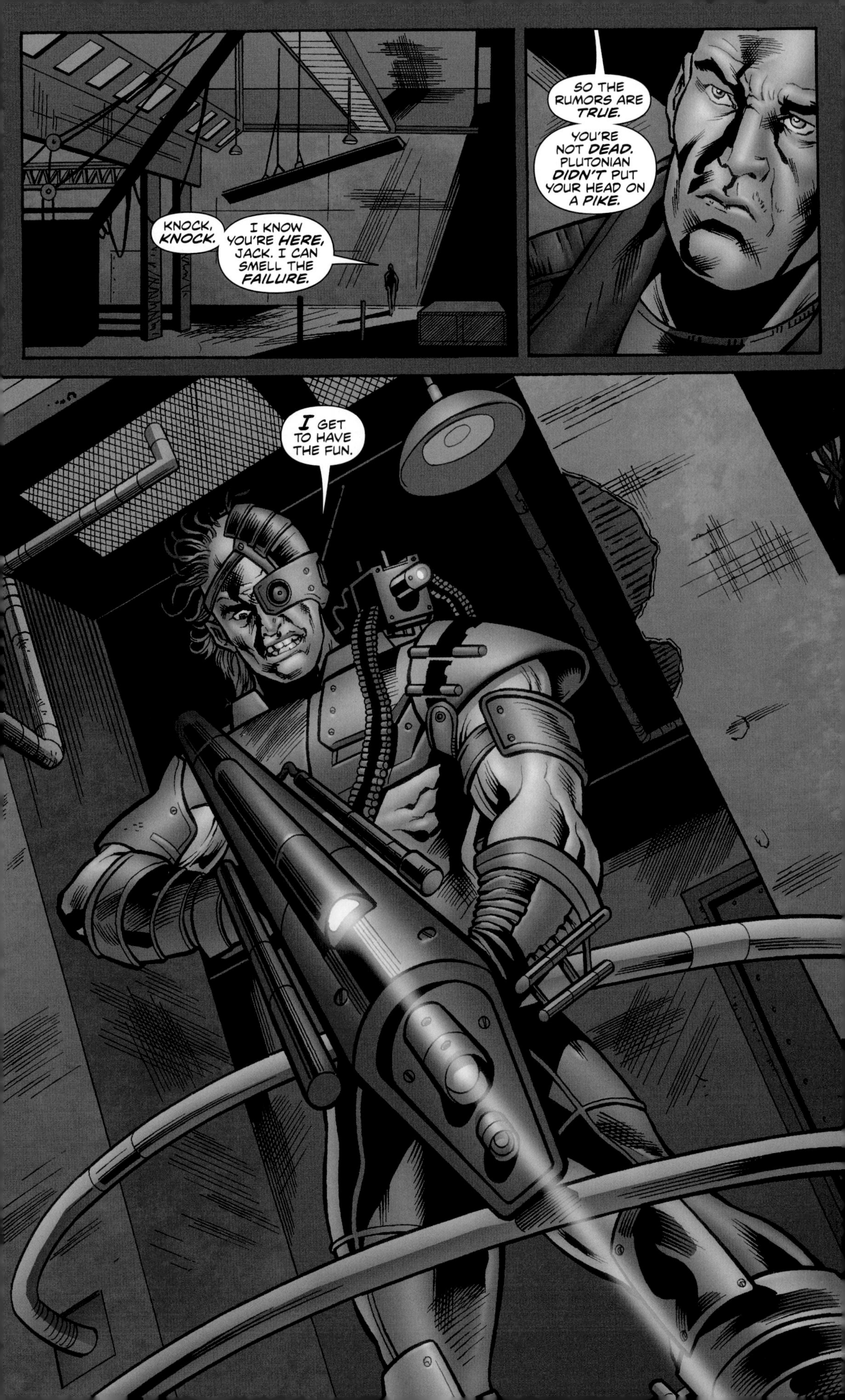
KNOCK, KNOCK.
I KNOW YOU'RE HERE, JACK. I CAN SMELL THE FAILURE.
SO THE RUMORS ARE TRUE.
YOU'RE NOT DEAD. PLUTONIAN DIDN'T PUT YOUR HEAD ON A PIKE.
I GET TO HAVE THE FUN.

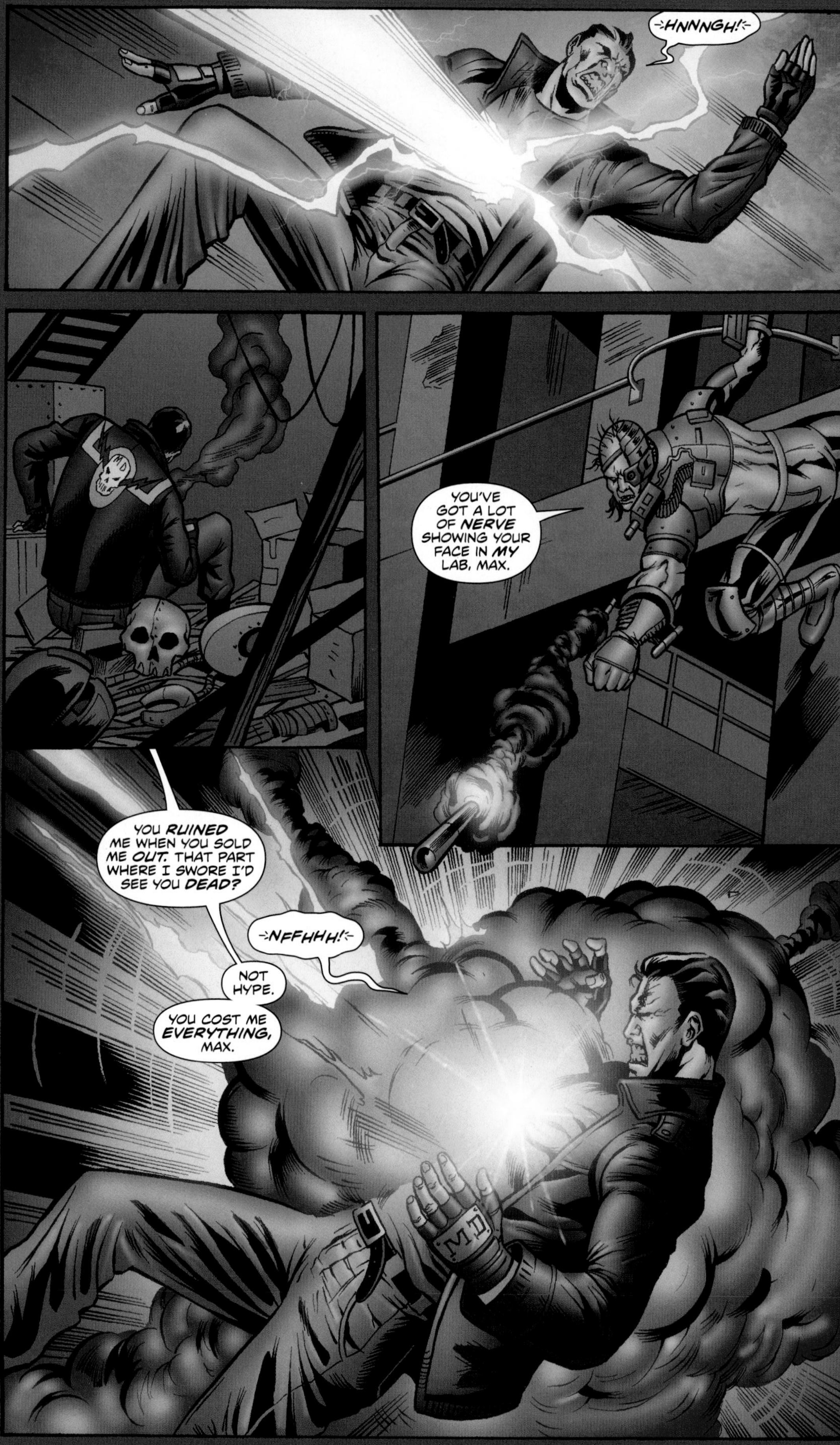

-HNNNGH!-
YOU'VE GOT A LOT OF NERVE SHOWING YOUR FACE IN MY LAB, MAX.
YOU RUINED ME WHEN YOU SOLD ME OUT. THAT PART WHERE I SWORE I'D SEE YOU DEAD?
-NFFHHH!-
NOT HYPE.
YOU COST ME EVERYTHING, MAX.

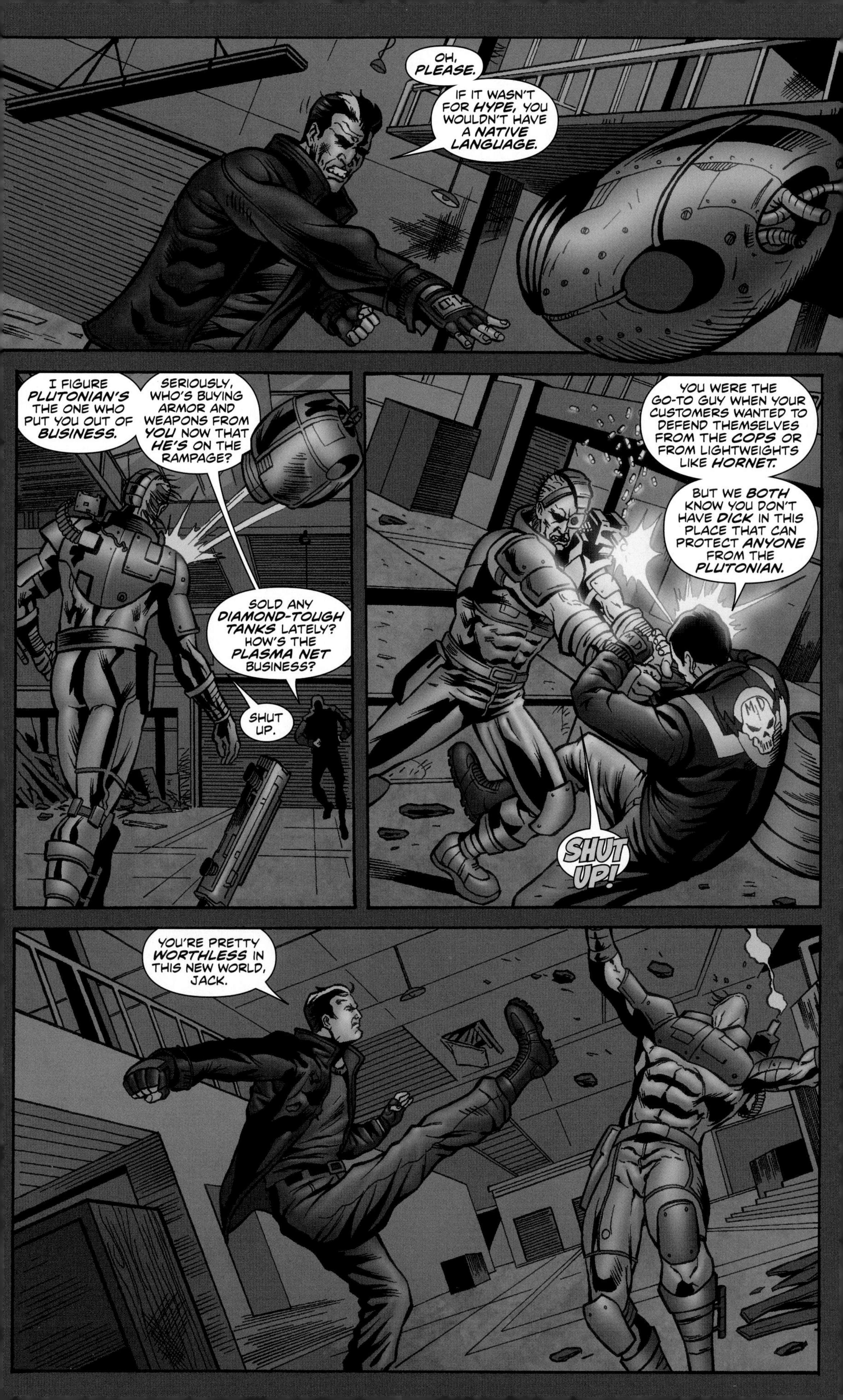
OH, PLEASE.
IF IT WASN'T FOR HYPE, YOU WOULDN'T HAVE A NATIVE LANGUAGE.
I FIGURE PLUTONIAN'S THE ONE WHO PUT YOU OUT OF BUSINESS.
SERIOUSLY, WHO'S BUYING ARMOR AND WEAPONS FROM YOU NOW THAT HE'S ON THE RAMPAGE?
SOLD ANY DIAMOND-TOUGH TANKS LATELY? HOW'S THE PLASMA NET BUSINESS?
SHUT UP.
YOU WERE THE GO-TO GUY WHEN YOUR CUSTOMERS WANTED TO DEFEND THEMSELVES FROM THE COPS OR FROM LIGHTWEIGHTS LIKE HORNET.
BUT WE BOTH KNOW YOU DON'T HAVE DICK IN THIS PLACE THAT CAN PROTECT ANYONE FROM THE PLUTONIAN.
SHUT UP!
YOU'RE PRETTY WORTHLESS IN THIS NEW WORLD, JACK.

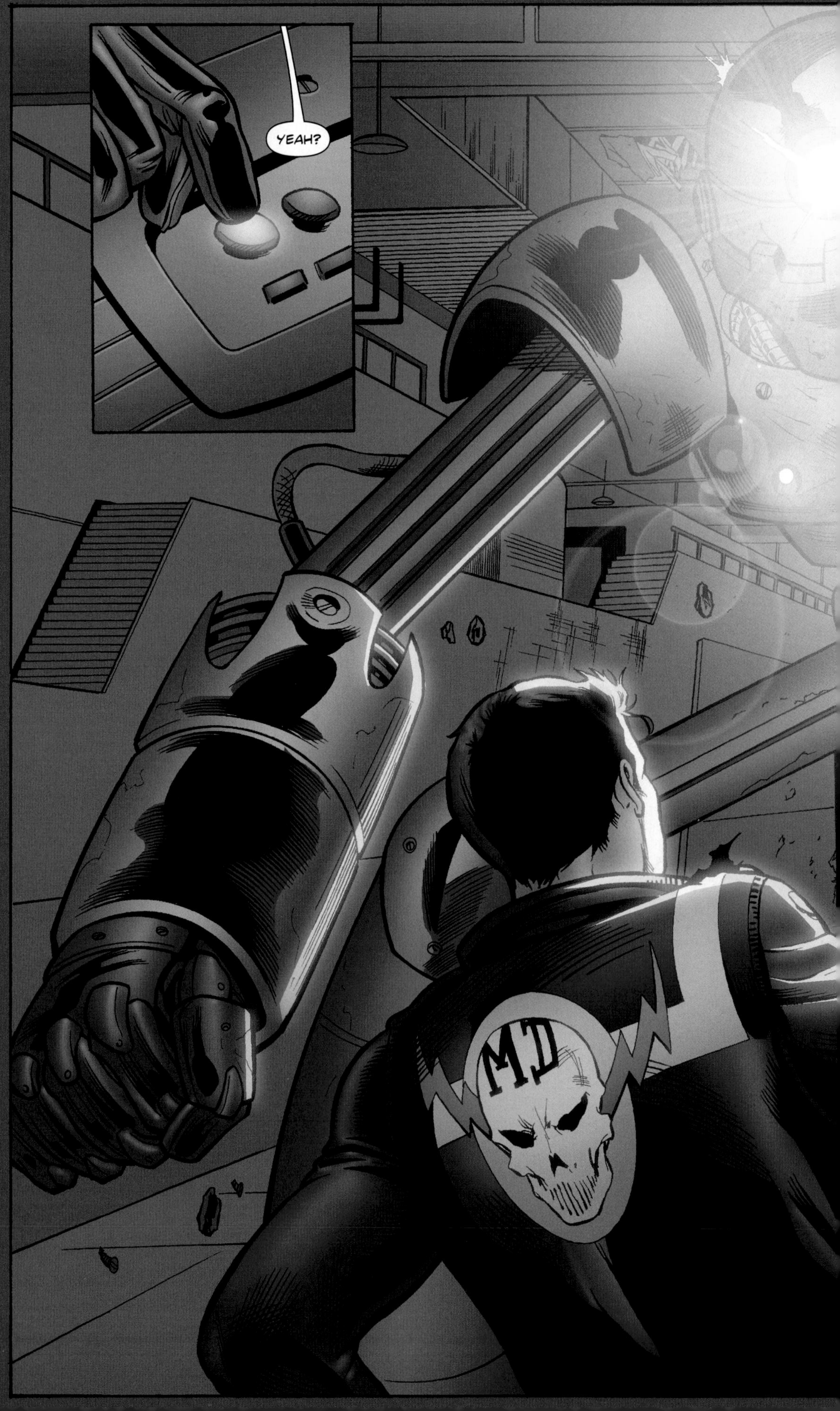
YEAH?
MD

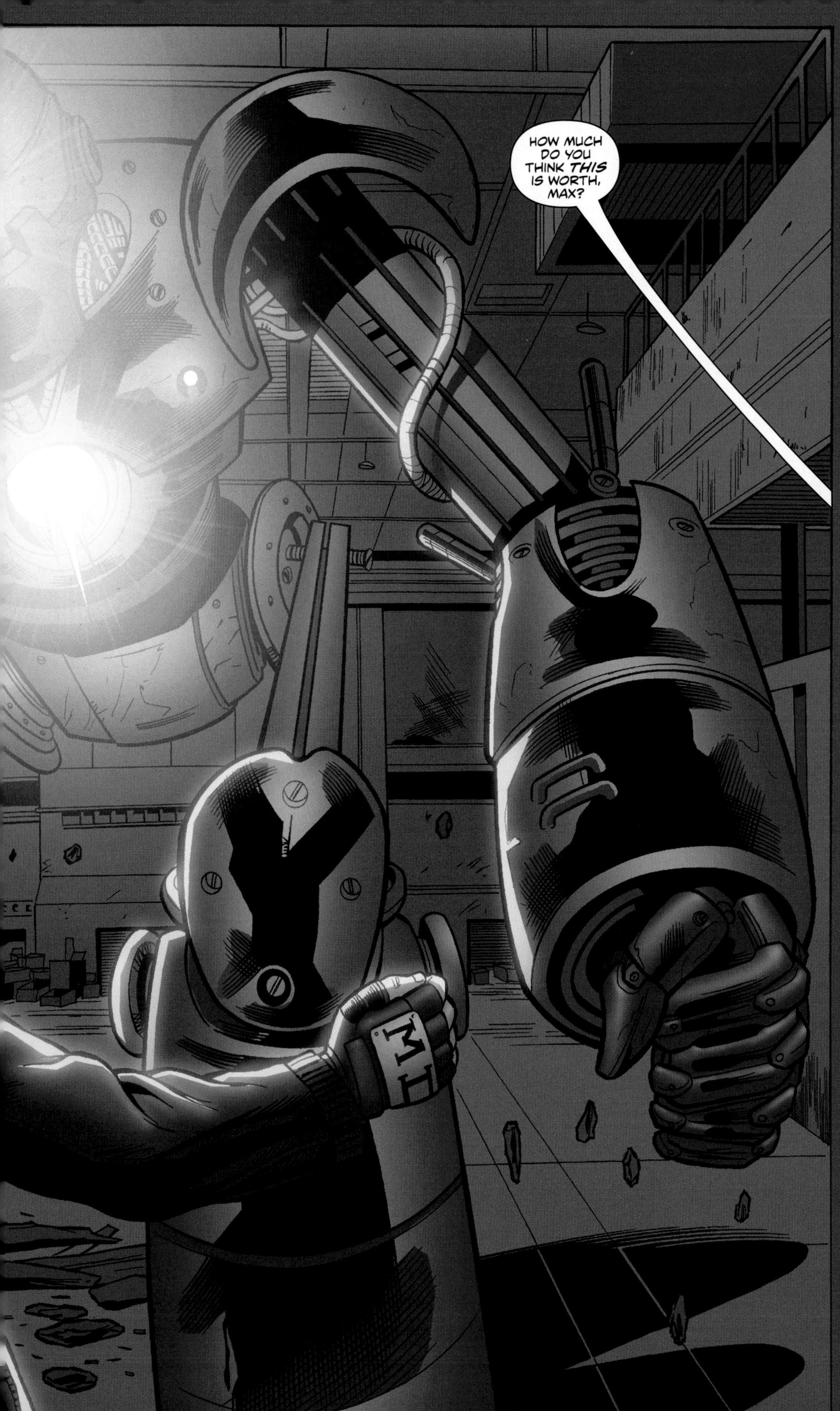
HOW MUCH DO YOU THINK *THIS* IS WORTH, MAX?

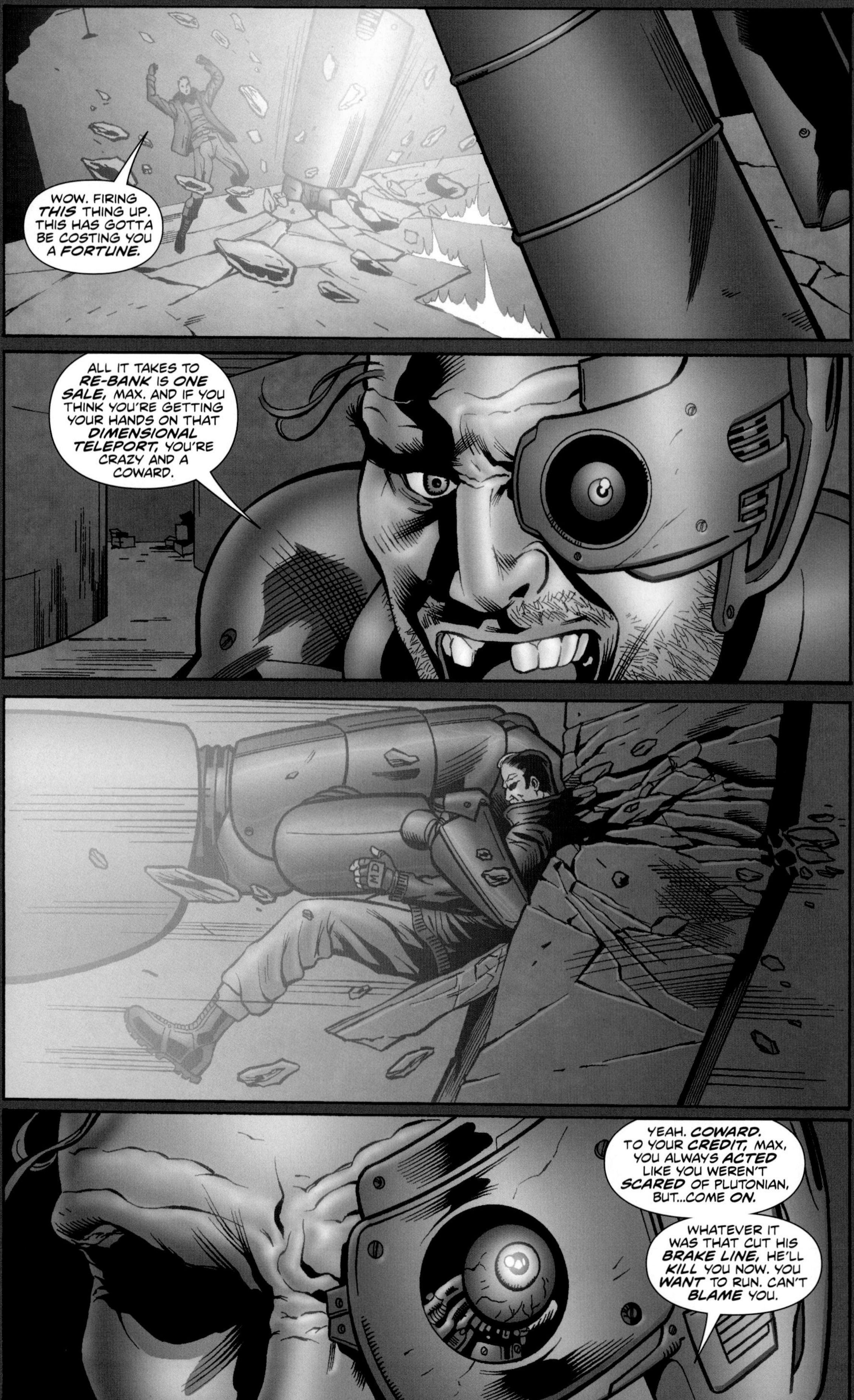
WOW. FIRING THIS THING UP. THIS HAS GOTTA BE COSTING YOU A FORTUNE.
ALL IT TAKES TO RE-BANK IS ONE SALE, MAX. AND IF YOU THINK YOU'RE GETTING YOUR HANDS ON THAT DIMENSIONAL TELEPORT, YOU'RE CRAZY AND A COWARD.
YEAH. COWARD. TO YOUR CREDIT, MAX, YOU ALWAYS ACTED LIKE YOU WEREN'T SCARED OF PLUTONIAN, BUT...COME ON.
WHATEVER IT WAS THAT CUT HIS BRAKE LINE, HE'LL KILL YOU NOW. YOU WANT TO RUN. CAN'T BLAME YOU.

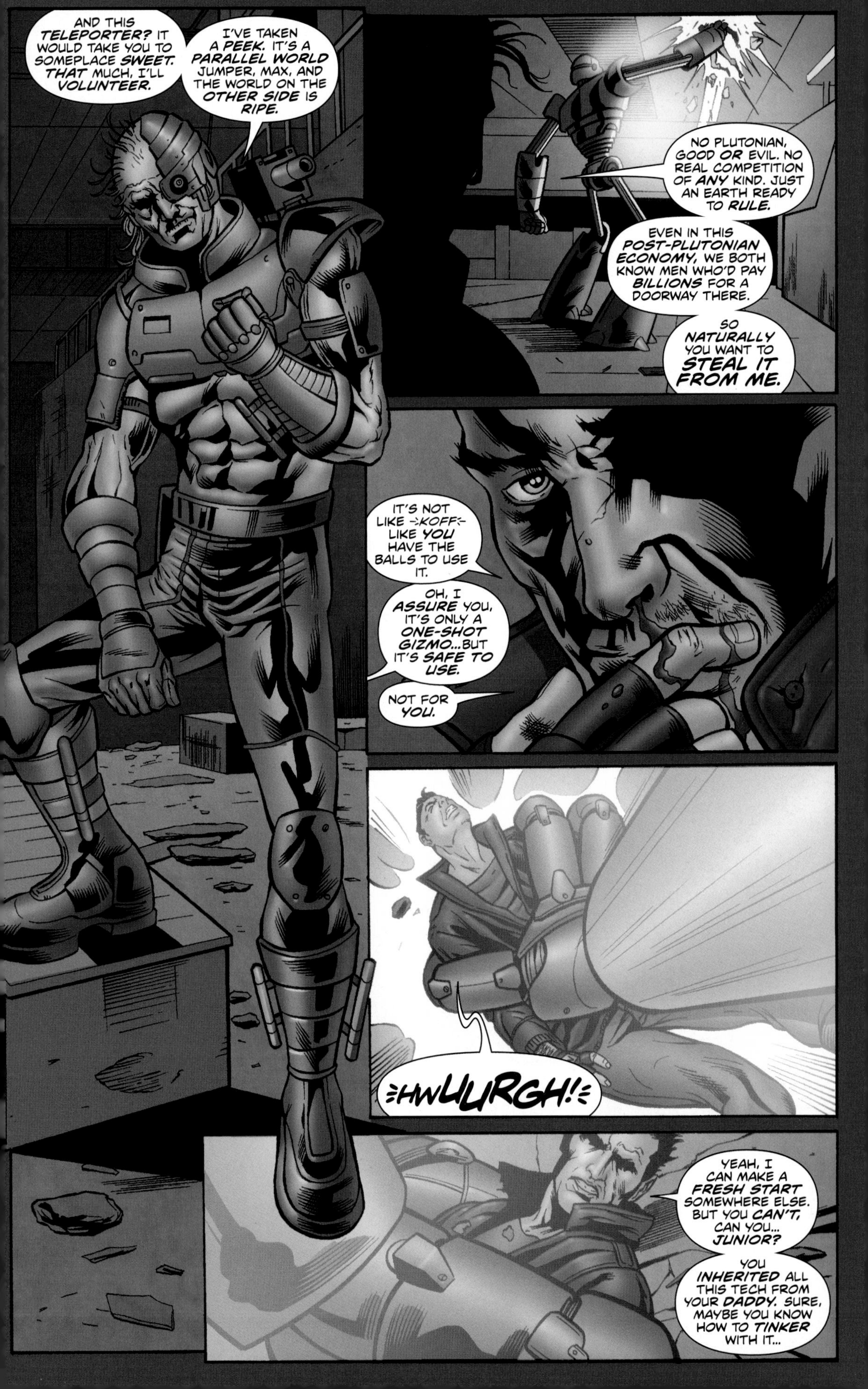

AND THIS TELEPORTER? IT WOULD TAKE YOU TO SOMEPLACE SWEET. THAT MUCH, I'LL VOLUNTEER.
I'VE TAKEN A PEEK. IT'S A PARALLEL WORLD JUMPER, MAX, AND THE WORLD ON THE OTHER SIDE IS RIPE.
NO PLUTONIAN, GOOD OR EVIL. NO REAL COMPETITION OF ANY KIND. JUST AN EARTH READY TO RULE.
EVEN IN THIS POST-PLUTONIAN ECONOMY, WE BOTH KNOW MEN WHO'D PAY BILLIONS FOR A DOORWAY THERE.
SO NATURALLY YOU WANT TO STEAL IT FROM ME.
IT'S NOT LIKE -KOFF- LIKE YOU HAVE THE BALLS TO USE IT.
OH, I ASSURE YOU, IT'S ONLY A ONE-SHOT GIZMO...BUT IT'S SAFE TO USE.
NOT FOR YOU.
HWUURGH!
YEAH, I CAN MAKE A FRESH START SOMEWHERE ELSE. BUT YOU CAN'T, CAN YOU... JUNIOR?
YOU INHERITED ALL THIS TECH FROM YOUR DADDY. SURE, MAYBE YOU KNOW HOW TO TINKER WITH IT...

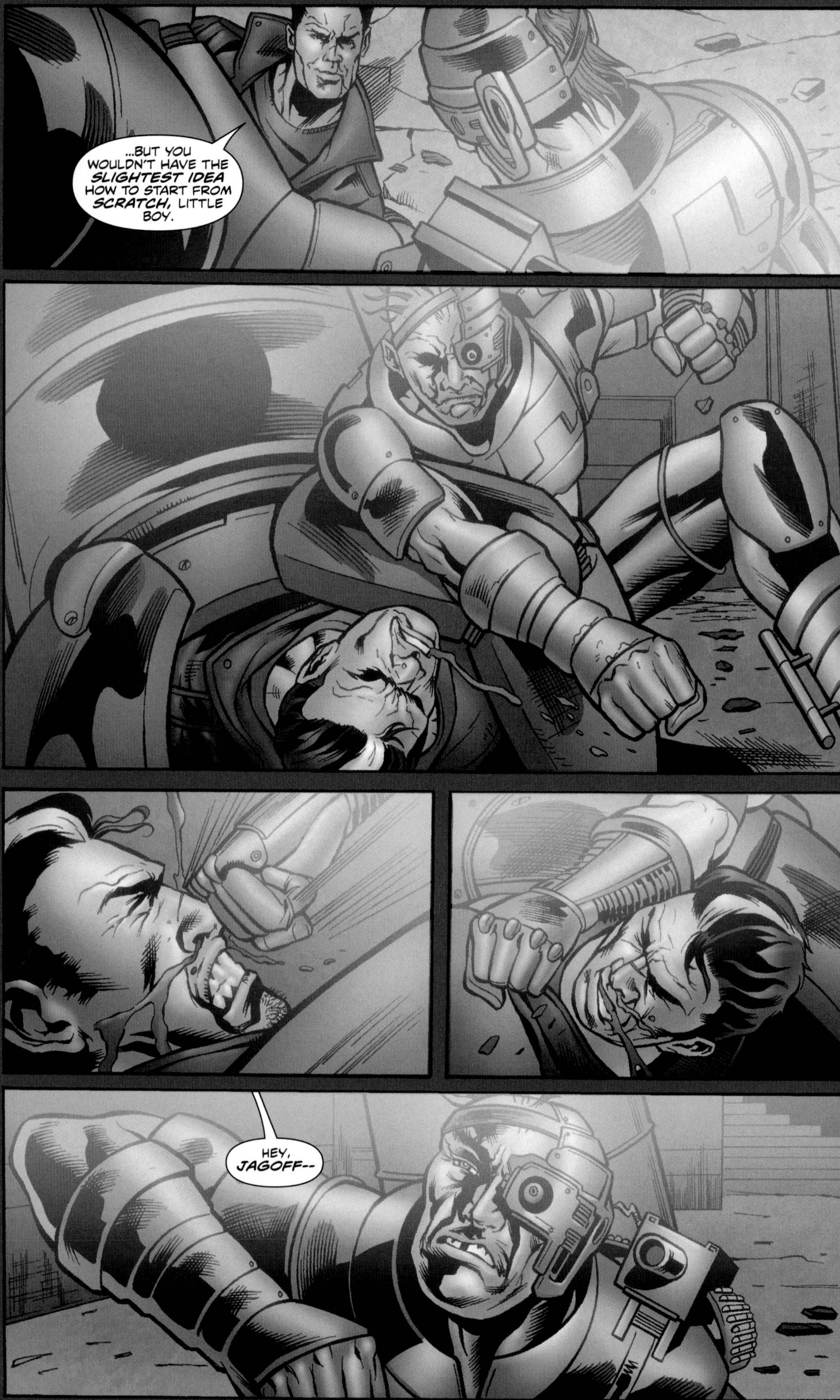

...BUT YOU WOULDN'T HAVE THE SLIGHTEST IDEA HOW TO START FROM SCRATCH, LITTLE BOY.
HEY, JAGOFF--

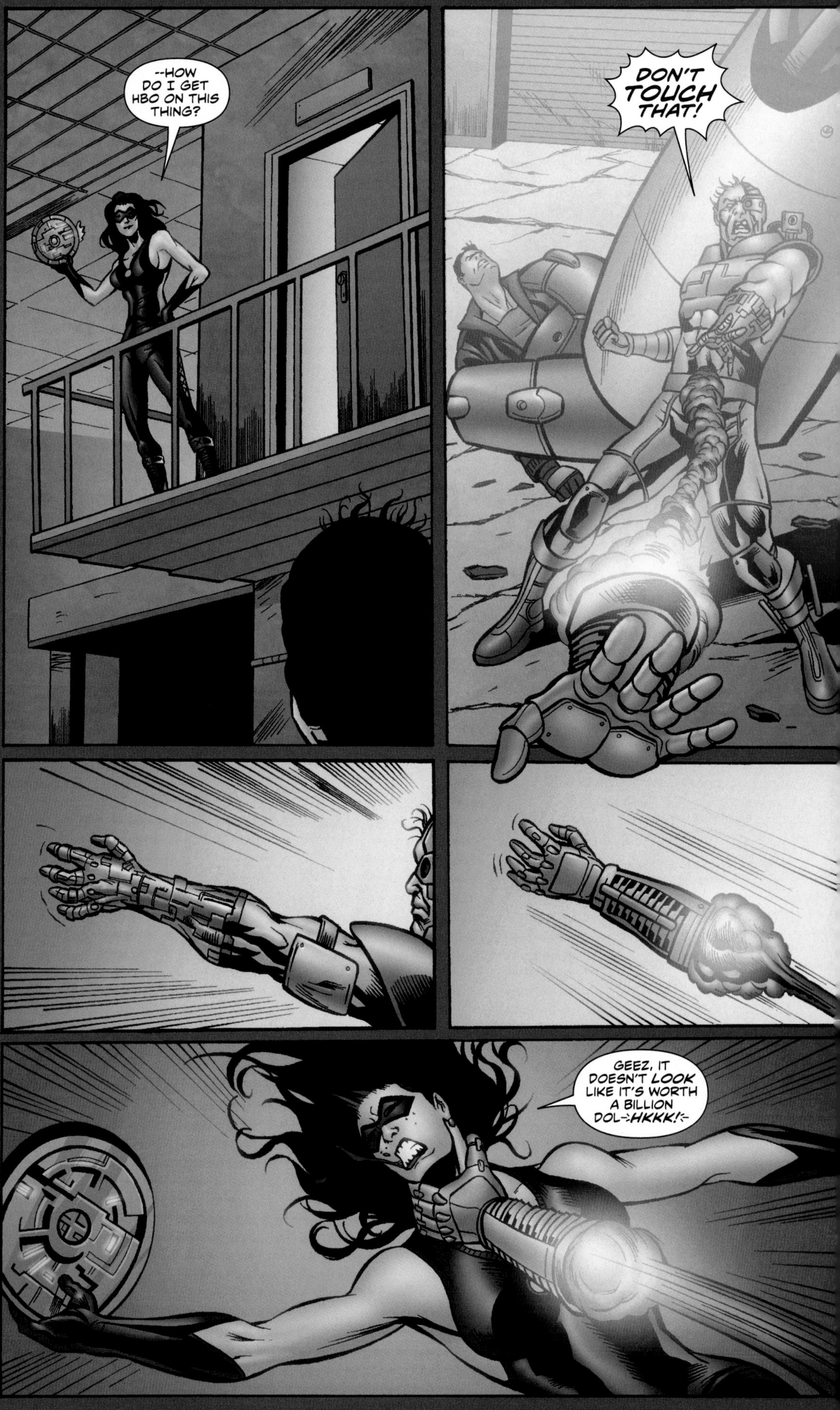
--HOW DO I GET HBO ON THIS THING?
DON'T TOUCH THAT!
GEEZ, IT DOESN'T LOOK LIKE IT'S WORTH A BILLION DOL--HKKK!

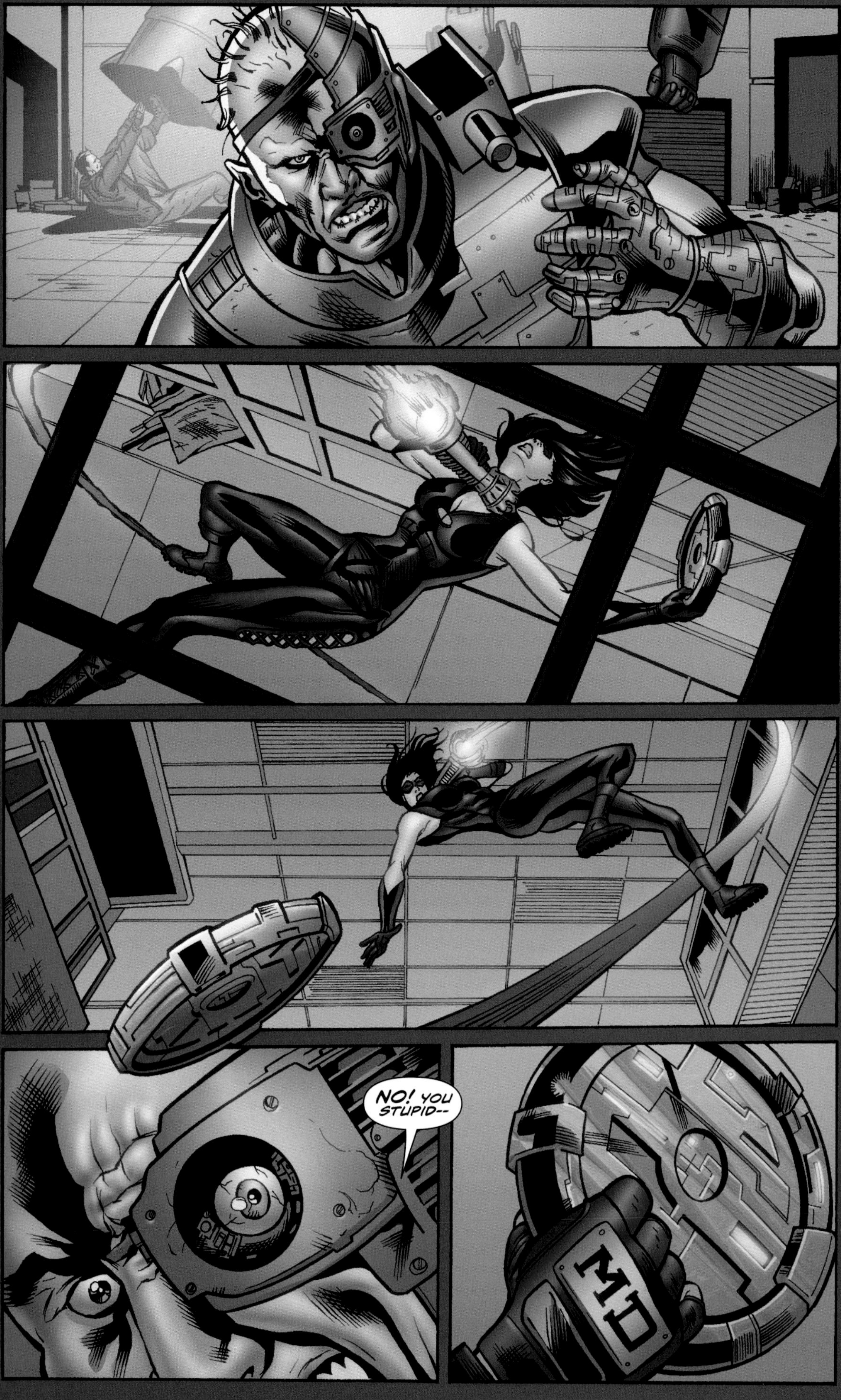
NO! YOU STUPID--
MD

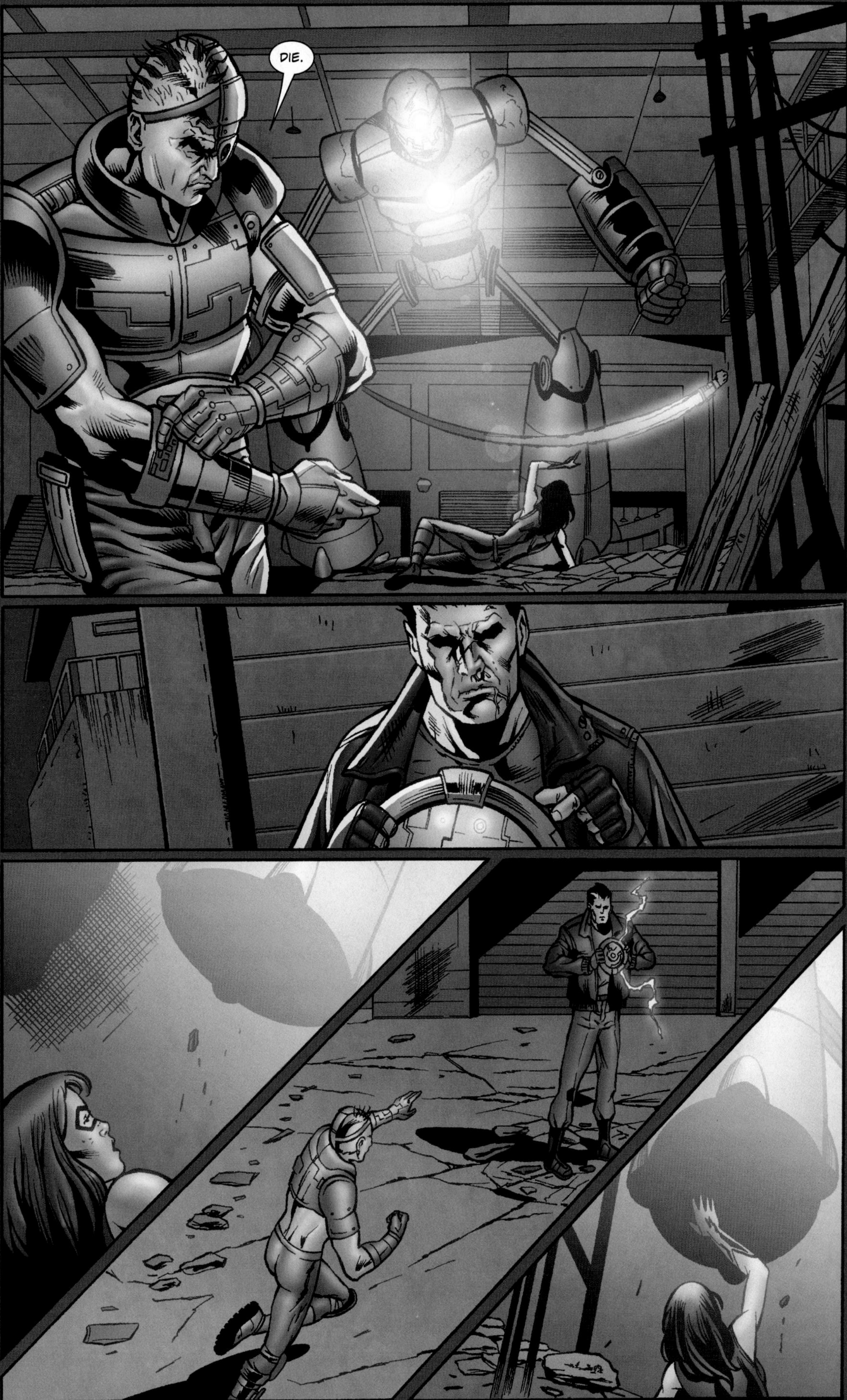
DIE.

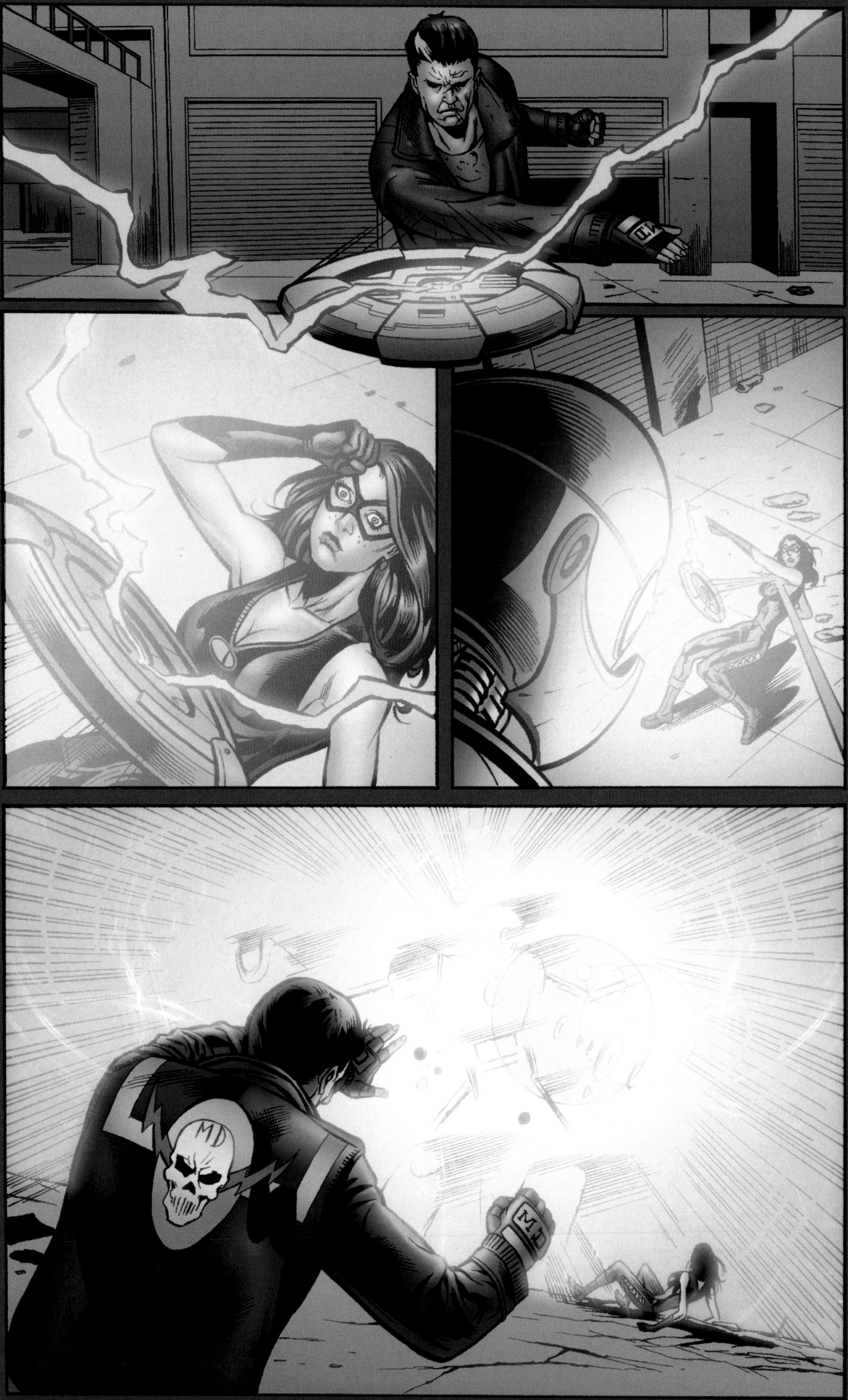

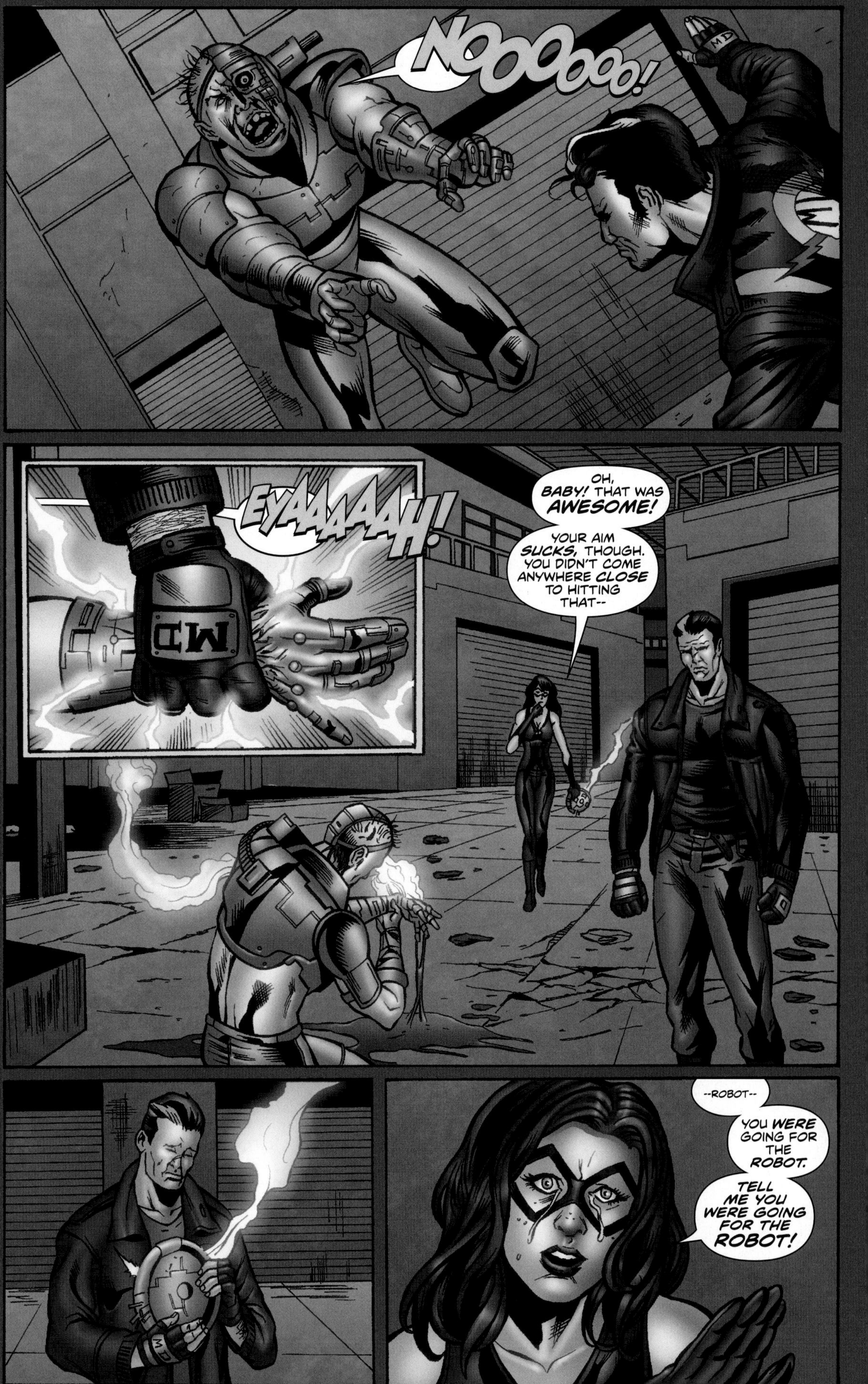
NOOOOOO!
EYAAAAAH!
OH, BABY! THAT WAS AWESOME!
YOUR AIM SUCKS, THOUGH. YOU DIDN'T COME ANYWHERE CLOSE TO HITTING THAT--
--ROBOT--
YOU WERE GOING FOR THE ROBOT.
TELL ME YOU WERE GOING FOR THE ROBOT!

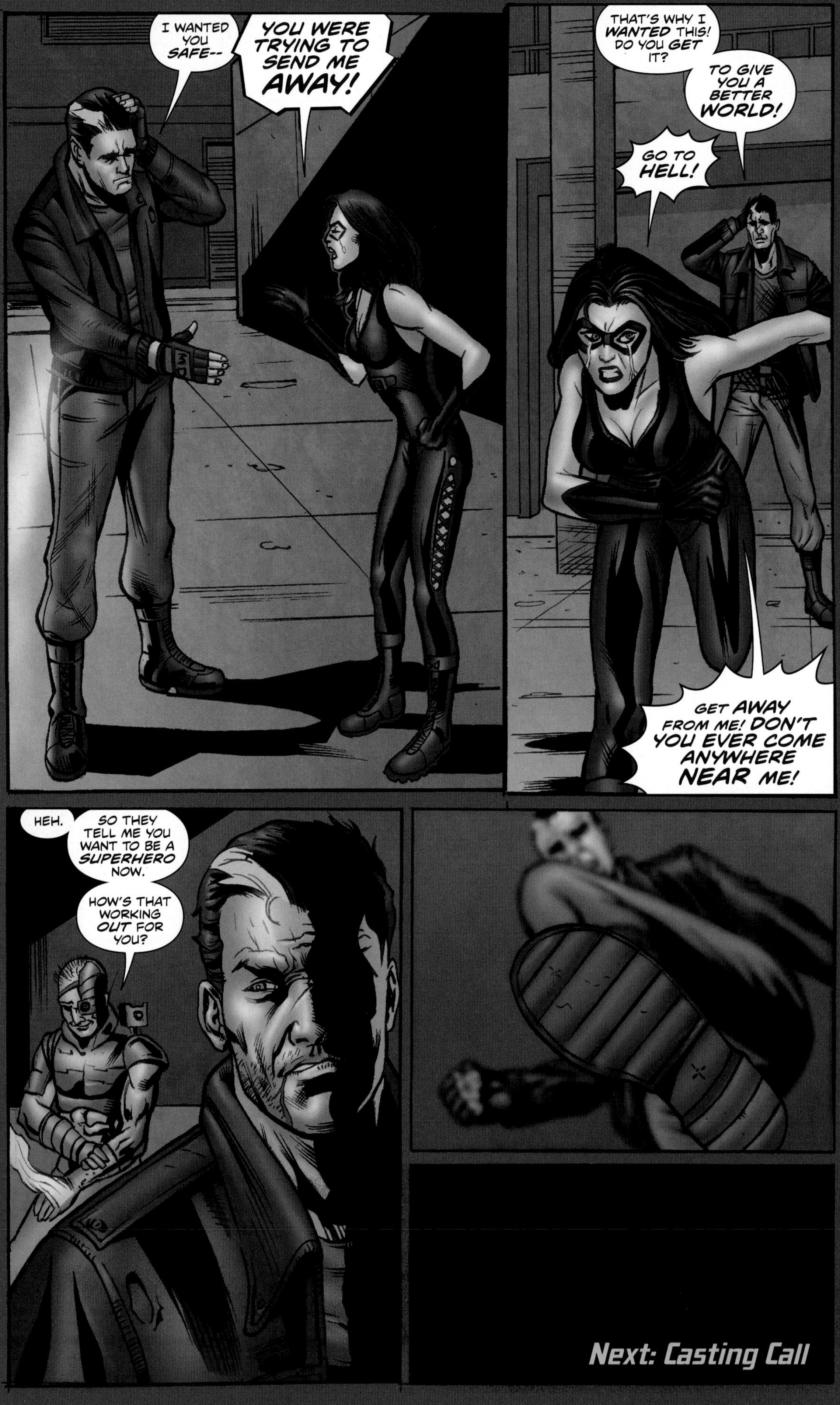
I WANTED YOU SAFE--
YOU WERE TRYING TO SEND ME AWAY!
THAT'S WHY I WANTED THIS! DO YOU GET IT?
TO GIVE YOU A BETTER WORLD!
GO TO HELL!
GET AWAY FROM ME! DON'T YOU EVER COME ANYWHERE NEAR ME!
HEH.
SO THEY TELL ME YOU WANT TO BE A SUPERHERO NOW.
HOW'S THAT WORKING OUT FOR YOU?

Next: Casting Call

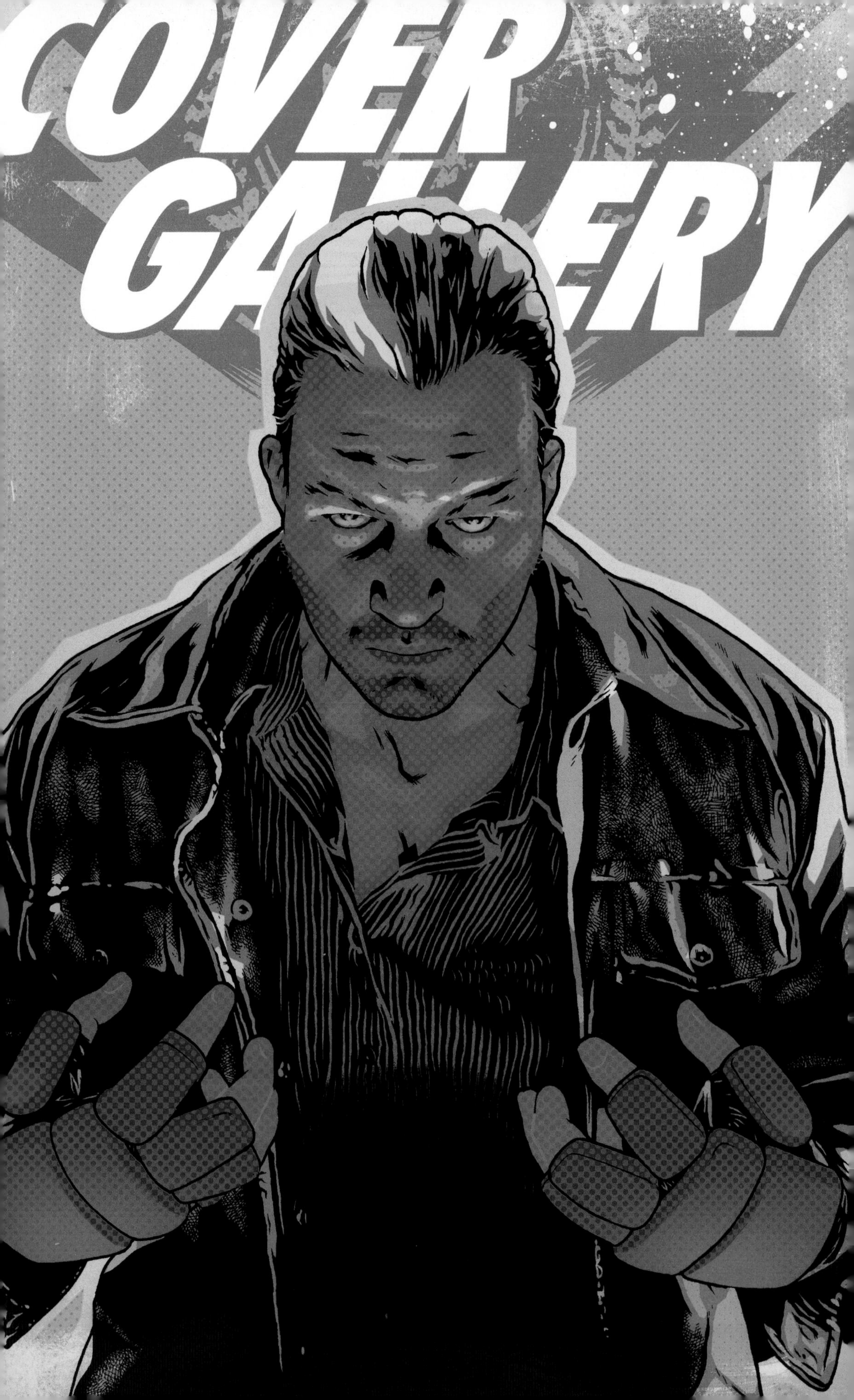
COVER
GALLERY

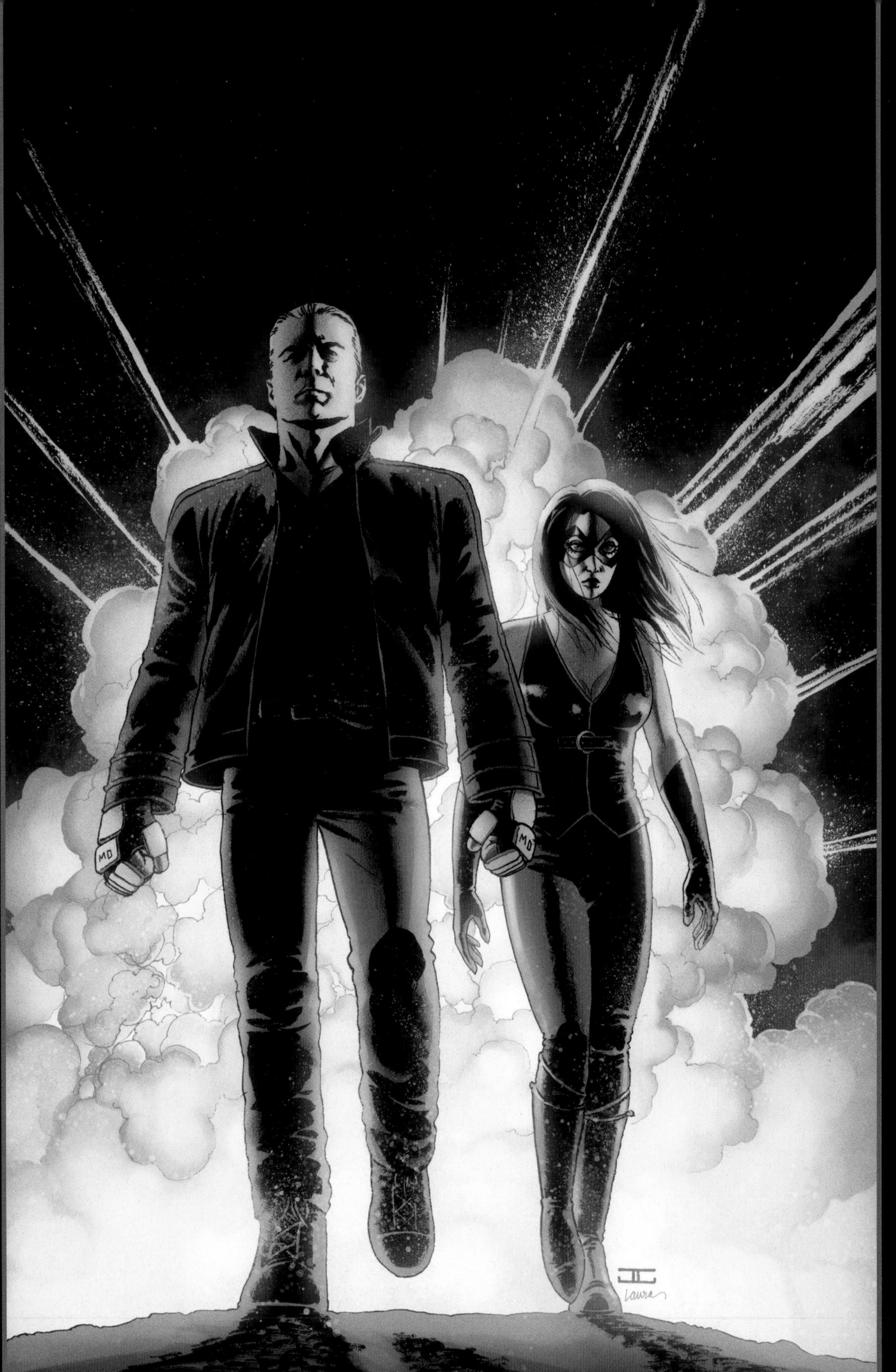
MD
MD
Laura

COVER 1A: JOHN CASSADAY
COLORS: LAURA MARTIN

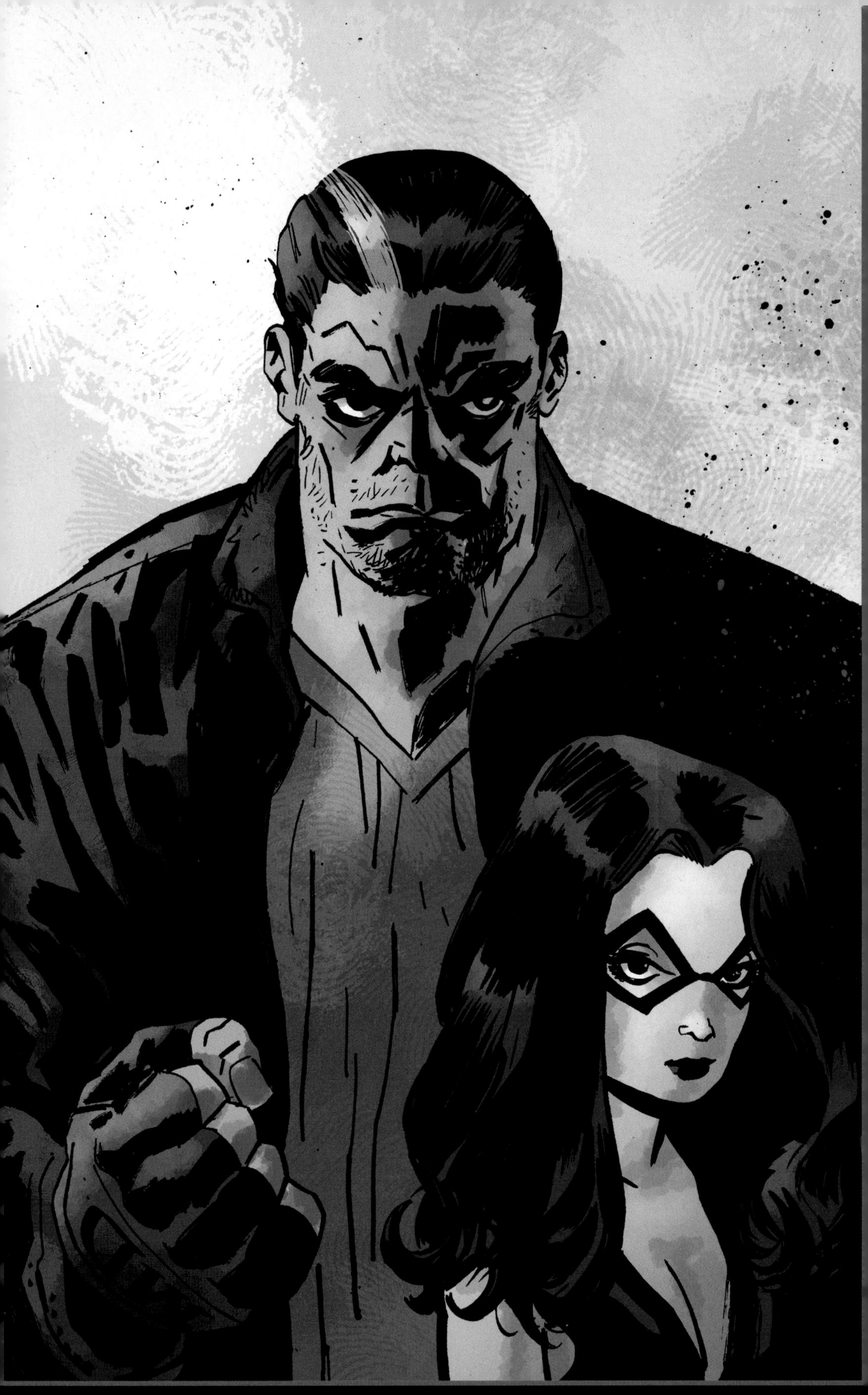

COVER 1B: TIM SALE
INKS: PAUL AZACETA, COLORS: MATTHEW WILSON

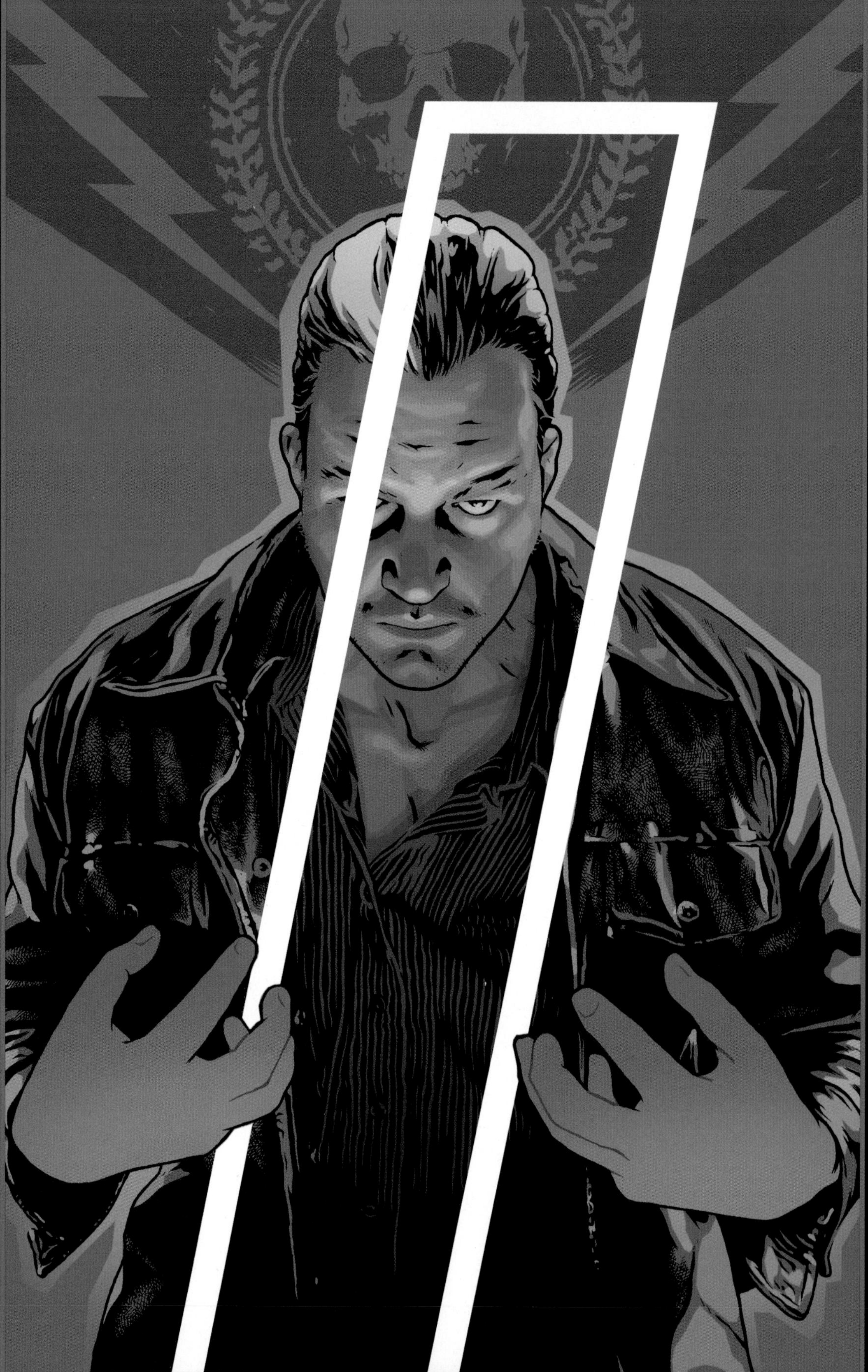

COVER 1C: JEFFREY SPOKES

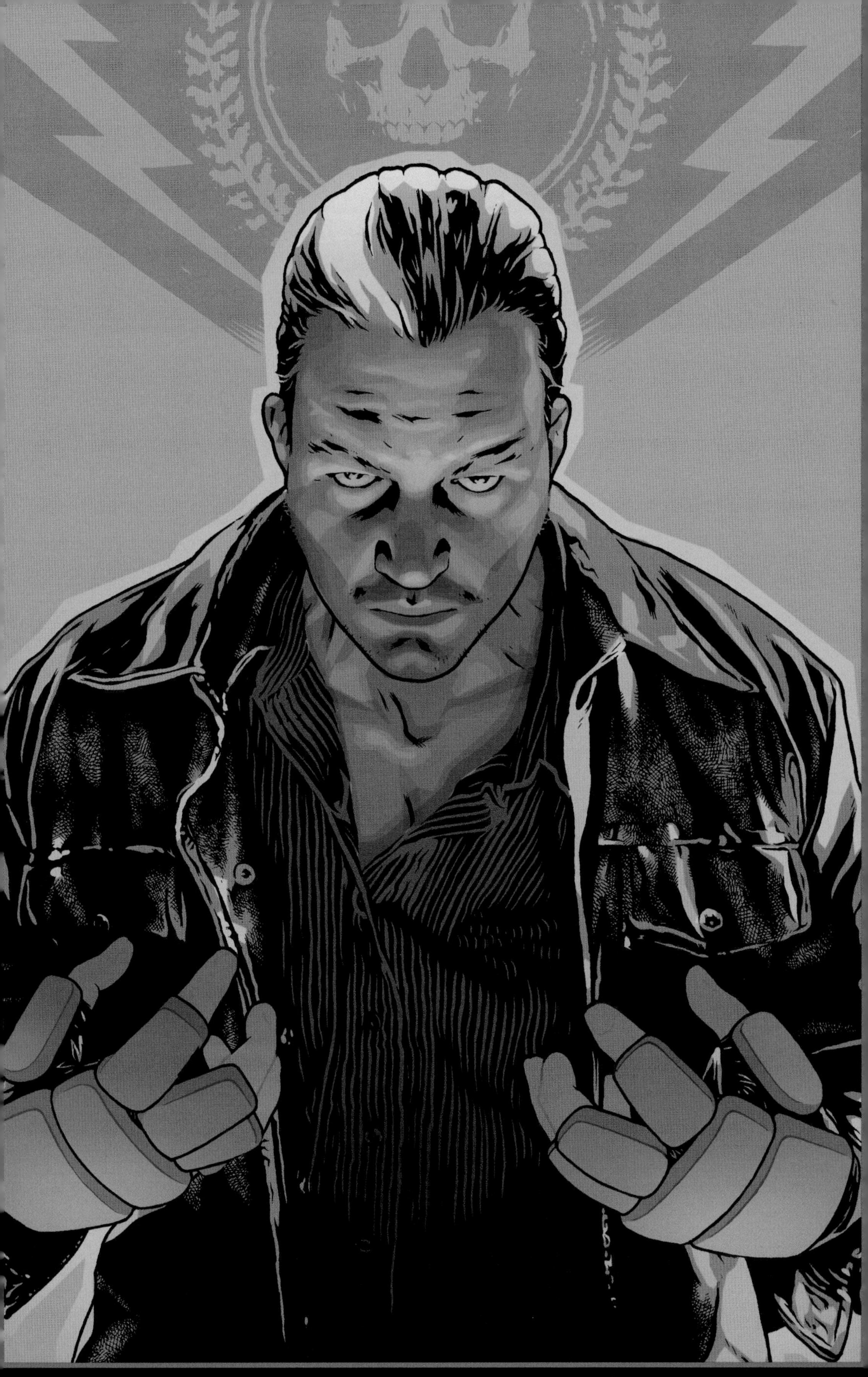

EMERALD CITY COMICON EXCLUSIVE: JEFFREY SPOKES

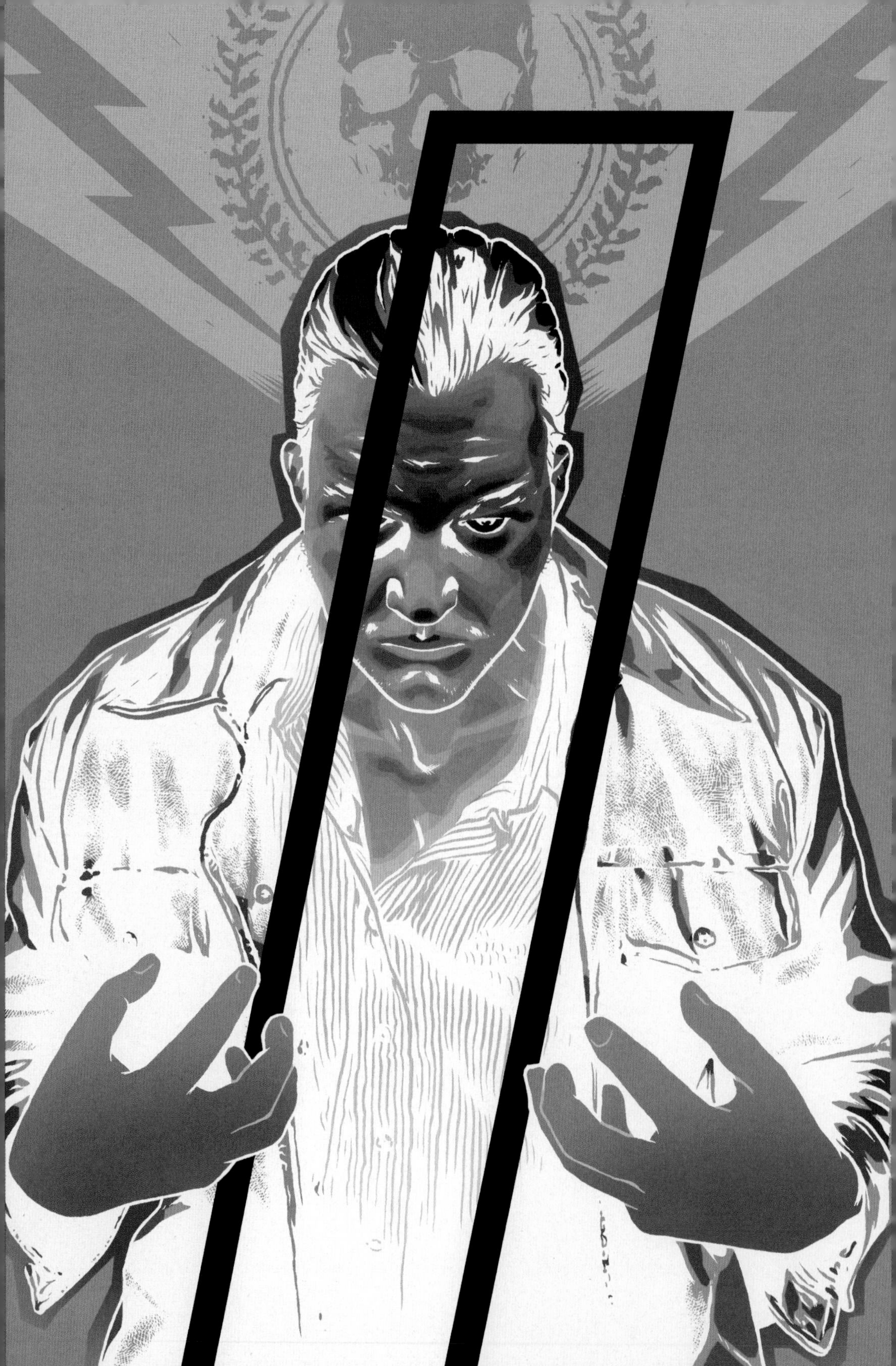

COMICS EX

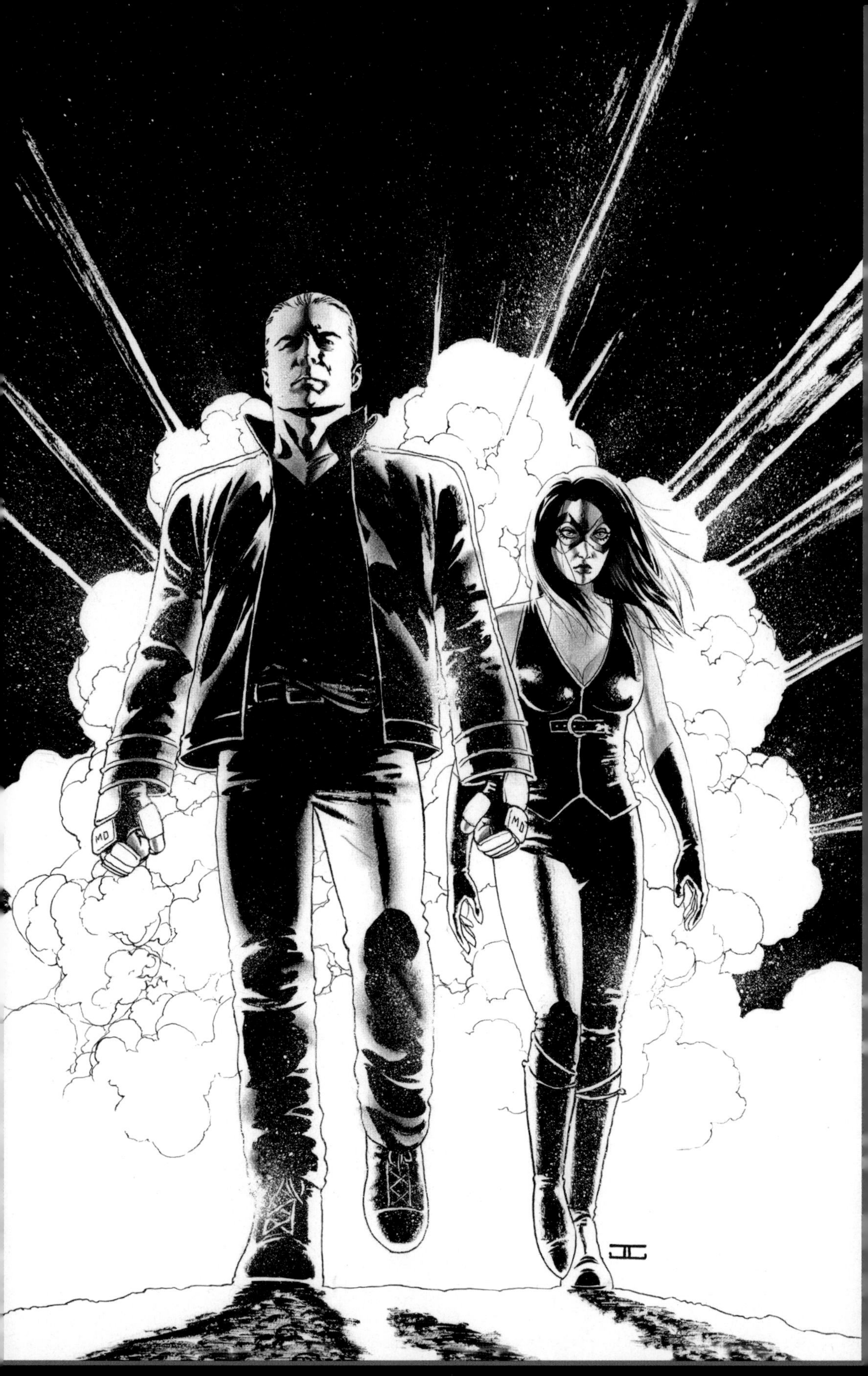

ISSUE 1 SECOND PRINT: JOHN CASSADAY

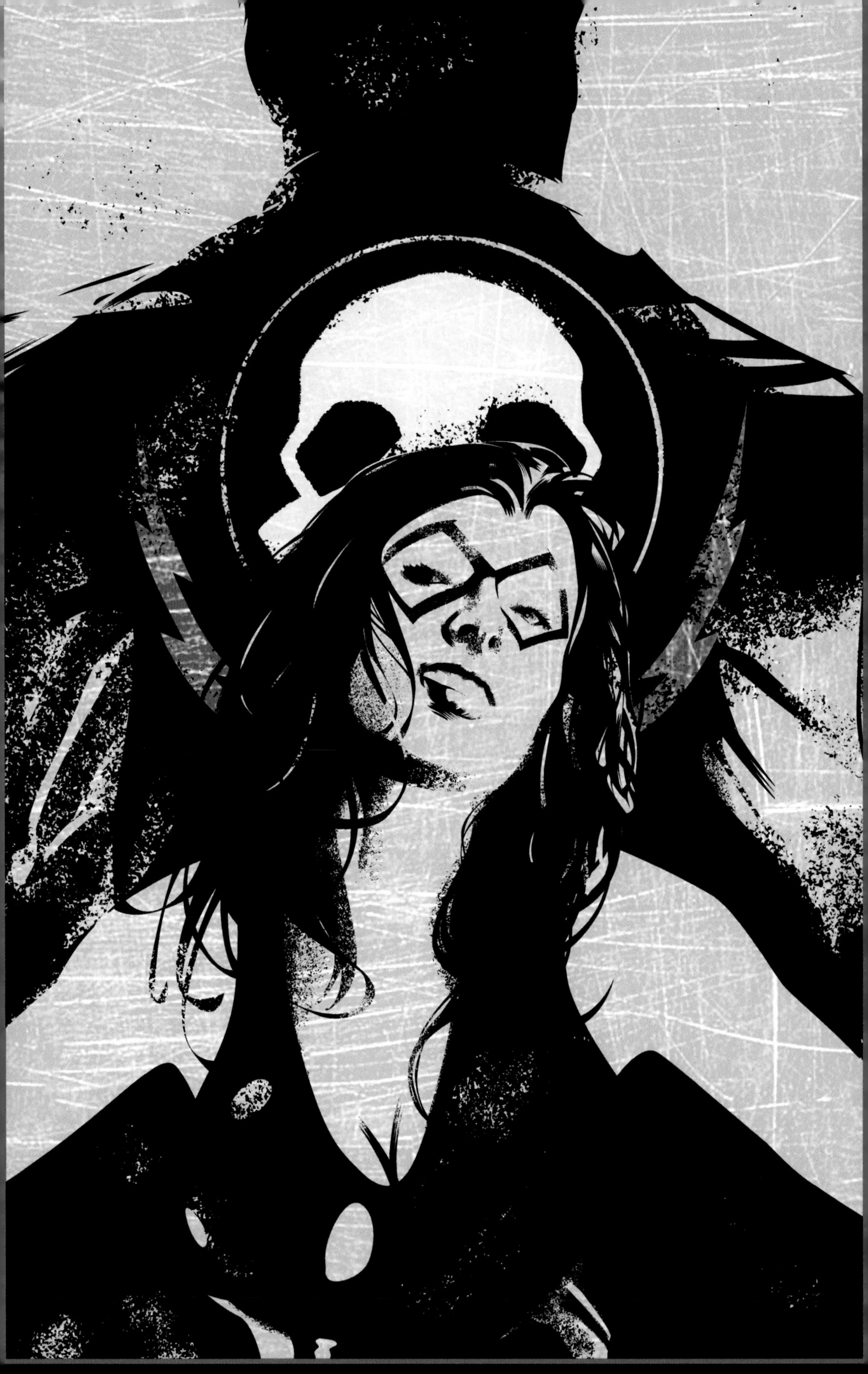

COVER 24: DENNIS CALERO

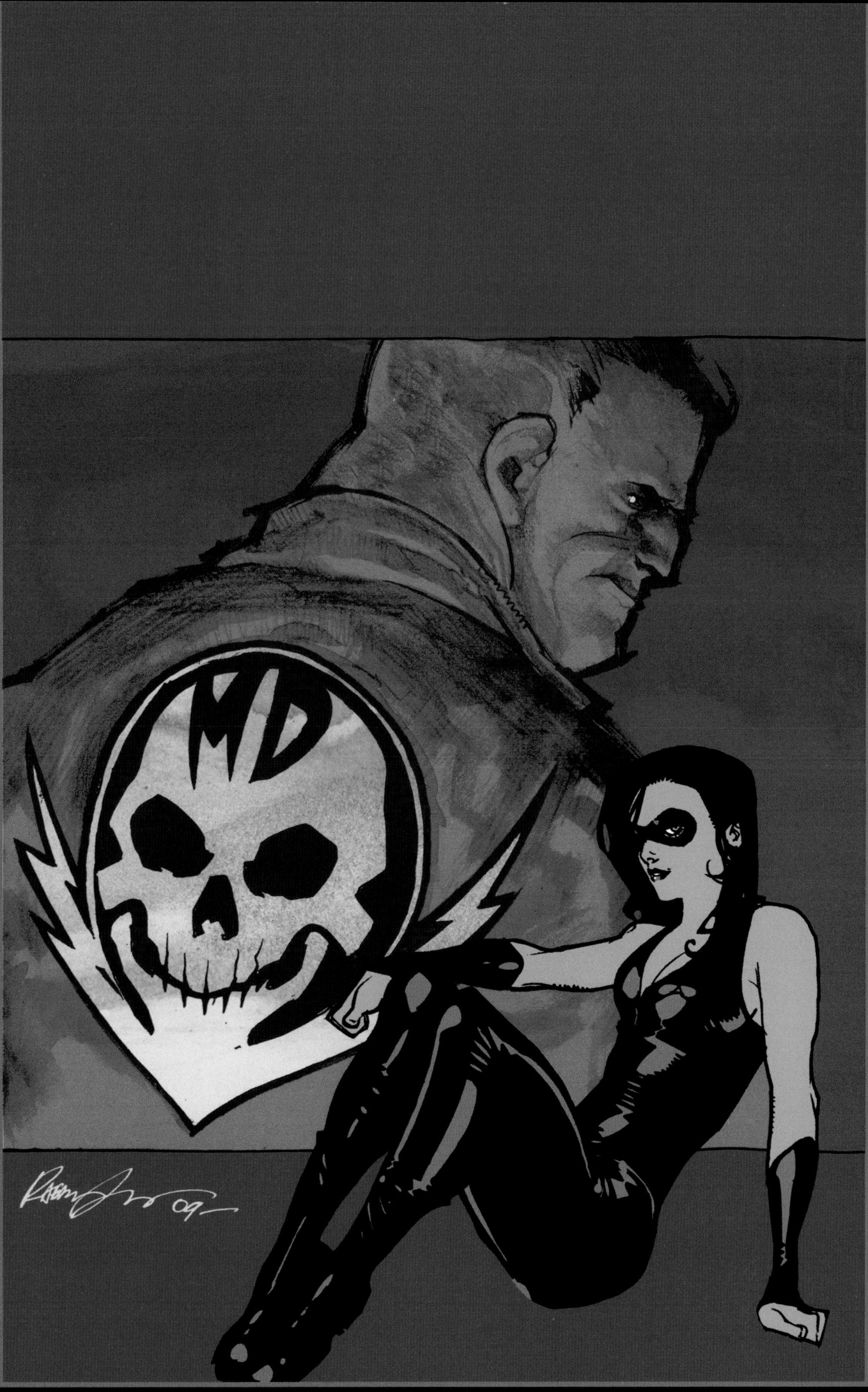
MD

COVER 2B: RAFAEL ALBUQUERQUE

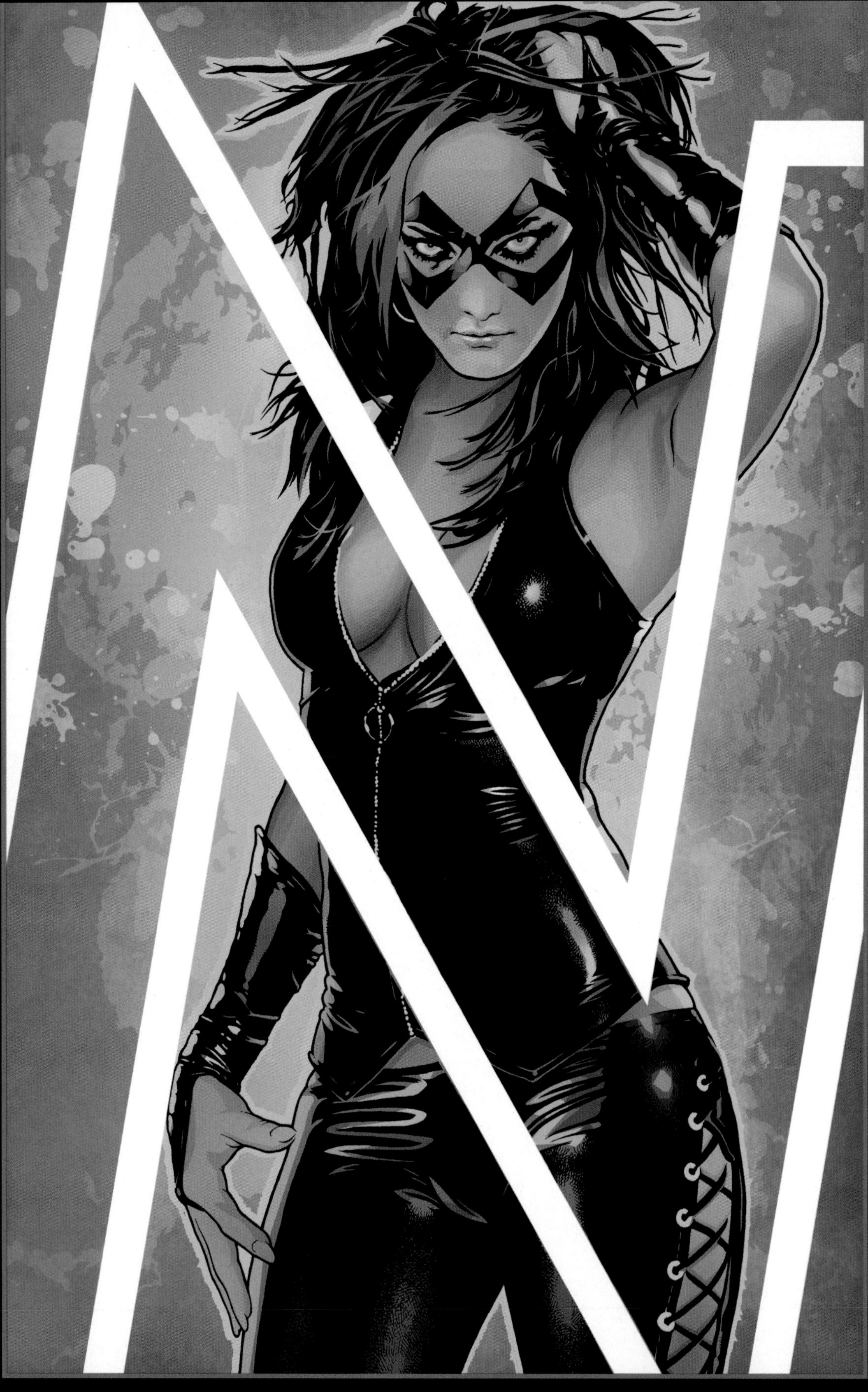
COVER 2C: JEFFREY SPOKES

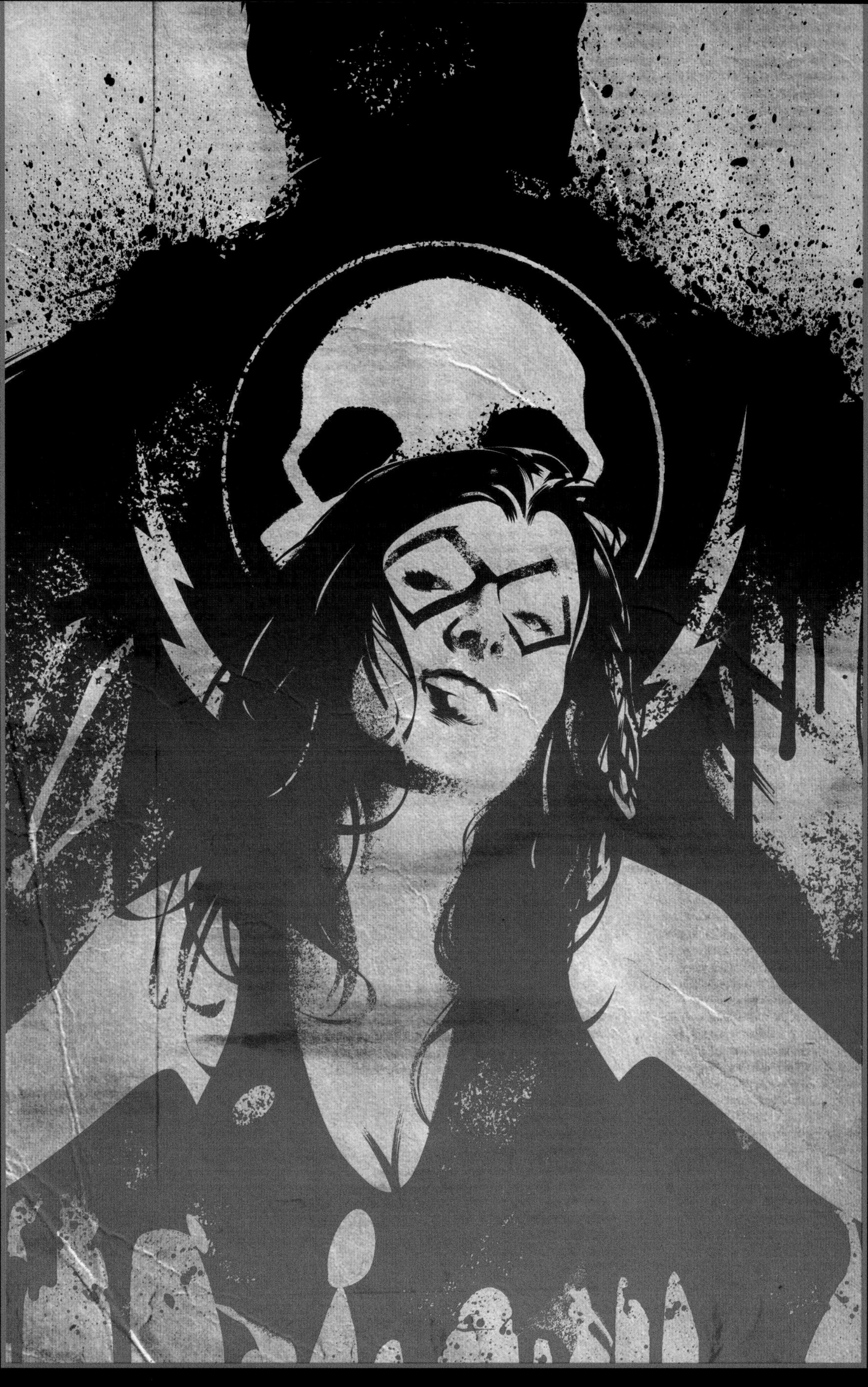

ISSUE 2 SECOND PRINT: **DENNIS CALERO**

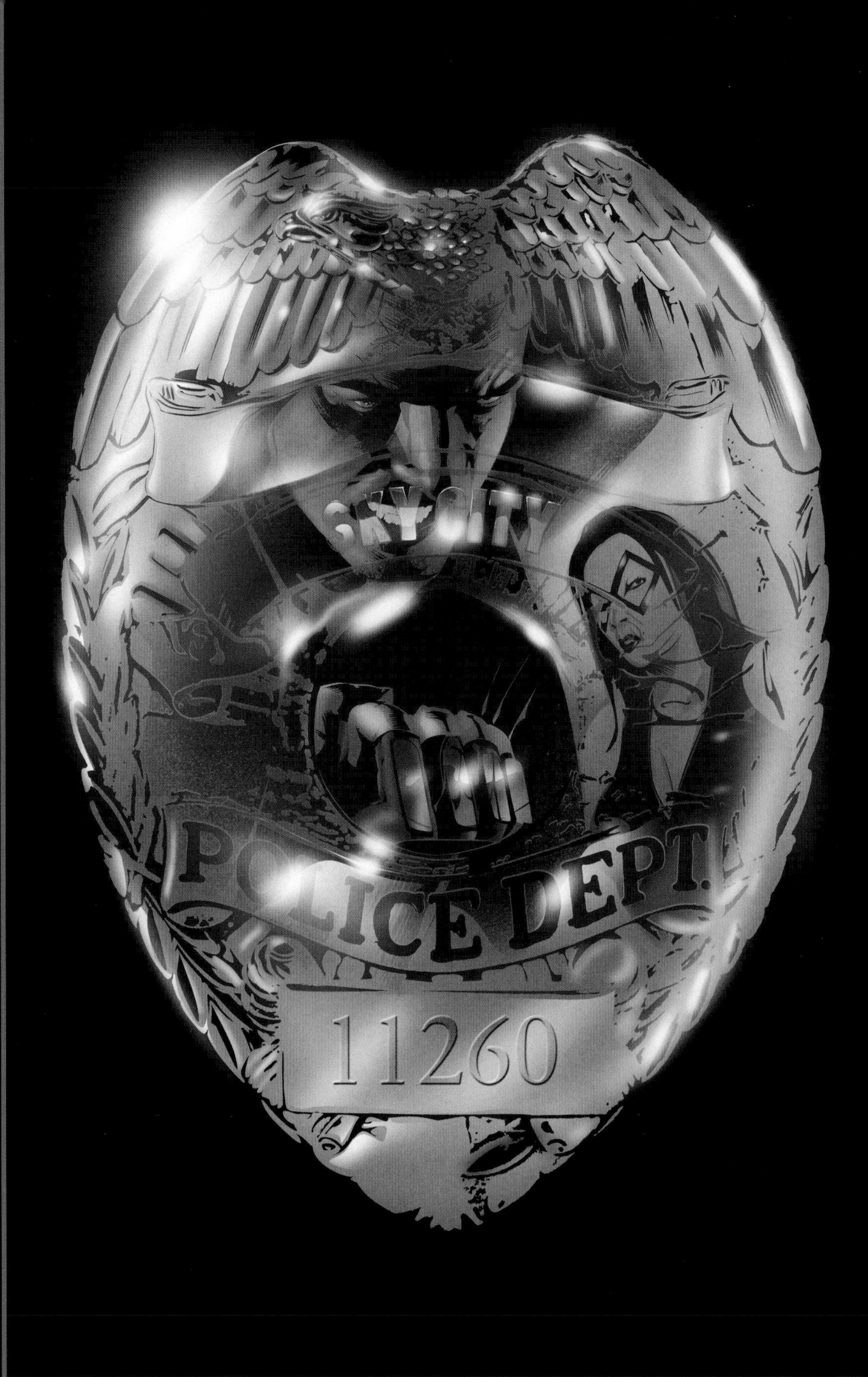
SKY CITY
POLICE DEPT.
11260
COVER 3A: DENNIS CALERO

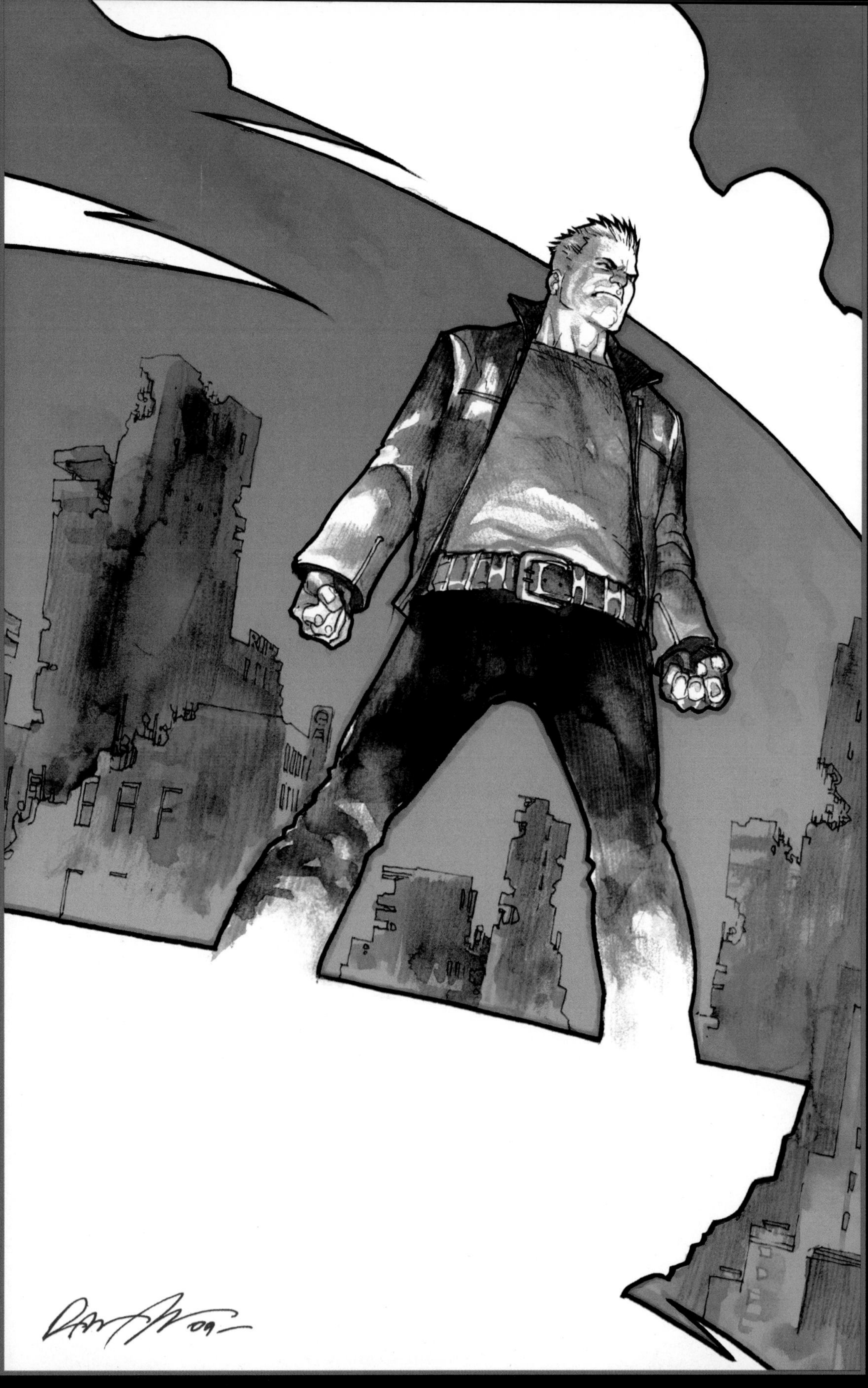

COVER 3B: RAFAEL ALBUQUERQUE

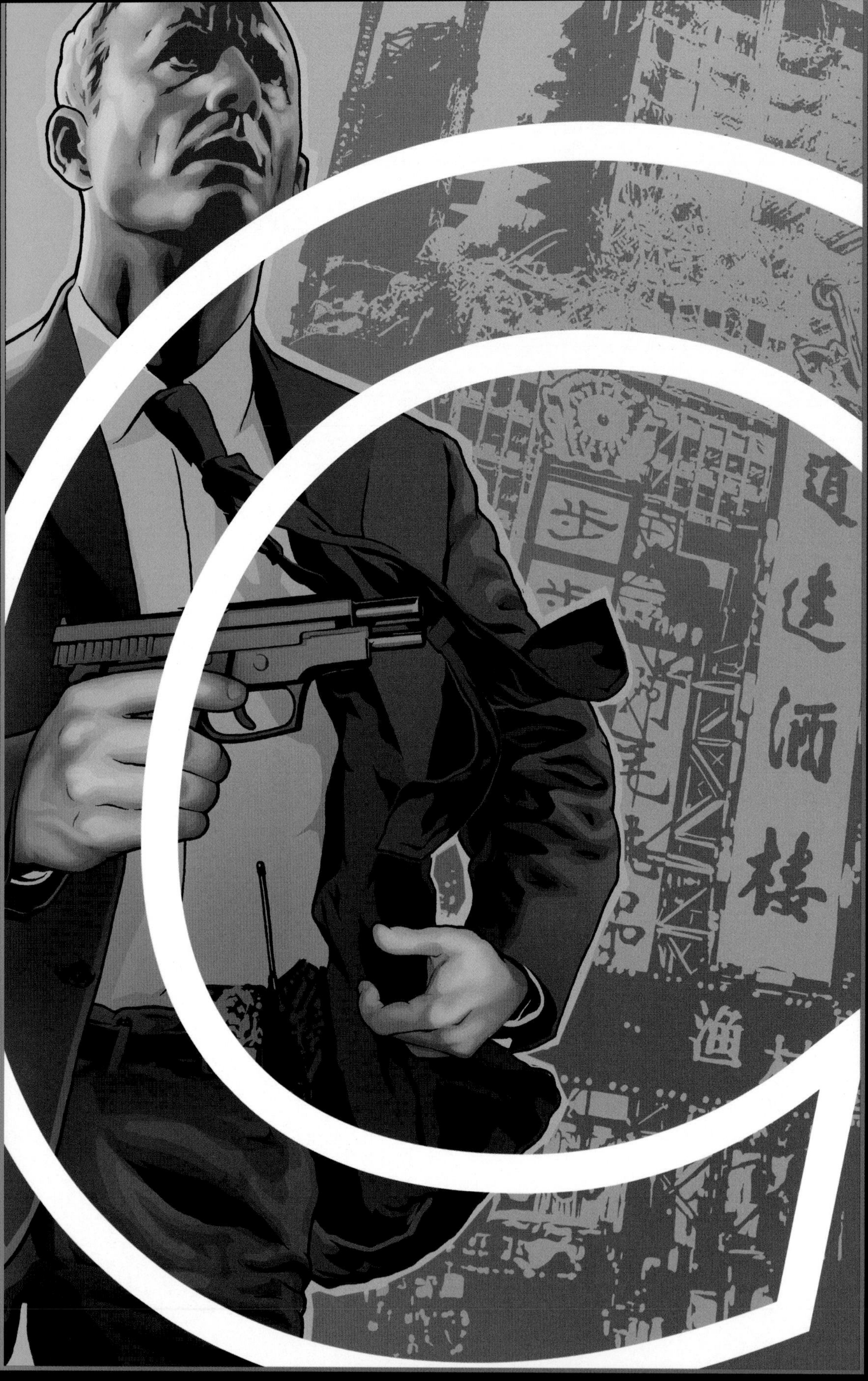

COVER 3C: JEFFREY SPOKES

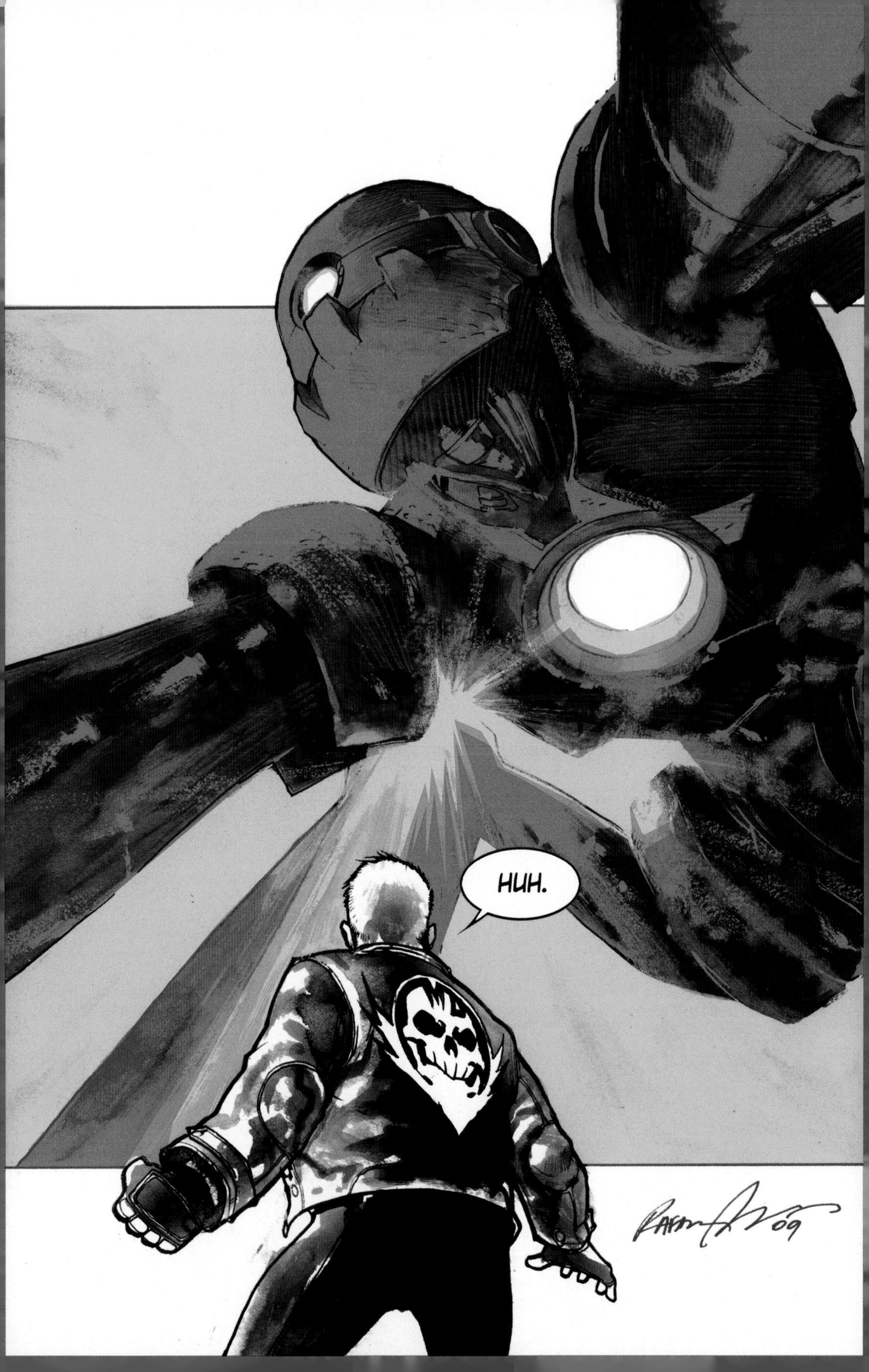
HUH.

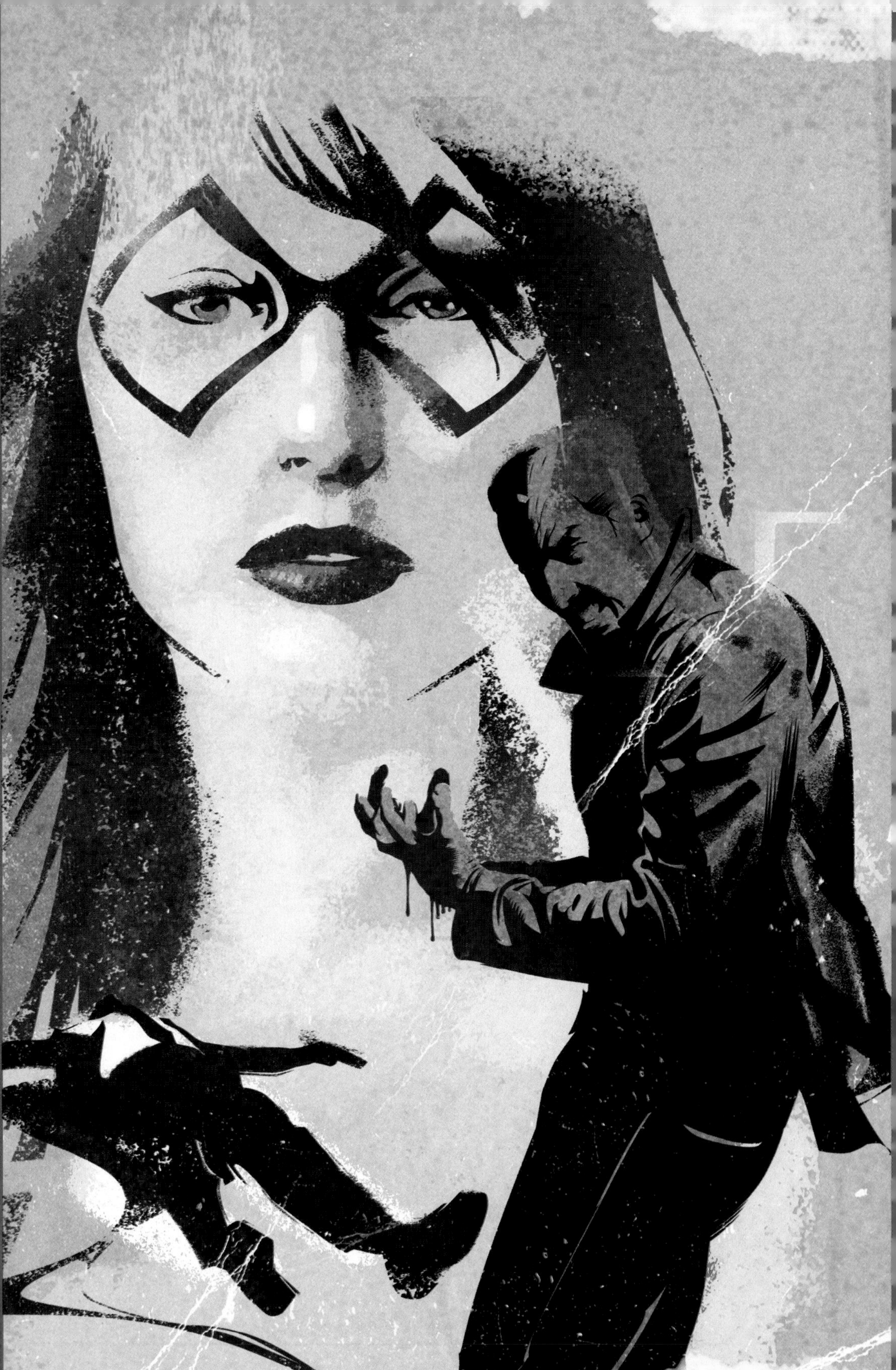

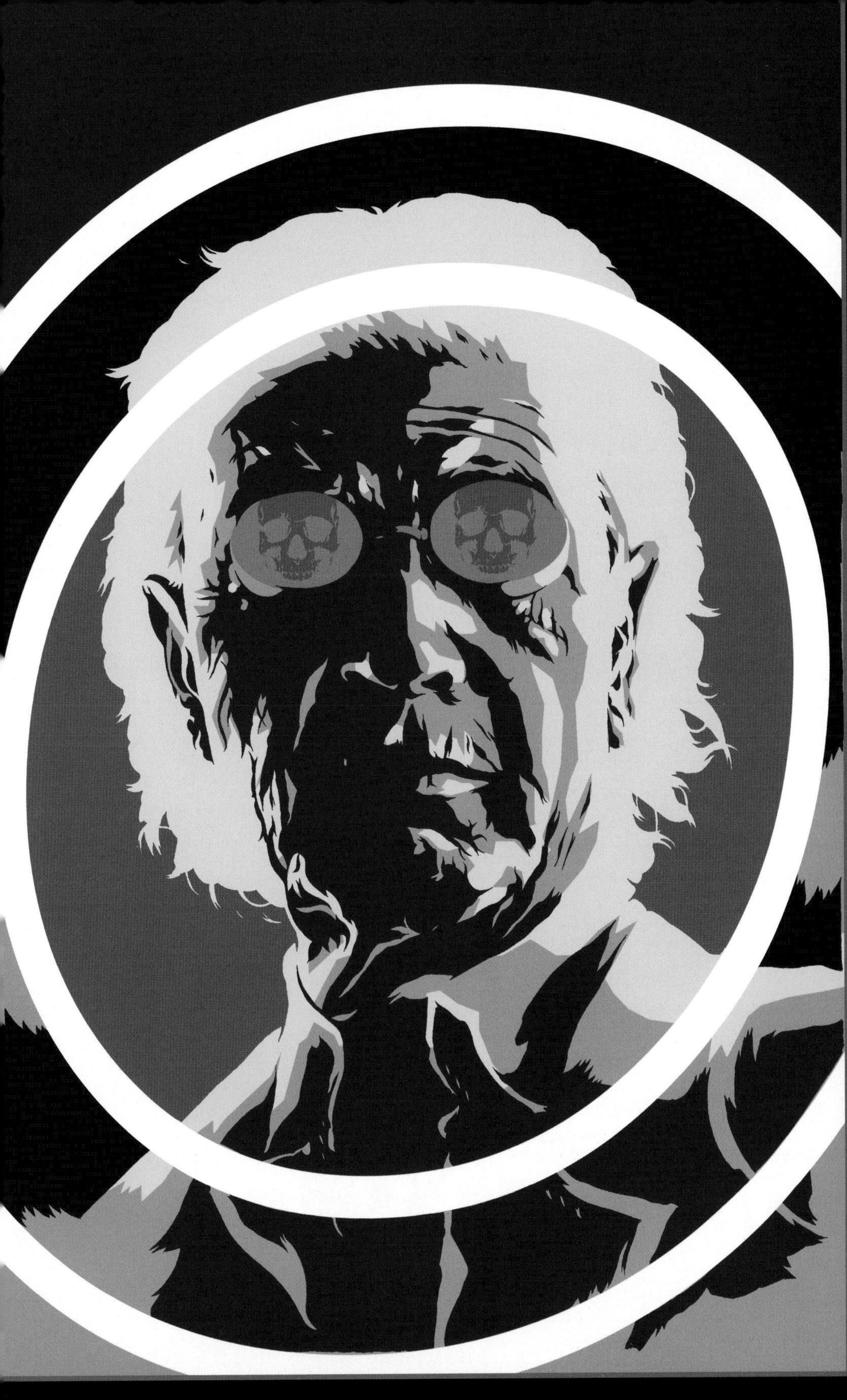

COVER 4C: JEFFREY SPOKES

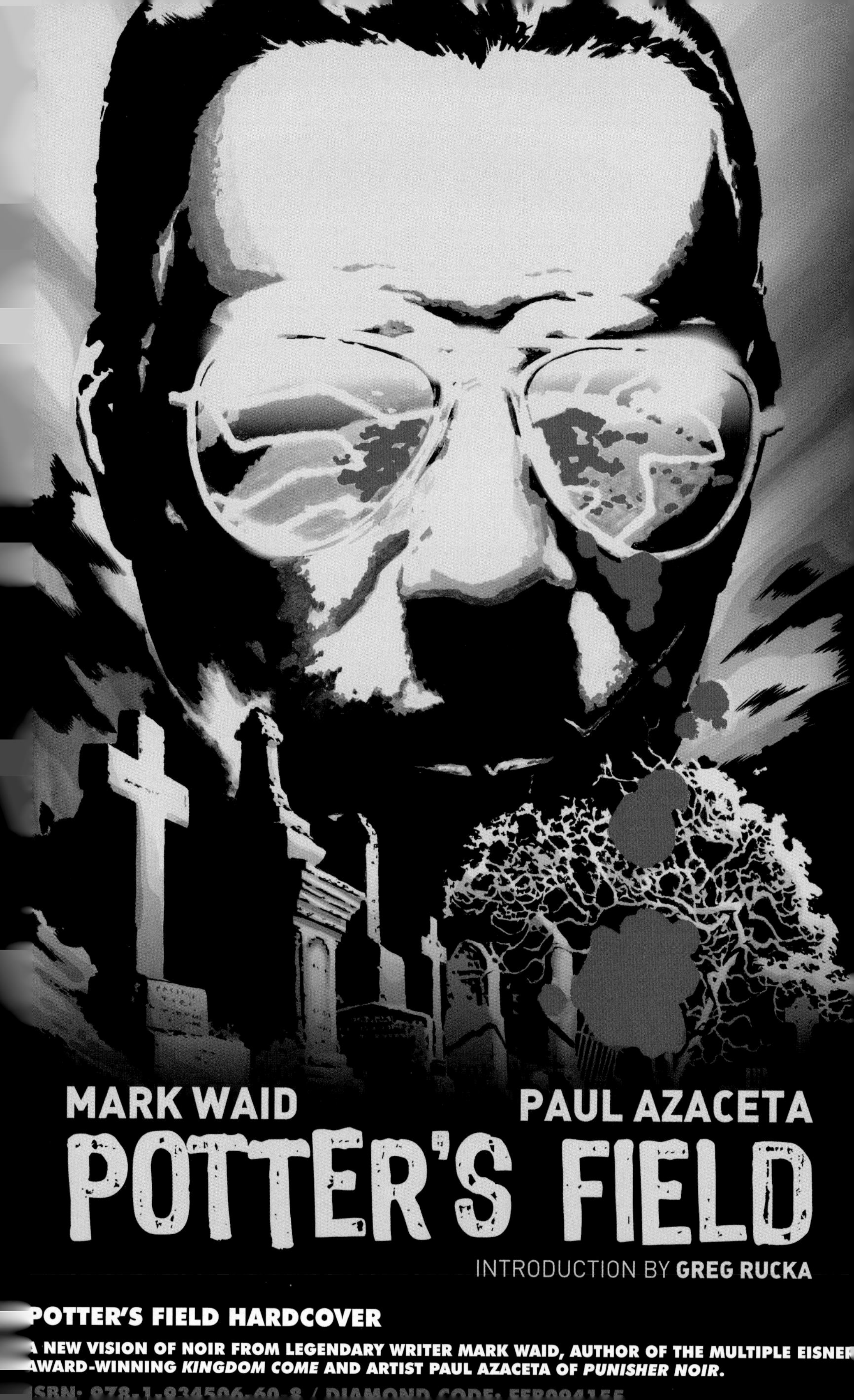
MARK WAID
PAUL AZACETA
POTTER'S FIELD
INTRODUCTION BY GREG RUCKA

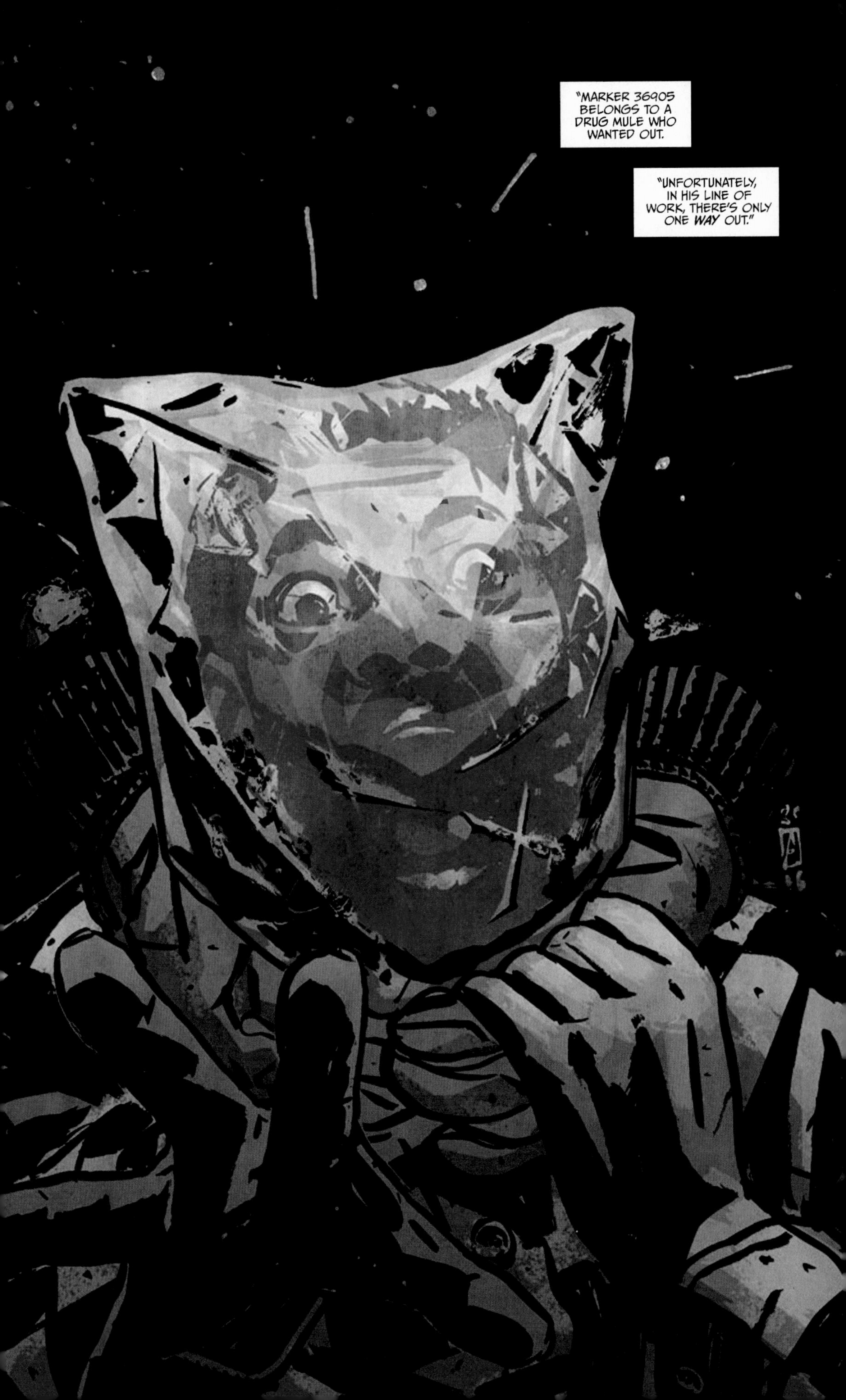
"MARKER 36905 BELONGS TO A DRUG MULE WHO WANTED OUT.
"UNFORTUNATELY, IN HIS LINE OF WORK, THERE'S ONLY ONE *WAY* OUT."

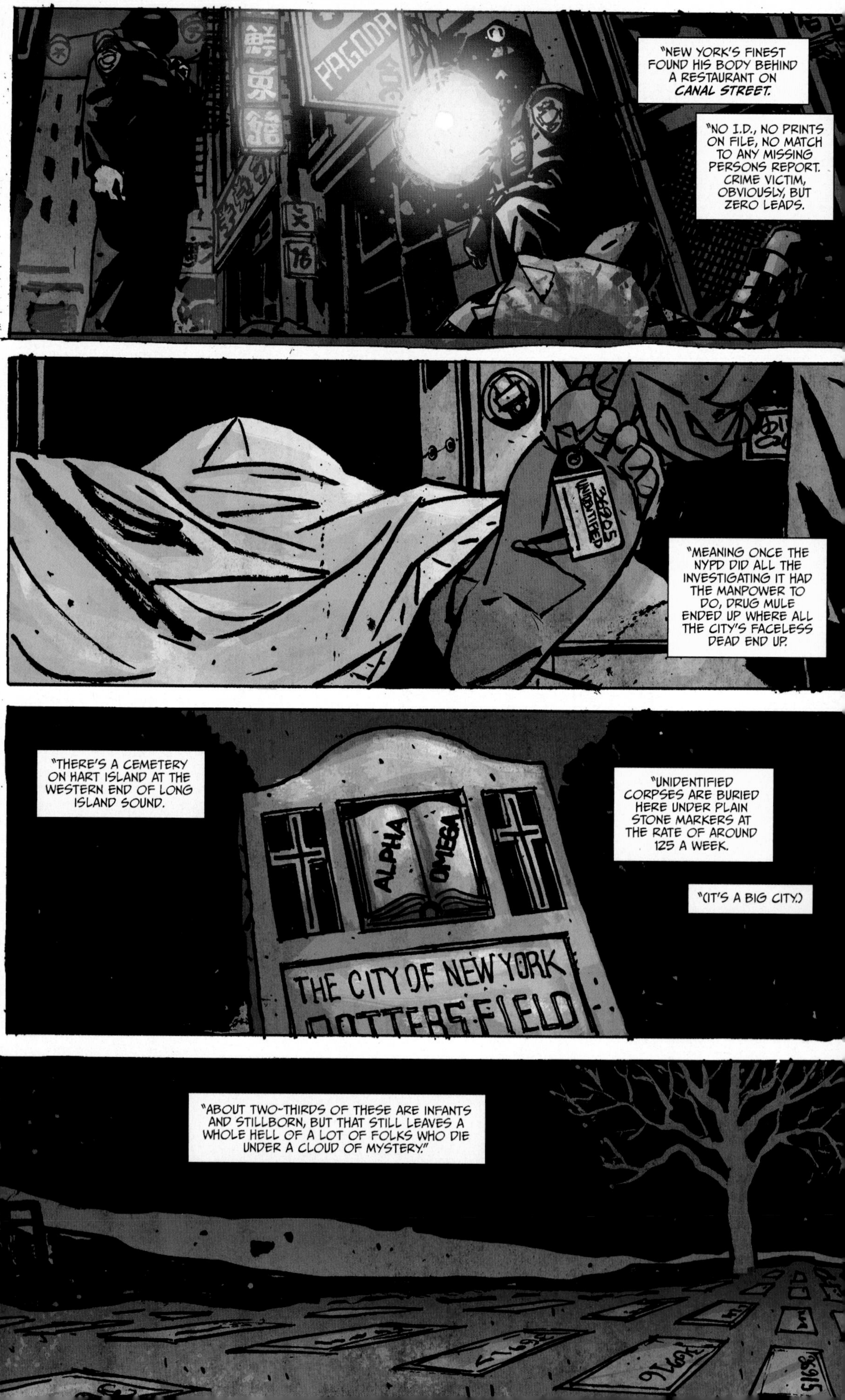

PAGODA
"NEW YORK'S FINEST FOUND HIS BODY BEHIND A RESTAURANT ON *CANAL STREET.*
"NO I.D., NO PRINTS ON FILE, NO MATCH TO ANY MISSING PERSONS REPORT. CRIME VICTIM, OBVIOUSLY, BUT ZERO LEADS.
UNIDENTIFIED
"MEANING ONCE THE NYPD DID ALL THE INVESTIGATING IT HAD THE MANPOWER TO DO, DRUG MULE ENDED UP WHERE ALL THE CITY'S FACELESS DEAD END UP.
"THERE'S A CEMETERY ON HART ISLAND AT THE WESTERN END OF LONG ISLAND SOUND.
ALPHA
OMEGA
THE CITY OF NEW YORK
"UNIDENTIFIED CORPSES ARE BURIED HERE UNDER PLAIN STONE MARKERS AT THE RATE OF AROUND 125 A WEEK.
"(IT'S A BIG CITY.)
"ABOUT TWO-THIRDS OF THESE ARE INFANTS AND STILLBORN, BUT THAT STILL LEAVES A WHOLE HELL OF A LOT OF FOLKS WHO DIE UNDER A CLOUD OF MYSTERY."

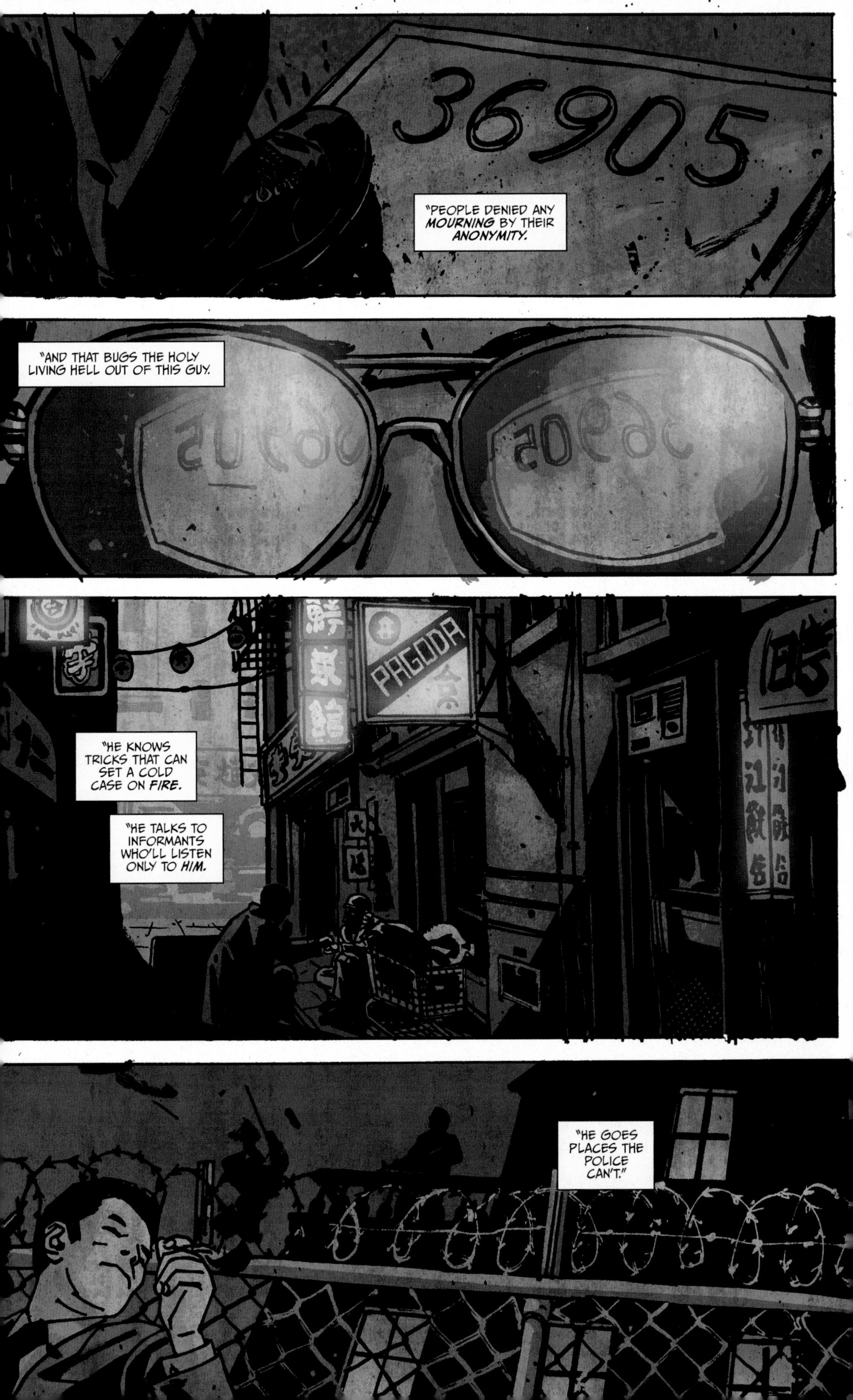
36905
"PEOPLE DENIED ANY *MOURNING* BY THEIR *ANONYMITY.*
"AND THAT BUGS THE HOLY LIVING HELL OUT OF THIS GUY.
PAGODA
"HE KNOWS TRICKS THAT CAN SET A COLD CASE ON *FIRE.*
"HE TALKS TO INFORMANTS WHO'LL LISTEN ONLY TO *HIM.*
"HE GOES PLACES THE POLICE CAN'T."

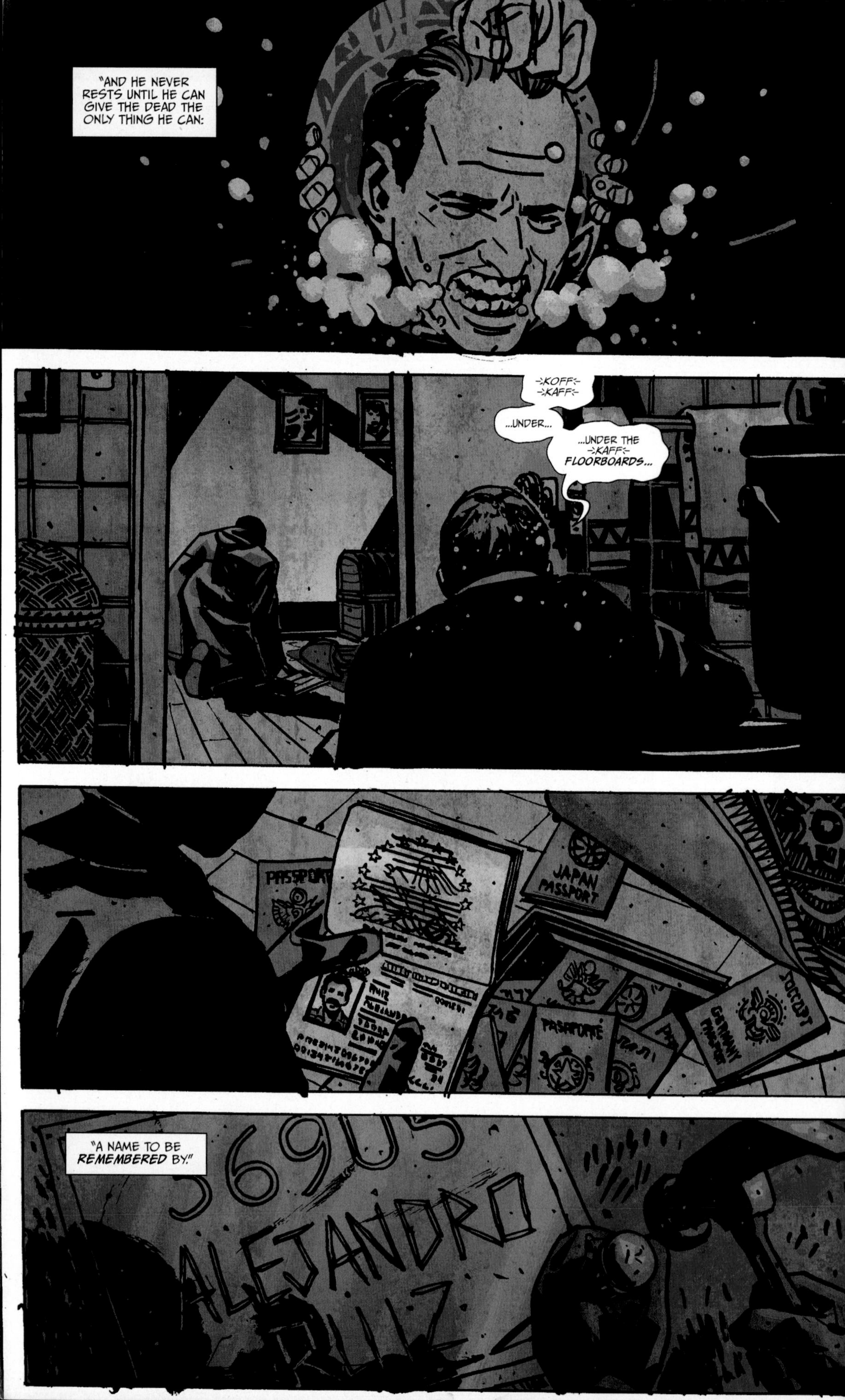
"AND HE NEVER RESTS UNTIL HE CAN GIVE THE DEAD THE ONLY THING HE CAN:
-KOFF- -KAFF-
...UNDER...
...UNDER THE -KAFF- FLOORBOARDS...
PASSPORT
JAPAN PASSPORT
PASAPORTE
"A NAME TO BE *REMEMBERED* BY."
56905
ALEJANDRO

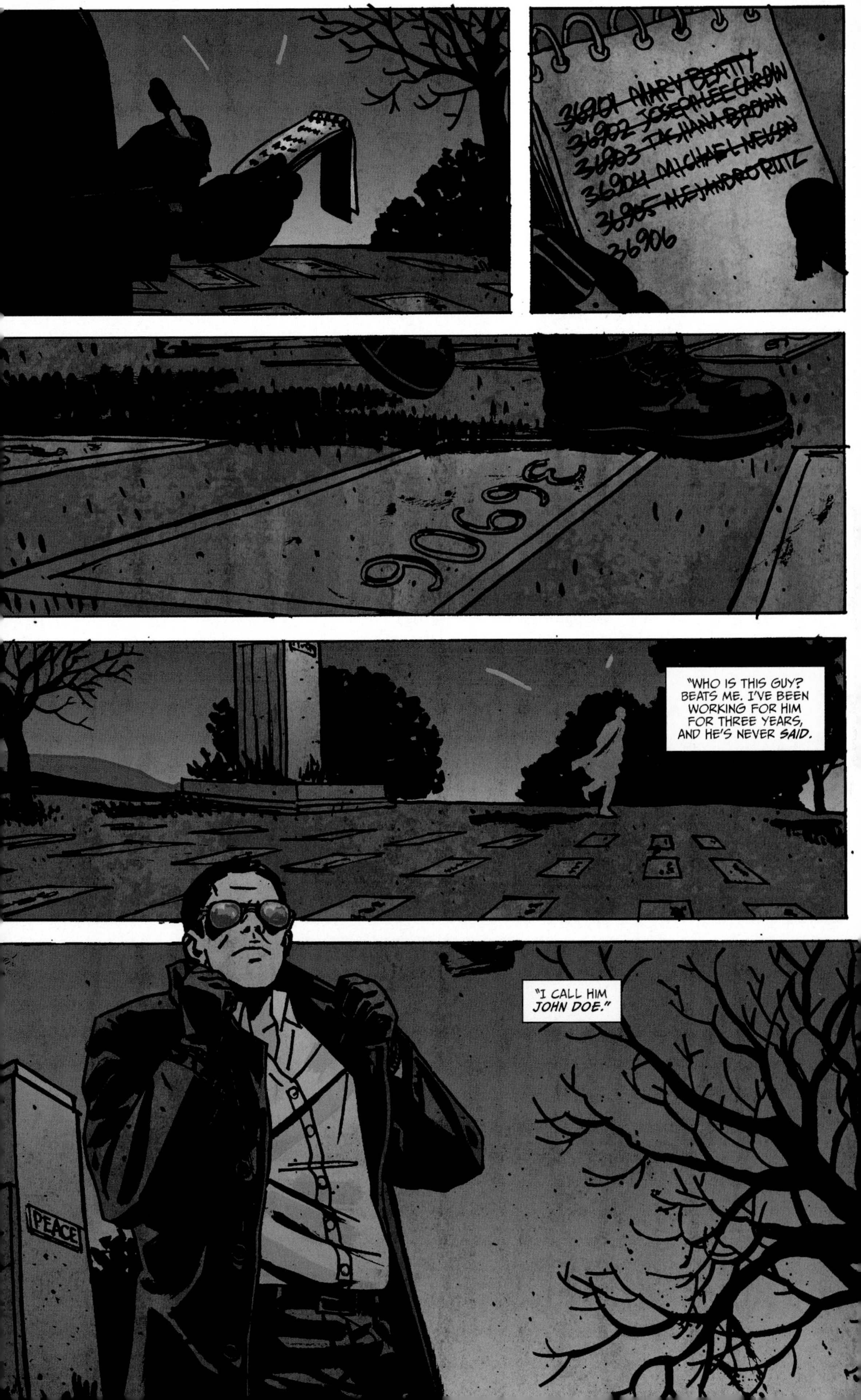
36901 MARY BEATTY
36904 MICHAEL NELSON
36905 ALEJANDRO RUIZ
36906
"WHO IS THIS GUY? BEATS ME. I'VE BEEN WORKING FOR HIM FOR THREE YEARS, AND HE'S NEVER *SAID*.
"I CALL HIM *JOHN DOE*."
PEACE

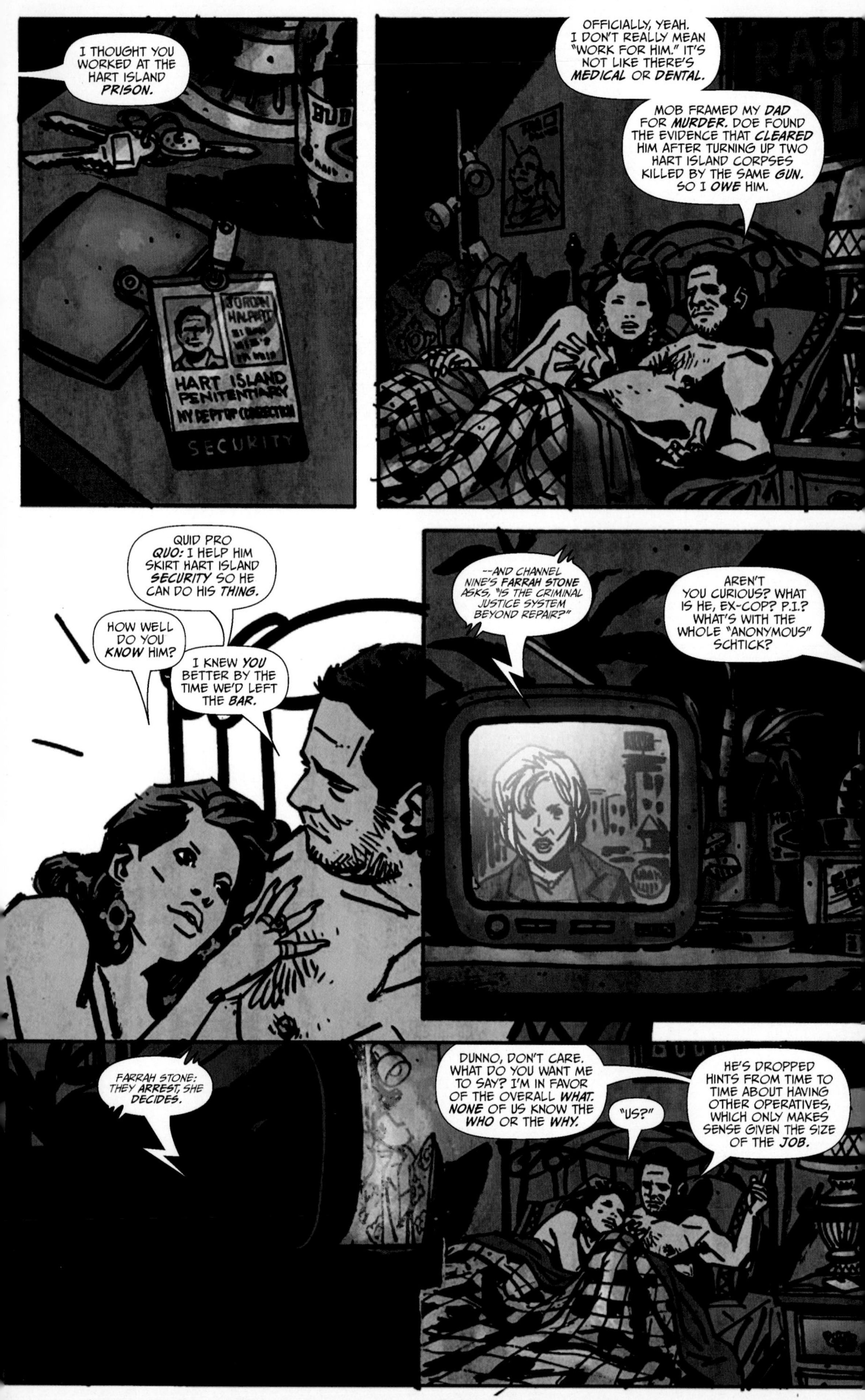
I THOUGHT YOU WORKED AT THE HART ISLAND PRISON.
HART ISLAND PENITENTIARY
SECURITY
OFFICIALLY, YEAH. I DON'T REALLY MEAN "WORK FOR HIM." IT'S NOT LIKE THERE'S MEDICAL OR DENTAL.
MOB FRAMED MY DAD FOR MURDER. DOE FOUND THE EVIDENCE THAT CLEARED HIM AFTER TURNING UP TWO HART ISLAND CORPSES KILLED BY THE SAME GUN. SO I OWE HIM.
HOW WELL DO YOU KNOW HIM?
QUID PRO QUO: I HELP HIM SKIRT HART ISLAND SECURITY SO HE CAN DO HIS THING.
I KNEW YOU BETTER BY THE TIME WE'D LEFT THE BAR.
--AND CHANNEL NINE'S FARRAH STONE ASKS, "IS THE CRIMINAL JUSTICE SYSTEM BEYOND REPAIR?"
AREN'T YOU CURIOUS? WHAT IS HE, EX-COP? P.I.? WHAT'S WITH THE WHOLE "ANONYMOUS" SCHTICK?
FARRAH STONE: THEY ARREST, SHE DECIDES.
DUNNO, DON'T CARE. WHAT DO YOU WANT ME TO SAY? I'M IN FAVOR OF THE OVERALL WHAT. NONE OF US KNOW THE WHO OR THE WHY.
"US?"
HE'S DROPPED HINTS FROM TIME TO TIME ABOUT HAVING OTHER OPERATIVES, WHICH ONLY MAKES SENSE GIVEN THE SIZE OF THE JOB.

"I TAKE IT HE'S GOT INSIDE AGENTS ALL OVER THE *CITY.*"

AUTOPS
ROOM

CORONER

PAXTIN, JAMES

"--ACT MIGHTY *NERVOUS* FOR AN *INNOCENT MAN,* MR. TRENDLE. MAYBE THE D.A. BUYS YOUR STORY, BUT MY VIEWERS KNOW THE *TRUTH.*"

WHY NOT JUST COME *CLEAN,* SIR?

BECAUSE HE'S NOT *GUILTY,* YOU SANCTIMONIOUS *HARRIDAN!*

SHE MAKES ME *ILL.* HOW DOES BEING A FORMER *CRIME VICTIM* GIVE YOU THE RIGHT TO PLAY JUDGE *AND* JURY ON THE PUBLIC AIRWAVES?

THIS IS *NEW YORK.* FIND ME SOMEONE WHO'S *NOT* A CRIME VICTIM! I'D CALL FARRAH STONE AN *HARPY,* BUT THAT'S AN INSULT TO HARPIES *EVERYWH--*

WAIT. SHE AND I AREN'T IN THE SAME *FRATERNITY,* ARE WE?

CHK

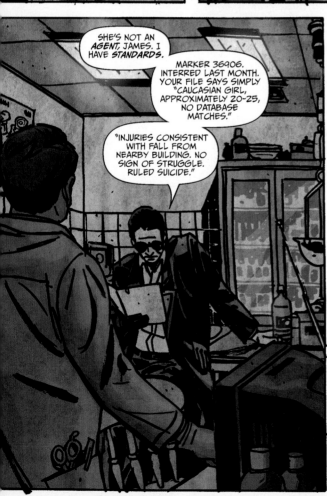

SHE'S NOT AN *AGENT,* JAMES. I HAVE *STANDARDS.*

MARKER 36906. INTERRED LAST MONTH. YOUR FILE SAYS SIMPLY "CAUCASIAN GIRL, APPROXIMATELY 20-25, NO DATABASE MATCHES."

"INJURIES CONSISTENT WITH FALL FROM NEARBY BUILDING. NO SIGN OF STRUGGLE. RULED SUICIDE."

THIS IS A PHOTO OF HER PERSONAL EFFECTS?

SUCH AS THEY *WERE,* BOSS. NO WALLET, NO I.D.

WHAT DID YOU MAKE OF THE *WALKMAN?*

WE CALL THEM *IPODS* NOW, GRAMPA.

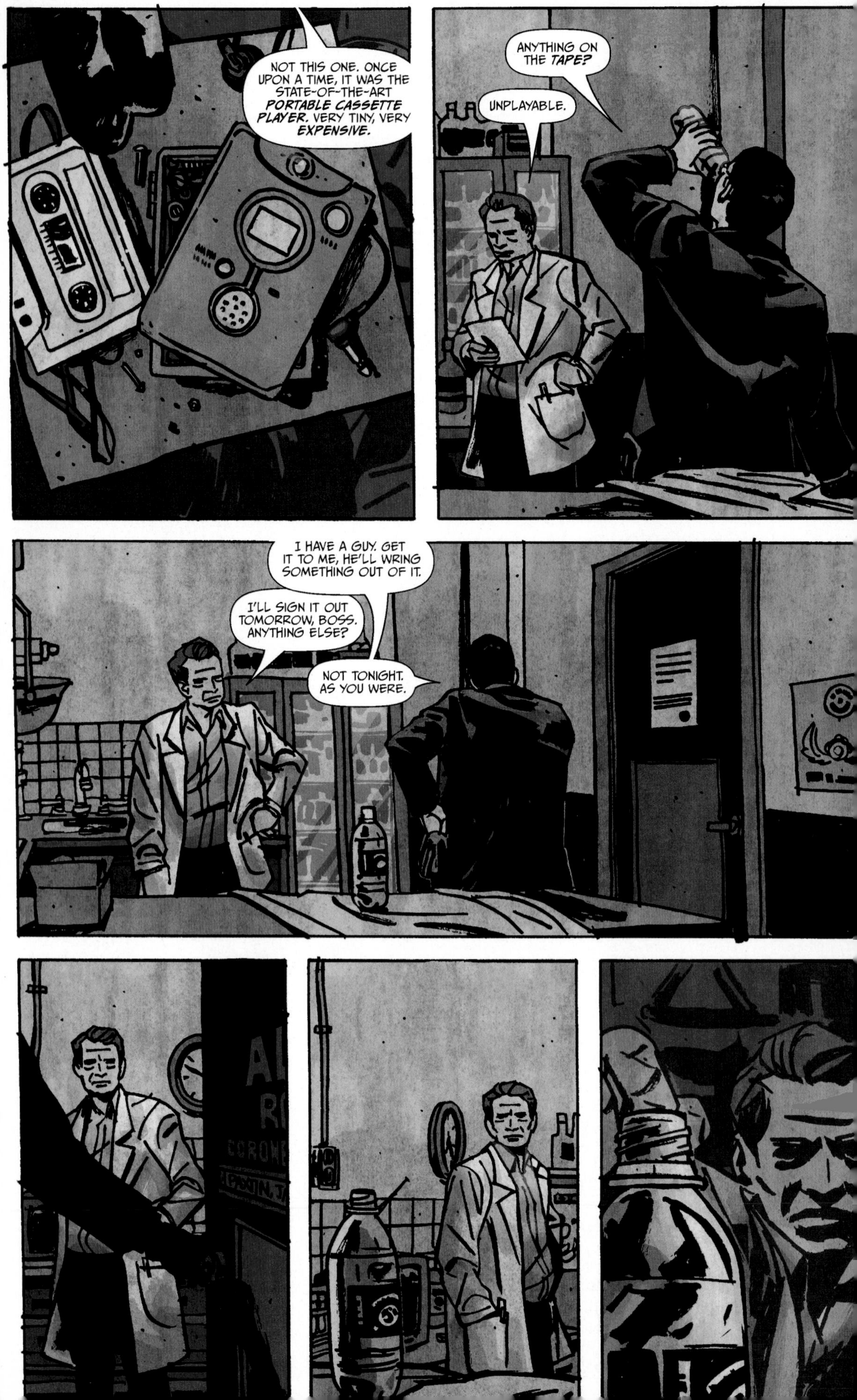
NOT THIS ONE. ONCE UPON A TIME, IT WAS THE STATE-OF-THE-ART *PORTABLE CASSETTE PLAYER.* VERY TINY, VERY *EXPENSIVE.*
ANYTHING ON THE *TAPE?*
UNPLAYABLE.
I HAVE A GUY. GET IT TO ME, HE'LL WRING SOMETHING OUT OF IT.
I'LL SIGN IT OUT TOMORROW, BOSS. ANYTHING ELSE?
NOT TONIGHT. AS YOU WERE.

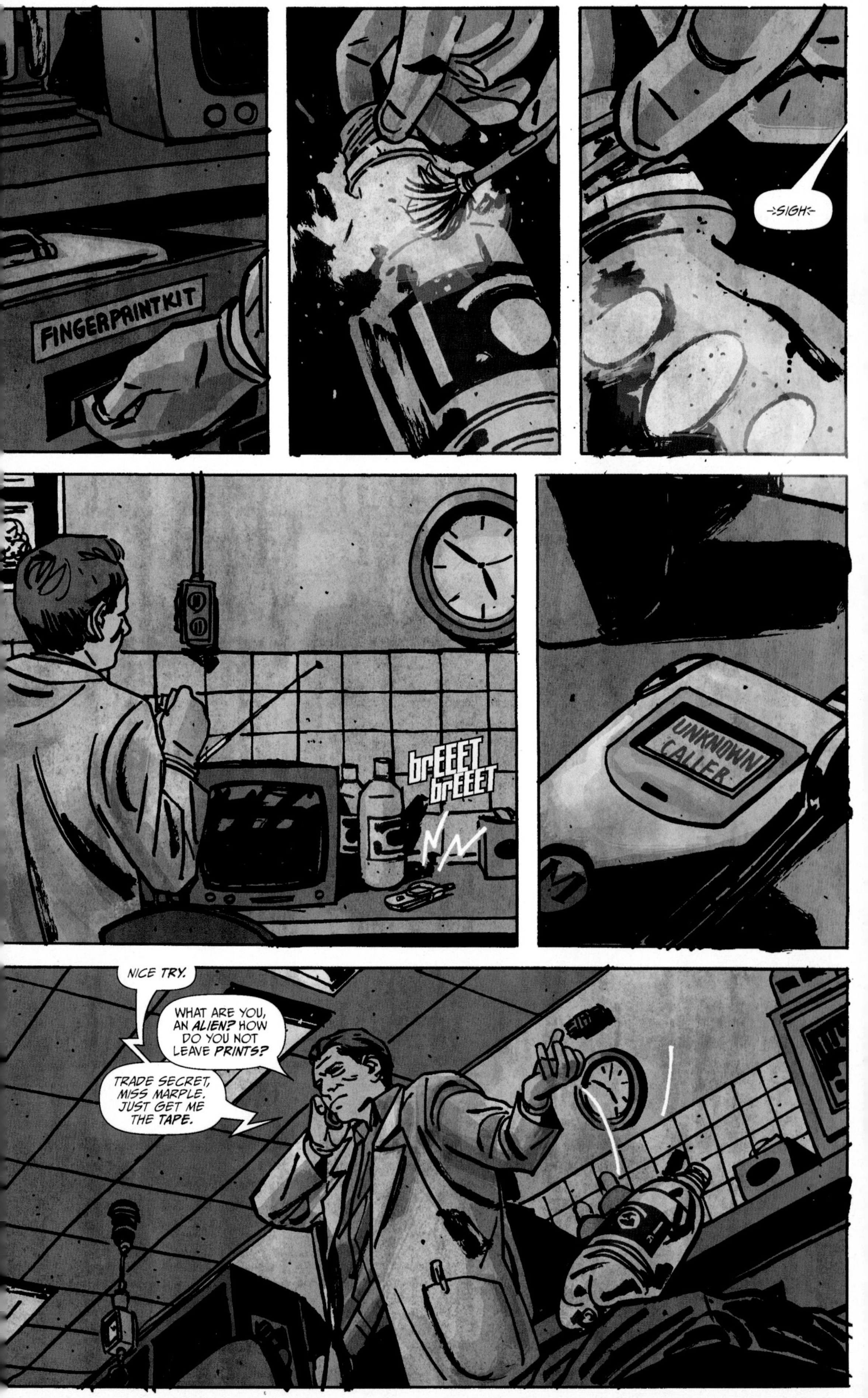
FINGERPRINT KIT
-SIGH-
brEEET brEEET
UNKNOWN CALLER
NICE TRY.
WHAT ARE YOU, AN ALIEN? HOW DO YOU NOT LEAVE PRINTS?
TRADE SECRET, MISS MARPLE. JUST GET ME THE TAPE.

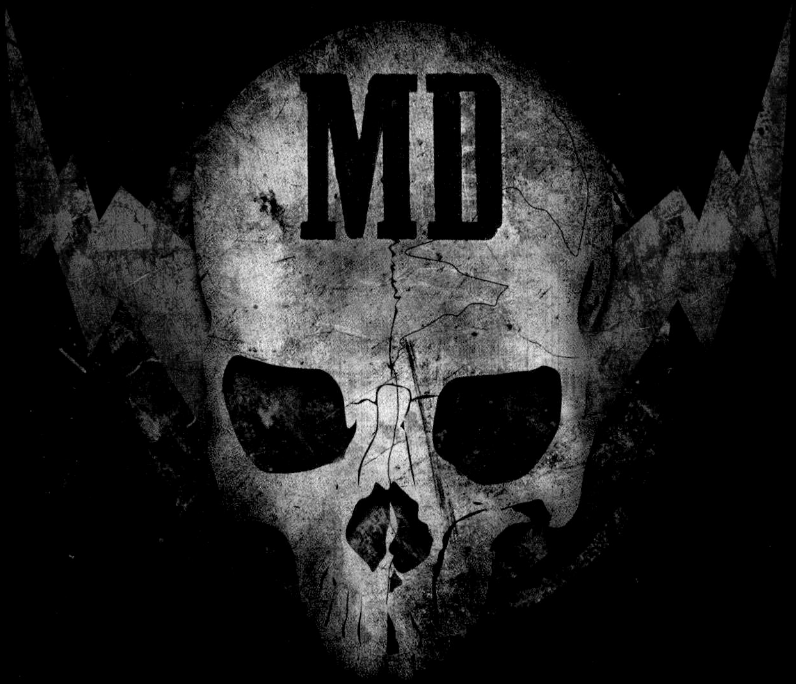
MD